Clarita's
Cooking
Lighter

· · · · · · · · · · · ·

Clarita Garcia

Publishing, Inc.

Cover and Book Design:
Robyn Voshardt

Editorial Assistance:
Sara Kennedy
Janet de Guehery

Cover Art:
Peggy Hering

For special group discounts or retail information contact:
Seaside Publishing, Inc.
P.O. Box 14441, St. Petersburg, Florida 33733
Toll Free Number: 1-888-FLA-BOOK

TABLE OF CONTENTS

DEDICATION

*I dedicate this book to my grandchildren for their unlimited
and unselfish love they have given me throughout
these many wonderful years...*
Gina Marie
Melissa Maria
Manny John
Forrest Manuel (my "Bo")

For patiently testing and tasting...
Tony Pace, executive chef (and more!) of our
great restaurants in Central Florida
His wife, Rosanne
Manny John
Manny and Gerry
Carmen

*For editorial assistance and typing my recipes
over and over again...*
Janet de Guehery

*For her loving patience editing and tasting,
my friend...*
Sara Kennedy

*For her faith in my ability...
My dear friend and publisher,*
Joyce LaFray

FOREWORD

I wanted to write this book because I hoped to share recipes left out of my first book, *Clarita's Cocina*. I also hoped to help you reduce fat, sodium and cholesterol in recipes without destroying quality and taste. And to chat, *aqui estoy - otra vez, mis amigas y amigos* – in the privacy of your kitchen.

Since my first book was published, friends, relatives and my good friend and editor, Joyce LaFray, had encouraged me to revise it – we got that done in 1989 with the addition of a Tapas chapter. Now, I'd like to take you to the "light" side of my kitchen.

Of course, you will notice a pronounced Spanish influence, often paired with American-style cooking, in many of my recipes. The reason? Because it was in a Spanish kitchen with my gentle, patient and loving mother, that I first learned the art of cooking.

My mother's kitchen was a shrine in our spacious home, the warmest and most hospitable room. It was not only a kitchen with perpetually enticing aromas, it was also our homework room, our family counseling room, our get-together room. Here decisions were made, recipes created, quarrels and disagreements settled; it was the emotional focus of my family.

How well I remember the wooden stove against one wall of the kitchen, where soups and potages slowly and lazily simmered away. In the wintertime, we roasted chestnuts there, and put potatoes in to bake that delighted my brother and me; then there was the magnificent gas range on the opposite wall, used only on special occasions.

As a child, I was the youngest of three and the only girl. Mother encouraged me to help prepare meals. It was sheer joy to be with her in the kitchen, watching how skillfully she prepared even very simple entrees. Once in a while, however, disaster upset the meticulous routine: Such as the day she had string beans with ham hocks cooking on the beautiful gas stove. She asked me to watch and stir; she had a chore to do.

A few minutes later, my brothers, who were outside playing baseball, needed an outfielder. So, I volunteered my service...forgetting the beans. There I was in the middle of an exciting game, when I remembered the beans! I dashed back into the house and there was Mother, staring at the horrible black pot. Inside the pot were the beans, standing at attention, crisply burned to perfection.

How could I redeem myself? What could I say to my sweet and wonderful mother? I burst into tears and ran upstairs to my room. Moments later, she was there beside me, and very gently, but firmly, spoke to me about the importance of responsibility, a lesson I have never forgotten. Cooking with Mother was always fun, and I enjoyed every phase of it, even the clean-up because she insisted on the "clean-as-you-go" method. A messy kitchen was not tolerated in our home.

I remember the simple perfection of white rice. A cup of long-grain rice was first washed in a colander, then poured into a pot filled with two cups of boiling salted water; the water was then again brought to a boil, the heat lowered and the pot covered. When the water was totally consumed by the rice, the pot was removed from the heat.

She would then pour two tablespoons of olive oil and two crushed garlic cloves into a skillet. When the oil was hot and the garlic crisp, she discarded the garlic and poured the hot oil over the cooked rice, together with two tablespoons of finely minced fresh parsley. With two forks, she fluffed the rice lightly, covered again, and allowed to stand 15 minutes before serving. Never have you tasted white rice so delectable!

Today, it is indeed heartening to see the trend toward better and healthier ways of cooking. When I wrote my first cookbook, I concentrated on the importance of basic preparation in cooking; in other words, cooking from scratch. Today young adults seem to be developing a new interest in home-cooking that is not only emotionally rewarding because it is a group activity, but nutritionally rewarding as well because in so doing, they are eliminating harmful pre-servatives and additives that are proving hazardous to their health. It is more economical to prepare an entree from scratch than to use convenience foods.

Still, I have no quarrel with convenience foods. They are helpful in emergencies; I use them myself occasionally. The late professor Vance Christian, who taught at the Hotel and Restaurant School at Cornell University, once said in an interview: "Convenience food is like a woman without make-up!" Convenience foods can be glamorized so effectively that it takes an expert to determine the original ingredients. And it is so quick to use! However, it is more satisfying to be able to say, "I made this white sauce from scratch; it is not a canned cream soup masquerading as a dignified bechamel." Here, time is irrelevent.

To be creative in your kitchen is so gratifying. How many times have I been asked by my late husband Manuel or my children, Carmen and Manny, "This is terrific; but, what's in it that makes it so special?" And many times I have truth-fully answered, "I really don't know!" simply because I im-provise as I go along. However, I do not want to give you the impression that I am the ultimate chef; far from it! The constantly changing modern world of ours keeps throwing out new and exciting challenges!

My dear ones, don't lose heart if your first attempt at cooking does not turn out perfectly as you imagined it would. Fortunately, in cooking, one learns through experience. You can always remedy whatever goes wrong on the second try, *no es verdad?* Remember, you can only improve by first committing errors. Isn't this true with most endeavors in life?

When you cook, instill your personality into the recipe. Learn your family's likes and dislikes, and if there is an ingredient in a recipe that you know your family will dislike, leave it out and substitute your own. Nine chances out of ten, the entree will be better.

When I am in my kitchen, stirring my bechamel sauce or watching zealously that the hollandaise does not curdle, I feel as if I am in a world all my own. I also feel as if the room is alive and watching. I know one thing is certain: If something goes wrong, that room will say nothing to anyone. Ah, but if all goes well, it will rejoice with me! It's a warm, fanciful feeling...

And so, my friends, I hope you enjoy these recipes. If I can be of any help to you, let me know through Seaside Publishing in St. Petersburg, Florida. I will do my best to assist you. And remember: Cook well and conscientiously. The reward arrives in the long run when you are hailed by those whom you love as the "world's greatest" – what joy! *Dios te bendigo* (God bless you)!

Tu amiga,
Clarita

INTRODUCTION

Hola Amiga,

In this book, I have attempted to compile recipes that will give you the most healthful possible way of preparing foods, without forsaking the beauty of traditional home-style cooking.

The trend in the culinary world of today is to be on guard against those "evil agents": Fat, cholesterol and sodium. However, in so doing, are we skimping on flavor and quality that is one of the great joys of life? Please read me correctly, the big three should be watched carefully, but we should not become paranoid with every morsel we consume! The answer is moderation, or in the wise words of my Mother, *todo en moderacion y nada en exceso* (all in moderation and nothing in excess).

In following her simple advice, I have been able to adjust very well to the lighter way of preparing meals, without suffering. The reduction of fat, sodium and cholesterol in a recipe is known basically as eating healthfully *pero bien*, and this can be done with most recipes in cookbooks throughout the nation, including my very own.

There are ways to preserve the good taste and quality in cooking, by depending on a good rich stock, be it chicken, beef, a combination of both, and of course, a nutritious fish fumet. My late husband's words come to mind: "A good rich stock is the soul of the kitchen."

To eliminate unwanted fat, stock should be cooked the day before or early in the morning. A variety of fresh vegetables should accompany the meat, poultry or fish. These will simmer lazily (after skimming), in a good-sized stock pot with a good tight lid, cooled, then completely chilled. The "blanket" of fat that accumulates and comes to the surface can easily be removed with a large kitchen spoon, skimmer or degreaser. Now you have defatted stock that has not lost its ability to enhance any number of soups, entrees and good hearty sauces.

Undoubtedly there will be traces of fat and cholesterol to deal with, but a definite percentage of these will be eliminated as it chills. Stock can be prepared in large quantity, then poured into various containers, frozen and used as needed. Of course, like in any important endeavor in life, it is time-consuming, but, my friends, it is well worth the effort.

I hope you enjoy these recipes in good cheer – and in parting – here's to good, healthful cooking, the Spanish way. And now, here are some wonderful appetizers and dips I'm sure you'll enjoy!

Hasta la vista!

Clarita

APPÉTIZERS

Apertivos

Aperitivos are similar to those famous "little" dishes of Spain, but they are not as hearty. I am speaking of *tapas*, the delicate hors d'oeuvres that are served to stave off hunger until the late dinner hour arrives. The most appropriate food for appetizers are chips, vegetables and dips, cheeses, anchovies and salsas. You will find a fantastic selection here, including light dips and tangy salsas to serve with cocktails before guests arrive. Friends will love these specialties, which provide something munchy, spicy or smooth, and signal the welcome beginning of a festive social event.

Appetizers also provide the added benefit of being manageably small enough to eat while one chats; they can serve as a colorful, exotic snack for finicky children; or, for those watching and counting calories, they take the edge off so one doesn't overeat during the main course. Still, appetizers are designed to only tease the palate, not satisfy it: You certainly do not want to interfere with the fabulous main dishes to come!

For a cocktail party alone, use the more substantial recipes from this chapter, such as those featuring tuna or salmon. Or, serve a nice mixture of lighter recipes, like the spinach or avocado dips, interspersed with heavier ones, like tuna and salmon recipes -- and let your guests choose which ones they prefer. Some people can eat a dozen appetizers, and still finish the entire main course without feeling the slightest pang of discomfort. So come along with me and try some of these recipes, which tantalize the palate the way a lovely little piano prelude pleases the ear. *Buen provecho!*

Recipes

Three-Cheese Spinach Dip

Cheese Stuffed Mushrooms

Watercress and Pine Nuts Dip

Avocado Salsa Dip

Chunky Delicious Salsa

Eggplant Appetizer

Artichoke Dip

Stuffed Belgian Endive Leaves

Sensational Dip

Unforgettable Tuna Canape

Tidbit Salmon Surprises with Mustard Sauce

Smoked Salmon Thumb-bits

Tidbit Salmon Surprises

Simple Salmon Molds

Salmon Mousse

Cheese Yogurt

Fresh Vegetables Vinaigrette

Vinaigrette Sauce

Three-Cheese Spinach Dip
Tres Quesos - Salseo De Espinaca

A wonderful way with spinach. A crunchy, zesty but filling dip that will satisfy your friends until dinner is ready; it is high in Vitamin A and calcium.

1/2 cup part-skim ricotta
1/2 cup low-fat cottage cheese
1/4 cup fresh grated Parmesan cheese
1 – 10 ounce package frozen spinach, thawed
1 onion, finely chopped
2 garlic cloves, pressed
2 tablespoons fresh lemon juice
Hot sauce to taste
Salt to taste
1/2 cup toasted and chopped pine nuts

Combine three cheeses in a bowl. Squeeze out excess liquid in spinach by hand; cut up and add to cheese. Add onion, garlic and lemon juice. Add hot sauce and salt *al gusto*.

Stir all ingredients, and put in the container of an electric blender or food processor; pulse about 3 seconds. Return mixture to bowl; correct seasoning. Sprinkle with pine nuts and fold into mixture. Chill. Serve with julienned raw vegetables, or low-sodium chips.

Serves: 6 to 8.

Cheese Stuffed Mushrooms
Champiñones al Queso

Make sure mushrooms are uniform in size, and free of blemishes. Choose nice, large ones rather than smaller ones, and clean them gently to remove dirt and blemishes; treat them with utmost care. They bruise easily. For an attractive appetizer, try this very satisfying recipe.

1 pound mushrooms, cleaned

Stems of mushrooms, chopped

2 tablespoons extra virgin olive oil, plus 2 tablespoons
    butter or margarine

2 tablespoons finely minced parsley

2 tablespoons finely chopped onion

2 tablespoons fresh minced basil

1/4 cup seasoned bread crumbs

1/4cup finely chopped walnuts

1/2 pound shredded Mozzarella or Swiss cheese

1 – 2 ounce jar pimientos, drained

Preheat oven to 375 degrees F.

Clean mushrooms gently; remove stems, and place mushrooms in a single layer on a flat pan or cookie sheet to drain. In a skillet, heat the oil and margarine; add stems, parsley, onion and basil, sauteing at low heat until onion is soft. Remove skillet from heat. Add bread crumbs, walnuts and cheese; stir to mix thoroughly. The heat from the sauté will soften the cheese somewhat.

Wipe a large baking pan free of moisture, and spray with olive oil; set aside. Pick up each mushroom head, and with a small spoon, fill it generously with stuffing, and set in baking pan, single layer, filled side up, of course. Bake 20 to 25 minutes, or until the cheese is melted.

Remove from the oven, sprinkle each with a little dry sherry and decorate each with a small strip of pimiento. Arrange upon a decorative round platter, then garnish with parsley or watercress bouquets.

Yield: 24.

Watercress and Pine Nuts Dip
Berros a la Mayonesa

When all the ingredients are blended, the result is a most intensely delectable and nutritious dip. Pine nuts give it crunch while the watercress and parsley provide a delicate flavor – for an outstanding dip.

1 bunch fresh watercress, chopped
1/4 cup toasted pine nuts
$1/2$ teaspoon butter
$1/2$ cup low-fat yogurt
$1/4$ cup low-fat mayonnaise
1 onion, finely minced
3 garlic cloves, minced
Juice of half a lemon
$1/4$ cup chopped parsley
1 teaspoon extra virgin olive oil
1 teaspoon rice vinegar
Louisiana hot sauce to taste
Dash of salt
1 tablespoon small capers

Carefully wash watercress and chop. Saute nuts in butter for a few minutes, until soft and set aside. In the container of an electric blender or food processor, put yogurt, mayonnaise, onion, garlic, lemon juice, parsley, watercress, olive oil, vinegar, hot sauce and salt; blend for 5 seconds, or until desired consistency is reached. Pour into a pretty bowl; correct seasoning. Fold in capers and pine nuts. Mix well and refrigerate for an hour. Serve with julienned raw vegetables or unsalted chips.
Serves: 6 to 8.

Avocado Salsa Dip
Salsa De Aguacate

A "must" for your dinner guests. Serve this dip with a good brand of saltless chips, or better still, julienned, crisp vegetables. Offer quality Spanish sherry, such as Manzanilla, Amontillado or Tio Pepe to complement the dip.

2 avocados, peeled and seeded
3 plum tomatoes, peeled, seeded and finely chopped
2 garlic cloves, pressed
1/2 cup finely minced onion
1 red bell pepper, pith and seeds removed, finely minced
2 tablespoons extra virgin olive oil
1/4 teaspoon cumin
2 tablespoons fresh minced oregano
3 ounces of feta cheese, crumbled
Juice of half a lemon
2 tablespoons rice or balsamic vinegar
Hot sauce to taste
1 teaspoon low-sodium soy sauce
1/2 cup low-fat sour cream

Prepare avocados; cut into a bowl, in chunks; add tomatoes. Add garlic, onion, pepper, olive oil, cumin and oregano, in order listed; toss to mix well.Sprinkle crumbled cheese over all, but do not mix yet. In a separate bowl, combine lemon juice, vinegar, hot sauce and soy sauce. Whisk to mix thoroughly. Pour over the avocado mix. Fold in sour cream and with 2 forks, mix lightly but well. Chill an hour or so, then remove from refrigerator. Let stand at room temperature for 30 minutes. Serve surrounded by crisp vegetables or plantain chips.
Serves: 4 to 6.

Chunky Delicious Salsa
Salsa Sabrosa

A salsa can be used in a variety of recipes -- it can helps chips or vegetables, enhance broiled fillet of fish, or even decorate a steak. Try it as a filling for a French omelette. Serve with unsalted or salted chips, whichever you prefer.

1½ pounds plum tomatoes, peeled, seeded and chopped
2 tablespoons fresh minced basil
2 tablespoons fresh minced oregano
2 tablespoons minced cilantro
2 garlic cloves, peeled and pressed
1 onion, minced
2 tablespoons minced green bell pepper
2 tablespoons minced red bell pepper
2 tablespoons chopped inner rib celery
1 hot chili pepper, finely minced
2 tablespoons rice vinegar
1 teaspoon small capers
½ teaspoon salt

In a deep mixing bowl, place coarsely chopped tomatoes; sprinkle with basil, oregano and cilantro. Force garlic through garlic press into bowl; add onion and remaining ingredients. Stir to mix well. Pour into an attractive chip-and-dip bowl, and serve *con gusto*. This salsa may be prepared ahead of time since it can marinate two or three hours in the refrigerator.
Serves: 6 to 8.

Eggplant Appetizer

Berenjena, Estilo Venecia Caponata

Caponata is probably the most popular of Italian appetizers. It is a mixture of eggplant, tomatoes, olives and savory herbs and spices. Prepare the day before you plan to serve it, so herbs have time to blend with other ingredients.

2 eggplants, peeled and cubed
3 tablespoons extra virgin olive oil
1 onion, finely chopped
3 garlic cloves, pressed
1 cup thinly sliced celery
3 cups ripe peeled and seeded plum tomatoes
3 tablespoons tomato sauce
1/4 cup (about 8), pimiento-stuffed olives
2 tablespoons small capers
1/4 cup fresh minced basil
2 tablespoons fresh minced oregano
2 tablespoons balsamic or rice vinegar
1 teaspoon butter or margarine
Louisiana hot sauce to taste
Dash of salt
1/2 cup toasted pine nuts
1/2 cup grated Parmesan cheese
2-ounce can imported anchovy fillets, drained and minced

Place eggplant cubes in a colander and sprinkle with salt. Cover and allow to "bleed" for 30 minutes. Meanwhile, heat 1 tablespoon olive oil in a large skillet. Add onion, garlic and celery; sauté until onion is soft. Add tomatoes and tomato sauce; cook until tomatoes are bubbly, about 10 minutes. Add olives, capers, basil, oregano and vinegar; stir to mix well. Cover and cook at low heat.

Toast pine nuts by sauteing in a teaspoon of butter. Now rinse eggplant thoroughly. In a separate skillet, heat remaining oil. Add eggplant and cook at moderately high heat until tender. Add to onion mixture, and mix all ingredients well, mashing as you stir. Add hot sauce and salt *al gusto*, and cook until all vegetables are done – about 15 or 20 minutes. Scatter pine nuts over all, and add cheese. Stir and mix well, cook about 2 more minutes. Add salt and hot sauce to taste, and cook another 2 minutes. Cool and refrigerate. May be served on toasted baguette rounds as an appetizer,or as a dip with unsalted chips. If you like anchovies, add some, well-drained and finely minced, an hour or so before serving. Anchovies are high in sodium, so take care!

Serves: 6 to 8.

Artichoke Dip
Aderezo De Alcachofa

Serve this dip, which is zesty and healthful too, to family and friends. If you don't tell, they'll never know it's heart-healthy – full of vitamins and calcium.

14-ounce can artichoke hearts, drained and finely chopped
1/2 cup pimiento-stuffed olives, finely chopped
2 tablespoons finely chopped onion
1/4 cup parsley, very finely chopped
2 garlic cloves, pressed
1/4 cups crumbled feta cheese
1/2 cup low-fat mayonnaise
1/2 cup plain low-fat yogurt
Dash of Louisiana hot sauce, or a chili pepper, finely minced
Dash of salt
2 tablespoons dry sherry

Put artichokes into a medium-sized bowl; add olives, onion, parsley, garlic and cheese in the order given. In another bowl, combine mayonnaise, yogurt, hot sauce or chili pepper, salt and dry sherry; stir until well-blended, and pour over artichoke mixture; mix well and serve with your favorite chips.

Serves: 6 to 8.

Stuffed Belgian Endive Leaves
Ojitas Rellenas

Belgian endive is an unusual vegetable that looks a little like a closed tulip. Yet the taste is most refined; I love the slightly bitter taste of the leaves, cut into green salad or stuffed. A number of mixtures can be used as stuffing; it produces a crisp, succulent and elegante dish.

3 Belgian endive tulips
1/2 cup reduced-fat cream cheese, room temperature
1/2 cup non-fat yogurt
3 tablespoons finely chopped onion
1 tablespoon olive oil
1 garlic clove, pressed
6 1/2 ounce can albacore tuna, packed in water
1 teaspoon fresh lemon juice
Dash of hot sauce
Pinch of salt
1 tablespoon fresh, finely chopped dill or parsley
Pimiento strips, sprigs of watercress or canned beets for garnish

You will need about three Belgian endive "tulips" to obtain 10 to 12 uniform leaves. Separate leaves carefully, and use only uniform lengths. Carefully wash and pat dry, and set aside. Save the rest to cut up in salads.

Cream the cheese with the yogurt until smooth and nicely-blended; pour into a mixing bowl. Add onion, olive oil and garlic; mix well. Drain tuna thoroughly, put in another bowl, and flake finely. Sprinkle with lemon juice, hot sauce and salt. Add dill or parsley, or both; stir to mix.

Add to the cream cheese mixture; stir to mix well. With a teaspoon, stuff endive leaves at the base with the tuna mixture.

Cut pimiento into strips, and arrange over stuffing. On a round platter, carefully set the leaves artistically, cartwheel fashion. In arranging endive on platter, leave space in the center and fill with crispy watercress sprigs; drain and dry slices of beets, and arrange between the leaves. Serve with *gusto*.

Serves: 4.

Sensational Dip
Un Queso Sensacionál

This is an exceptionally delicious dip. Served with julienned raw vegetables or low-salt chips, you will savor the flavor dill, basil and olives impart. Allow time for yogurt to drain overnight, however: You want to eliminate most of the liquid whey, or it might spoil what you're trying to create in salad dressings and sauces - That smooth consistency that mimics rich sour cream – without all the calories.

1 cup plain, low-fat yogurt
1½ – 8 ounce packages reduced-fat cream cheese,
    at room temperature
2 tablespoons skim milk
1 cup low-fat mayonnaise
1 tablespoon extra virgin olive oil
2 tablespoons finely chopped onion
1 tablespoon fresh minced dillweed
2 tablespoons fresh minced basil
½ cup minced pimiento-stuffed olives
¼ cup fresh finely minced parsley
2 garlic cloves, pressed
1 teaspoon light soy sauce
Hot sauce
Dash of salt

Drain yogurt of as much of whey as possible. To do this, line a colander with a triple layer of cheesecloth; pour in the yogurt and allow to drain overnight over a bowl.*

Next day: Place cream cheese and milk in a blender container and blend until smooth; pour into a mixing bowl. Add drained yogurt and mix thoroughly and well. Add the rest of the ingredients in order given; stir to blend well.

Correct seasoning. Transfer to a pretty bowl and serve as a prize-winning dip.

Yield: 6 to 8 servings.

*For more information about draining yogurt, see Page 322.

Unforgettable Tuna Canapé
Aperitivas De Tuna Inolvidable

Use this mixture either for appetizers, or double and use as a tuna salad for a bridge luncheon...it's flavorful, festive, filling and thrilling!

1 tablespoon finely chopped dark raisins

2 tablespoons light Bacardi rum

6½ ounce can albacore tuna, packed in water

1 inner stalk of celery, finely chopped

1 tablespoon minced Spanish onion

¼ cup finely chopped water chestnuts

2 tablespoons extra virgin olive oil

1 tablespoon rice vinegar

3 tablespoons low-fat mayonnaise

2 tablespoons low-fat plain yogurt

2 tablespoons finely chopped fresh parsley

Dash of hot sauce

Dash of salt

Roll of party rye bread rounds

Garnish with lettuce, sprigs of dillweed, basil or parsley

½ cup chopped walnuts

Soak raisins in rum for an hour. Preheat oven to 300 degrees F. Drain tuna well, flake and place in a large mixing bowl. Add celery, onion, water chestnuts, olive oil and vinegar, plus the soaked raisins, rum and all; toss to mix well. In another bowl, combine mayonnaise, yogurt, parsley, hot sauce and salt; mix well and pour over tuna. Toss thoroughly with two forks.

For canapés, use a round-shaped roll of party rye breads. Brush each round with melted margarine or butter. Place in single layer on a cookie sheet.

Toast in oven 4 to 5 minutes on each side. Allow to cool, then spread each round with a teaspoon of the tuna mixture. Place canapés upon a pretty platter, attractively garnished with fresh herbs, such as dillweed, basil and parsley sprigs.

For a luncheon salad, double the tuna, celery, mayonnaise and yogurt. Line six plates with crisp Boston bibb or romaine lettuce, and divide the tuna among the plates. Garnish lavishly with sliced beets, dried with paper towels, cornichon pickles, thin slices of pickled cucumbers. To top it off, sprinkle chopped walnuts over each salad.

Serves: 4 to 6.

Tidbit Salmon Surprises with Mustard Sauce

Sorpresas De Salmon Con Salsa De Mostaza

These bolitas are one of the most unusually delicious surprises you will evertaste. Bake or fry for a colorful start to any party, fancy or casual.

7¹/₂ ounce can red salmon

1 egg

1 teaspoon chopped onions

¹/₂ teaspoon pressed garlic

3 tablespoons toasted almonds

3 tablespoons seasoned bread crumbs

2 tablespoons minced fresh onion

¹/₂ teaspoon fresh lemon or lime juice

¹/₂ teaspoon light soy sauce

2 tablespoons low-fat mayonnaise

Olive oil spray

Preheat oven to 325 degrees F.

Drain salmon, and by hand pick out skin and bones, then discard them. Flake salmon into a mixing bowl. Beat in egg, then add the next 9 ingredients in order given, ending with mayonnaise. Mix well and thoroughly. Spray a cookie sheet with olive oil.

(continued...)

Take heaping teaspoons of the mixture and roll it in your hands until a small salmon ball is formed; drop on cookie sheet in a single layer. Bake until golden, 20 to 25 minutes. Serve hot or cold, with mustard sauce.

Mustard Sauce
Salsa De Mostaza

2 teaspoons Dijon mustard

1/4 teaspoon curry

1/2 teaspoon light soy sauce

1/2 cup low-fat mayonnaise

1/2 cup low-fat yogurt

1 teaspoon fresh lemon juice

1 teaspoon fresh, finely chopped dillweed

Pinch of salt

Mix all ingredients in order given. Beat well, cover and refrigerate for at least 2 hours before using.

Yield: 20.

Smoked Salmon Thumb-bits
Salmon en Tostadas

Thinly sliced smoked salmon makes a luscious appetizer and lends class to any table. For this recipe, you'll need two loaves of French bread, long "baguettes," cut into half inch thick slices and toasted to a golden goodness.

8 thinly cut slices smoked salmon

1 tablespoon extra virgin olive oil

1 tablespoon fresh lemon or lime juice

1/2 cup low-fat mayonnaise

1/2 cup reduced-fat cream cheese

2 loaves of French "baguette" bread, sliced into 1/2 inch rounds

A light spread of margarine or butter
16-ounce jar of hamburger dill pickles

Preheat oven to 300 degrees F. Place salmon slices in a dish. Combine olive oil and lemon juice; pour over the fish and set aside.

Cream the mayonnaise and cheese by hand until smooth; set aside also. Slice the French bread. Tease each round with a brush of butter or margarine.

Place rounds in single layer upon a cookie sheet, and bake 10 minutes, until golden and toasted. Remove from oven and cool completely. In the meantime, the salmon-and mayonnaise-mixture is deliciously marinating.

To assemble: Cut salmon to fit each bread round. Spread each round with the mayonnaise mixture. Place salmon over each round. Arrange these thumb-bits in an attractive platter. Sprinkle all with parsley and top with a crisp dill pickle chip.

Yield: 25 to 30.

Simple Salmon Molds
Moldes de Salmon

Excelente for a lady's luncheon. Not only do they make a beauteous presentation, but they taste delightful too!

1 pound poached pink salmon

1/2 cup low-fat mayonnaise

1/4 cup plain low-fat yogurt, drained of most of whey*

2 tablespoons dry vermouth

1/4 cup minced onion

1 inner celery rib, minced

1/4 cup, 6 to 8, minced Spanish olives

1 1/4 teaspoon Dijon mustard

1 – 1/2 ounce jar minced pimientos

1 tablespoon lemon juice

1 tablespoon small capers, well-drained

1 tablespoon finely minced dill pickle

(continued...)

*For more information about draining yogurt, see Page 322.

Wedges of hard-cooked eggs and cherry tomatoes for garnish
2 tablespoons fresh, finely minced dillweed

Into a deep bowl, finely flake salmon; set bowl aside. Prepare 6 or 8 custard molds by coating with vegetable spray. In a mixing bowl, combine mayonnaise, yogurt and next 9 ingredients in order listed, ending with dill pickle. Mix thoroughly. Add to salmon bowl. With 2 forks, incorporate ingredients with the flaked fish. Stir until well-blended.

Pack prepared molds; cover each with plastic wrap. Place in a shallow dish for refrigeration. Chill several hours. Unmold into individual platters lined with bibb lettuce. Bank salmon molds with wedges of hard-cooked eggs and cherry tomatoes for color. Sprinkle fresh minced dillweed over all.

Serves: 6 to 8, depending on the size of the molds.

Salmon Mousse
Salmon Terrine

Salmon, no matter how it is prepared, has so much dignity – no es verdad? Prepare this recipe for a special occasion. On a buffet table, it is oh, so very elegant.

1 – 16 ounce can and 1 – 10 ounce can pink salmon
2 tablespoons butter or extra virgin olive oil
¼ cup finely minced onion
¼ cup finely chopped red bell pepper
¼ cup stringed, finely chopped celery
1 egg, well-beaten
2 tablespoons fresh minced parsley
1 teaspoon Dijon mustard
¾ cup low-fat mayonnaise

½ cup plain low-fat yogurt

¼ cup defatted, low-sodium chicken stock

2 tablespoons very dry sherry

1 tablespoon fresh lemon juice

1 envelope unflavored gelatin

1 teaspoon Louisiana hot sauce

Dash of salt

1 egg white, beaten to meringue consistency

¼ cup toasted, finely chopped walnuts

¼ cup ripe olives, cut in the shape of truffles

1 whole orange, peeled and cut into rings

Watercress or parsley bouquets

Drain salmon, then skin and debone. Flake into a large mixing bowl. In a small skillet, heat butter or oil. Add onion, bell pepper and celery. Sauté until translucent, 2 to 3 minutes. Pour this over salmon. Add beaten egg and parsley.

Combine mustard, ¼ cup of the mayonnaise and ¼ cup of the yogurt. (When using yogurt in a recipe, I usually place it in a colander and drain some of the whey – but not all – unless you wish to make a most delicious yogurt cheese. In that case, the recipe follows); mix well and pour into salmon bowl. With 2 forks, toss ingredients until well-blended.

In a saucepan, heat chicken broth. Add sherry (I recommend Tio Pepe), lemon juice, and the gelatin. Cook at low heat until gelatin is completely dissolved. Add hot sauce; mix well. Cool. Add to salmon and stir lightly until ingredients are in complete harmony.

Put in the container of an electric blender or food processor, and in 2 batches, puree salmon mixture about 5 seconds per batch, or until thick and smooth, but still with character. Pour into original mixing bowl. Fold in the meringue until the white disappears (do not beat). Sprinkle with nuts, and gently fold them into mixture.

Spray with olive oil a 6½ cup copper fish mold; fit wax paper in bottom of mold and spray also. Pour mixture lightly into mold, fill to the top of the pan. Cover with plastic wrap or foil. Refrigerate until firm, about 3 hours or overnight.

(continued...)

To unmold, dip mold in hot water for a few seconds. Run a knife around edge of pan to loosen mousse. Drop onto a pretty, shallow serving platter. Carefully peel off wax paper. Combine remaining mayonnaise and yogurt.

Season to taste. Ice the mousse with this mixture. (This is called "poor man's truffles"). Place "truffles" artistically over icing. Cut orange rings in half; bank the salmon with them. Place bouquets of parsley or watercress a capricho, here and there. Pimiento strips will add color to the salmon mousse. You may have garnishing ideas of your own, so...*adelante!*

Serves: 6 to 8.

Cheese Yogurt
Queso de Yogurt

1 16-ounce container of plain, non-fat yogurt

First, read the label on the yogurt package. If the yogurt contains thickeners, such as vegetable gum or gelatin, do not use, as these interfere with the release of the whey. (It takes $2^1/_2$ cups plain yogurt to produce 1 cup of cheese).

Line a colander with two layers of cheesecloth. Spoon yogurt into the cheesecloth. Cover and place over a utensil to catch drippings. Let it drain 6 to 8 hours, or overnight. Turn over the yogurt after a few hours. The cheese should have the consistency of creamy cottage cheese when it has drained to the consistency that you want. Turn it into a bowl with cover and refrigerate. There are any number of ingredients that can be added to the cheese to make it ever so flavorful.

Yields: $^3/_4$ cup of cheese.

Fresh Vegetables Vinaigrette
Vegetales a la Vinagretta

Vegetables, when steamed just slightly (al dente) and then satu-rated with vinaigrette are an easy to prepare appetizer or salad for the busy host or hostess. Prepare ahead for your part. Let the marinade do its magic while you read the latest fashion or sports magazine!

2 cups broccoli flowerettes
2 cups cauliflower flowerettes
1 cup fresh sliced mushrooms
1 cup baby carrots, scraped and thinly sliced
1 red bell pepper, julienned
1 green bell pepper, julienned
½ cup pimiento-stuffed manzanilla olives, halved
½ cup pitted black olives, halved
19-ounce can garbanzo beans, drained
1 onion, sliced in rings

For the marinade
El adobo

2 tablespoons olive oil
2 garlic cloves, pressed
2 tablespoons rice vinegar
Juice of half a lemon
2 tablespoons dry sherry
1 teaspoon Dijon mustard
1 tablespoon fresh grated Parmesan cheese
¼ cup finely minced onion
¼ cup fresh minced parsley
2 tablespoons small capers
1 tablespoon fresh, finely minced dillweed
Salt and pepper

(continued…)

To prepare vegetables:

Put a couple of cups of water in a large steamer, and bring to a boil. Place broccoli, cauliflower, mushrooms and carrots in it, and steam scarcely 5 minutes; remove from heat and plunge vegetables under cold running water. Drain well. In a large wide bowl, put steamed vegetables. Add peppers, olives, beans and onion, and toss gently to mix; cover and refrigerate.

When serving time is near, prepare vinaigrette: Mix olive oil, garlic, vinegar, lemon, sherry, mustard cheese and onion; pour into a screw-top jar. Put the lid on tightly, and shake vigorously to form an emulsion. Now add parsley, capers and dillweed. Add a little salt, and shake gently.

Remove bowl from refrigerator and coat vegetables with vinaigrette. Cover and refrigerate until chilled, turning occasionally until ready to serve. To serve, line an inch-deep platter with lettuce, and spoon the vegetables over the lettuce.

Serves: 4 to 6.

Vinaigrette Sauce
Salsa Vinagretta

This tasty vinaigrette will glamorize any entree. It's ideal for marinating fish before baking to golden goodness. Over chicken, it's also a blue ribbon winner.

1/2 cup extra virgin olive oil
Juice of one lemon or lime
3 tablespoons rice vinegar
1 onion, finely chopped
2 garlic cloves, pressed
2 tablespoons fresh minced basil, or 1 tablespoon dried
2 tablespoons fresh minced oregano, or 1 tablespoon dried
1/2 teaspoon crushed tarragon
1 teaspoon Dijon mustard
1/4 cup grated Parmesan cheese
2 tablespoons finely minced parsley
Dash of salt
Dash of hot sauce

Put all ingredients in a mixing bowl, and whisk until well-blended; pour into a screw-top jar, cover tightly, and shake gently. Refrigerate at least 2 hours, but remove at least an hour before serving so it can return to room temperature.
Yield: About 1 cup.

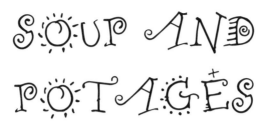

SOUP AND POTAGES

Sopas y Potajes

The recipes in this chapter are designed to use a minimal amount of vegetable oil and animal fat. Instead of plain water, I always use rich stock, thoroughly defatted, which produces low-fat goodness without sacrificing quality and excellent taste.

Soup, you will agree, is a wonderful beginning for any meal. Many times, if the soup is hearty enough, it does not take much more to complete a satisfying lunch or supper.

I use fresh seasonal vegetables in cooking. However, frozen vegetables, packed in plastic bags, are exceptionally good, and, of course, save time in the kitchen – so precious to the working person. So, do not hesitate to use the frozen variety (especially greens); *Pero*, whenever possible, *vegetales frescos por favor*, okay?

Also in this chapter is a selection of my favorite cream soups, usually prepared with rich, thick creams and butter: If you can tolerate the fat and cholesterol, you may prefer richer ingredients; however, since I cannot – or should not – indulge, I have devised an alternative I truly believe will win you over. I hope you enjoy the recipes as much as I have.

Recipes

Erica's Tropical Fruit Gazpacho

Clarita's Chicken Soup

Garlic Soup

Cabbage and Cannellini Bean Soup

Black Bean Soup

Spanish Bean Soup Number One

Spanish Bean Soup Number Two

Famous Bean Soup of Segovia

Pasta Lentil-Vegetable Soup

Mom's Magic Lentil Vegetable Soup

Fish Chowder with Corn

Clarita's Gumbo

Portuguese Fish Medley Soup

Split Pea Soup

Vegetable Soup with Vermicelli

Best Cream of Broccoli Soup

Cream of Celery and Carrots Soup

Cream of Mushroom Soup

The Original Vichysoisse

An Affordable Vichysoisse

Spanish Salad Soup

Collard Greens Soup

Vegetarian Potaje of String Beans

Pebbles Tomato Soup

Erica's Tropical Fruit Gazpacho

Erica, a very talented and gracious young chef at Manuel's On the 28th, one of our restaurants in Orlando shared this delightful gazpacho with me. Erica's aim as an accomplished and respected chef is to be creative – and that she is! This cooling soup is featured at the restaurant during the hot summer Florida months.

The menu at Manuel's is resplendent with innovations such as this. So you see, mi amiga, it is no wonder why the restaurant has received the Golden Spoon Award and is listed among the top ten best restaurants in our country – and maybe in the world!

Gazpacho

3 ripe papayas, peeled and diced

2 ripe mangoes, peeled and diced

1 pineapple, peeled, cleaned and diced

2 cups cold water

1/4 cup cottonseed oil

1/4 cup rice wine vinegar

1 tablespoon extra virgin olive oil

3 tablespoons chopped cilantro

2 tablespoons chopped chives

2 tablespoons diced red onions

Chipolte Creme Fraiche

1 chipolte pepper,* seeded and diced

1 cup creme fraiche**

1 tablespoon fresh lime juice

*available at most gourmet shops

**available at most gourmet shops, or you may prepare your own

(continued...)

Combine papayas, mangoes, pineapple, water, cottonseed oil, vinegar and olive oil in a food processor. Pulse for about a minute, or until the fruit has become a pureé with fruit chunks the size of a corn kernel. Then add cilantro, chives, and red onions. Replace the lid and pulse for approximately 5 seconds, just enough to blend the last ingredients into the first. Place in a container and chill for approximately 1 hour.

Whisk together the diced chipolte, creme fraiche, and lime juice in a bowl. Garnish the Gazpacho with this mixture, a few red raspberries and a sprig of fresh cilantro.

Clarita's Chicken Soup
Sopa de Pollo "Clarita"

This is a hearty chicken soup, and its most important ingredient is the rich chicken broth that is its heart and soul. Caldo De Pollo is a Spanish favorite. Fresh herbs add a magical flavor, but if you can not get cilantro or do not like it, substitute fresh basil instead. Avoid dried herbs in this dish – they do not produce the same effect.

1½ pounds chicken breast halves
1½ pounds chicken thighs
2 carrots, scraped and cut in halves
2 celery ribs plus leaves, snapped in halves
1 onion
1 bell pepper, cored and seeded
2 bay leaves, crushed
1 garlic clove, unpeeled and crushed
1 teaspoon saffron threads
Salt
¼ pound vermicelli
¼ cup fresh, finely chopped basil or cilantro
¼ cup grated Swiss cheese

*For more information about saffron, see Page 322.

Place chicken in a medium-sized Dutch oven with cover. Add carrots, celery, onion, pepper, bay leaves and garlic. Pour water into pot until it covers ingredients by 2 inches. Bring to a quick boil, and skim thoroughly for about 10 minutes. Lower heat. Add crushed saffron* threads, and stir well. Correct seasoning, cover and cook at moderate heat about 30 minutes. Remove pot from burner to cool. With a slotted spoon, remove chicken parts and carrots to separate bowls.

Skin and bone chicken, removing all visible fat. Cube meat; slice carrots thinly. Cover and refrigerate both bowls. Strain broth into a refrigerator bowl with cover, and discard remaining vegetables. Cover broth and refrigerate 3 or 4 hours, or overnight.

Remove bowls from refrigerator; allow to sit at room temperature 15 minutes. Remove all fat that has surfaced. Pour defatted broth into a 4- or 5-quart soup pot with cover. Bring to a boil. Snap vermicelli in half and add to broth. Lower heat, cover and cook at least 15 minutes. Now, add 2 cups of the cubed chicken, saving any leftovers for later use. Stir in sliced carrots. Cover and cook another10 minutes, stirring and correcting seasoning again.

Sprinkle basil or cilantro over hot soup, followed by cheese. Stir gently. Cover and simmer at low heat 2 minutes before serving.

Serves: 4 to 6.

This is a hearty chicken soup, and its most important ingredient is the rich chicken broth that is its heart and soul.

Garlic Soup
Sopa De Ajo

We all know how beneficial garlic is for our health and we're not just talking about those pills they promote on the electronic media. This recipe uses the one-of-a-kind taste of garlic to its best advantage. If it seems as if it will be too strong for your taste, experiment the first time with a little less garlic, then each time you cook it, you may want to gradually add more until you reach the full amount I recommend in the ingredient list. But keep in mind, garlic loses some of its strength during the process of sautéing, and adds a uniquely pleasant taste to the sopa.

1 loaf day-old French bread, crust removed

2 tablespoons extra virgin olive oil

1 head of garlic, 10 to 15 cloves, peeled and finely minced

¼ cup fresh minced parsley

2 plum tomatoes, peeled, seeded and chopped

½ cup chopped bell pepper

½ cup chopped onion

1 teaspoon Spanish paprika

5 cups defatted, low-sodium chicken broth*

2 tablespoons dry sherry

Salt to taste

Hot sauce to taste

½ cup plain, low-fat yogurt

*For instructions on how to make broth, see Page 318.

Slice bread thinly, then cube. Heat oil in a soup kettle with cover, add cubed bread and sauté slowly, at low heat, until golden. Add garlic to bread in kettle. Add parsley, tomatoes, pepper and onion. Sauté at low heat, stirring to insure garlic does not burn. When onion is transparent, add paprika, and sauté another minute.

Add broth and sherry. Bring to a boil, and add salt and hot sauce to taste. Lower heat and cover; cook 30 minutes. Remove from heat and cool. In electric blender or food processor, blend in batches until nice and smooth. To the last batch, add yogurt.

Return to soup kettle to reheat, but do not boil.

Serves: 4 to 6.

Cabbage and Cannellini Bean Soup
Sopa De Coles y Judias

If you like cabbage, and I hope you do because it's so good for you, you will love this combination. Cannelli beans and cabbage are amicable partners; try it and see – dinner is ready in less than an hour!

2 tablespoons extra virgin olive oil
2 finely chopped onions
1 finely chopped green bell pepper
3 garlic cloves, minced
$1/2$ cup lean diced ham
2 thinly sliced carrots
2 bay leaves, crushed
2 tablespoons fresh minced basil
$1^1/_2$ pounds white cabbage
5 red potatoes, scraped and cubed
4 cups defatted, low-sodium chicken broth*
2 tablespoons finely chopped fresh parsley
Juice of half a lemon
2 – 19 ounce cans cannellini beans

*For instructions on how to make broth, see Page 318.

In a 4-quart Dutch oven or soup kettle, heat oil. Sauté onion, pepper and garlic until onion is transparent. Add ham, then carrots, bay leaves and basil. Mix well and cover. Sauté at low heat 2 or 3 minutes.

(continued...)

Cut cabbage in half, and remove core; shred, and add to soup pot. Press to mix with ingredients. Add potatoes and broth. Don't worry about an overpacked pot: The cabbage will cook down. Add parsley and lemon juice.

Cover pot and cook about 30 minutes, until potatoes are soft, but still firm. Add beans; stir thoroughly. Cook another 15 minutes. Serve hot.

Serves: 6 to 8.

Black Bean Soup
Frijoles Negros

Black beans demand quite a bit of olive oil during cooking; most beans do. In this recipe, I have drastically reduced the oil, and increased herbs and spices. The result is amazingly delicious. Allow time to soak beans overnight.

3 – 12 ounce packages black beans

3 tablespoons extra virgin olive oil

2 finely chopped onions

1 finely chopped green bell pepper

5 garlic cloves, minced

3 bay leaves, crushed

1/2 cup fresh minced oregano, firmly packed

1 teaspoon cumin

2 tablespoons minced cilantro

2 whole ripe tomatoes

1/4 cup minced fresh parsley

1/4 cup wine vinegar

1 tablespoon Louisiana hot sauce, or to taste

1 tablespoon salt

Remove any dirt or foreign particles, and wash beans thoroughly in a colander. Transfer beans to a large 4- or 5-quart soup kettle, with a lid; use only a wooden spoon to stir beans. Add water until beans are covered by 2 inches. Cover pot, and soak overnight.

The next day, do not drain beans; they will have absorbed most of the water. Simply add more water again until they are covered by 2 inches. Bring beans to a boil; A grayish foam will surface. Lower heat, and skim with skimmer or large spoon until no more foam rises.

In a large skillet, heat olive oil. Add onions and peppers, and sauté until onion is soft. Add garlic, bay leaves, oregano, cumin and cilantro. Sauté 3 minutes, stirring continually. Pour into bean pot. Add tomatoes and parsley, and bring to a boil again. Cover, lower heat and cook until beans are soft, but still firm. (It could take as long as 2 hours.) Add more water, sparingly. Stir beans at intervals to prevent sticking.

Remove what's left of tomatoes. Add vinegar, hot sauce and salt. Stir gently so as not to bruise the beans. Cover and cook another 30 minutes, or until beans are "butter-soft." Allow to rest at least one hour. Serve over steamed long-grain rice with chopped onions. A chopped dill pickle goes well with the beans. *Frijoles* freeze well; in fact, they are even tastier once they are frozen.
Serves: 12 to 15.

Spanish Bean Soup Number One
Potaje De Garbanzos Numero Uno

This soup is so popular in the Spanish kitchen, but it requires an excellent stock and the traditional chorizo, or Spanish sausage, which adds a sharp note to many Spanish recipes. In preparing this version of the famous soup, I have eliminated a good portion of the fat by using the chilling process as explained in the introduction of the book. Just follow the recipe closely, and enjoy the spectacular outcome. Beans must soak overnight, so start ahead.

1 – 1 pound package dried garbanzo beans (chick peas)
1 ham bone, all visible fat removed
1 large ham hock
2 pounds beef ribs, trimmed of all visible fat,
    or 2 pounds lean London broil
2 chorizos, degreased*
2 celery ribs with leaves
½ onion
½ bell pepper
1 ripe tomato
1 garlic clove, crushed
1 teaspoon salt
Defatted, low-sodium beef stock
1 teaspoon saffron threads, toasted**
5 boiling potatoes, cubed
5 carrots, scraped and cut in three
2 bay leaves
Sprig of Italian parsley
2 garlic cloves, unpeeled and crushed

*For instructions on how to degrease chorizos, see Page 318.
**For instruction how to toast saffron, see Page 322.

Remove any dirt or foreign particles from garbanzos and wash thoroughly in a colander. Place in a large, deep bowl and add salted water until it covers beans by 3 inches. (They expand like crazy!) Set aside and soak overnight.

Remove all visible fat from ham, ham hock, ribs or London broil, and chorizos, and place in a large pot with lid together with celery, onion, pepper, tomato and garlic. Add salt. Add water until it covers ingredients by 2 inches. Bring to a quick boil. Then lower to moderate heat. Skim several times, but do not cover with lid until stock is thoroughly skimmed.

Cover pot and cook until meat is tender, about one hour. (Don't forget to pierce the chorizos because a lot of the fat contained in the sausage will be eliminated in the cooking process. Cool slightly, then strain stock into a large refrigerator container with cover.

Remove meat to another bowl with cover. Discard vegetables and bones. Remove all visible fat from the meat and cube. Thinly slice chorizo. Add to bowl, cover and refrigerate together with the stock.

The next day, remove stock from refrigerator. Uncover, and you will see on its surface a thick blanket of unwanted fat; with a skimmer or degreaser, remove fat completely. Pour defatted stock into a soup kettle. Bring to a boil. Add garbanzos, cover and place the saffron, packaged in a little brown paper square, on the lid to toast. Cook beans an hour or so, or until tender but still firm. Now add the potatoes, carrots, bay leaves, parsley and garlic, plus the saffron. Bring to a boil, then lower heat, cover and cook 25 to 30 minutes, or until vegetables are cooked and beans are tender.

Remove meat from refrigerator, add to soup, and heat thoroughly. Serve hot. When I cook Spanish bean soup, I usually include a 2-pound London broil together with the beef ribs. This fortifies and enriches the stock, and I have shredded beef for Ropa Vieja another day. So there you have it...the taste is there, but much of the fat is not.

Serves: 6 to 8.

Spanish Bean Soup Number Two
Sopa De Garbanzo, Numero Dos

What can I say about this soup? Full of nutrients and muy sabroso. This soup is without a doubt an excellent introduction to the world of vegetables. I remember, as a child, my aversion to certain vegetables, specifically spinach! Mother circumvented this by cooking four or five vegetables, spinach included, in a soup kettle with a little of this and a little of that. The result...unbelievably tasty!

Here, then, is one of her unforgettable concoctions, one that inspires for me nostalgic memories.

½ pound lean ground top round

2 tablespoons extra virgin olive oil

1 onion, minced

2 or 3 garlic cloves, pressed

2 ripe tomatoes, peeled, seeded and chopped

2 bay leaves, crushed

2 tablespoons fresh minced thyme

2 tablespoons fresh minced basil

Pinch of saffron, toasted*

4 cups hot defatted, low-sodium beef broth

2 potatoes, peeled and cubed

3 carrots, scraped and sliced

2 zucchini, scraped and thinly sliced

Salt

Hot sauce to taste

12 cups fresh spinach leaves, washed and dried

1 tablespoon rice vinegar

2 – 19 ounce cans garbanzo beans (chick peas)

*For instructions how to toast saffron, see Page 322.

Ask for very lean meat at the market, then have the meat specially ground, once only. In a soup kettle with cover, brown meat until red disappears; drain. Add olive oil, along with onion, garlic, tomatoes, bay leaves, thyme and basil. Stir and gently sauté until onion softens.

Add saffron to hot beef broth. Mix well and pour over ingredients in kettle. Add potatoes, carrots and zucchini. Bring to a boil, cover, lower heat and cook until vegetables are partly cooked, about 25 minutes. Check seasonings; add salt and hot sauce. Add spinach, vinegar and garbanzo beans. Again, bring to a boil, cover and cook at medium heat, 20 to 25 minutes. You may need more stock. If so, a can of defatted chicken or beef stock will do just fine. However, if you have frozen stock, thaw and use it.

Serves: 6 to 8.

Famous Bean Soup of Segovia
La Famosa Fabade Segoviana

High upon the slopes of La Sierra de Guadarrama nestles the quaint and historic town of Segovia, an hour's drive from Madrid. Besides its impressive aqueduct built by Romans 2,000 years ago, there was another attraction that drew a staggering number of tourists every year.

El Meson de Candido was a restaurant to remember. Its colorful owner, the late Candido, had mastered the art of cooking with so much pride. To meet him in itself was a treat; he had a reputation as the greatest innkeeper in Castillo. Upon greeting his guests, he wore a broad, friendly smile and his eyes gave the impression of a kind and benevolent man.

Among the items that appeared on the menu at his restaurant, the Fabada and El Cochinello were indeed outstanding. The fava European bean is the one used in the preparation of this recipe. These broad beans are similar to large lima beans, but not as flat. They compare to the cannellini bean.

(continued...)

1 pound great northern white beans, in lieu of favas

1 ham hock

1/4 pound slab bacon or salt pork

1/2 pound lean beef

2 chorizos, degreased*

2 morzilla sausages, degreased*

1 whole ripe tomato

1 onion or large scallion, cut in two

3 unpeeled garlic cloves, crushed

Sprig of fresh rosemary

1/2 green pepper

2 bay leaves, crushed

3 potatoes, peeled and cut in small cubes

Salt to taste

Hot sauce

Use a Dutch oven or soup kettle suitable for refrigeration. Discard imperfect beans and any foreign particles; wash well. Place beans in pot. Fill with water until it reaches 3 inches above the beans. Soak overnight. Do not drain soaking water.

The next day, add to the beans all ingredients in order up to and including bay leaves. Beans will have absorbed much of the water, so again add water, covering ingredients by 2 inches. Bring to a brisk boil. Skim several times to remove scum. Cover pot, lower heat and cook until beans are tender and meat is cooked, approximately 1 hour. Remove and discard what is left of the vegetables cooked with the beans, except bay leaves. Remove cooked meat to platter. Slice sausages in rounds and cube meat into small serving pieces. Return prepared meat to beans and add potatoes to pot.

(Okay, the original *Fabada Asturiana* recipe does not call for potatoes. Traditionally it is strictly beans and meat, of which the most important is sausage. However, my mother, upon occasion, would add potatoes; and if you want to know the truth, I think potatoes complement the *fabada*. Your choice!) Cook until potatoes are fully cooked and all is tender. Allow to rest 20 or 30 minutes. Again check for excess fat that may have surfaced. Skim off all!

Serves: 6 to 8.

*For instructions on degreasing sausages, see Page 318.

Pasta Lentil-Vegetable Soup
Sopa De Lentijas

This is a marvelous, rich, filling soup. A good source of iron and vitamins...so economical too. Did you know that lentils are the only beans that do not require prior soaking?

1 – 14 ounce package lentils
7-9 cups defatted, low-sodium chicken broth*
1 tablespoon extra virgin olive oil
1 onion, finely chopped
2 carrots, scraped and chopped
2 very ripe tomatoes, peeled, seeded and chopped
4 garlic cloves, finely minced
2 bay leaves, crushed
Dash of hot sauce, or to taste
1/4 pound angel hair pasta or vermicelli
2 tablespoons rice or balsamic vinegar

Discard all foreign particles from lentils and wash thoroughly in colander. Use a large soup pot with cover. Pour 5 cups of the chicken stock into soup kettle, and bring to a boil; reserve the rest. Add lentils, cover and cook at low heat, stirring at intervals. Meanwhile...

Heat oil in a large skillet. Add onion, carrots and tomatoes. Sauté until onion is transparent. Add garlic and bay leaves. Cook a couple of minutes longer, then add to soup pot, cover and cook until lentils are soft. Add reserved 2 cups of broth if needed, but don't overdo.

Snap vermicelli into 2-inch lengths. Add to lentils, together with extra broth and vinegar. Bring to a frisky boil, stirring to prevent pasta from sticking, then cover and lower heat to simmer until vermicelli is cooked. Serve piping hot!

The soup may be puréed in an electric blender or food processor, and served with toasted, seasoned croutons.

Serves: 4 to 6.

*For instructions how to make broth, see Page 318.

Mom's Magic Lentil Vegetable Soup
Sopa de Lentejas con Vejetales

This soup is chock full of good, vitamin-packed ingredients with a minimum of fat. When you serve it to your family members, they will marvel at Mom's kitchen magic.

1 tablespoon extra virgin olive oil

1 onion, finely chopped

1/2 green bell pepper, minced

1/2 red bell pepper, minced

3 garlic cloves

3 carrots, scraped, then thinly sliced

2 celery ribs, chopped

2 very ripe tomatoes, peeled, seeded and chopped

1 cup dry lentils

2 bay leaves

2 tablespoons fresh minced oregano crushed

4 or 5 cups defatted, low-sodium beef broth

1/2 pound fresh spinach, chopped

5 red potatoes, cubed

Salt

Hot sauce

Use a large soup pot with cover. Heat olive oil and sauté onion and bell peppers until onion is transparent. Add garlic, carrot, celery and tomatoes; cook, stirring carefully, to coat all vegetables with oil. Stir in lentils, bay leaves and oregano. Add beef stock. Bring to a boil, and cook until lentils are soft. If you need more stock, cautiously add more.

Thoroughly scrub and trim spinach and potatoes, and add to the pot; bring to a boil. Add salt and hot sauce. Again bring to a boil, cover, then lower heat and cook approximately 30 minutes, or until all vegetables are done.

Serving suggestions: Cook 1 cup long-grain rice* and serve a generous tablespoon with each bowl. To add nutritional value, finely chop 2 tablespoons fresh parsley and 2 tablespoons toasted almonds or walnuts. Sprinkle over rice, and fold into soup – delicious! Enjoy!

Serves: 6 to 8.

*For instructions on cooking rice, see Page 321.

Fish Chowder with Corn
Sopa de Pescado y Maiz

Until recently, the Spanish regarded corn derogatorily as food for cattle (comida para ganados). Now, it's a different story. Corn is a well-accepted vegetable and used in any number of recipes in the Spanish kitchen. This recipe produces a thick, crunchy and filling dish with elegant bits of white fish to give it punch. I want to share this recipe with you and sincerely hope you enjoy it as much as I do.

1 pound white firm-flesh fish such as orange roughy or grouper,
    cut into 1-inch pieces
4 corn husks, to produce 3 to 4 cups kernels
3½ cups defatted, low-sodium chicken broth
Pinch of saffron strands
2 slices lean bacon
1 tablespoon extra virgin olive oil
2 cups finely minced onion
2 celery ribs, thinly sliced
3 garlic cloves, minced
2 tablespoons fresh finely minced thyme
2 tablespoons finely minced cilantro
2 tablespoons fresh finely minced oregano

(continued...)

4 new potatoes, peeled and cubed

2 cups 1% milk

¼ cup light cream

1 teaspoon cornstarch

Hot sauce to taste

Salt to taste

¼ cup dry white wine

1 – 2 ounce jar minced pimientos, drained

¼ cup toasted, chopped almonds

Carefully clean the fish and cut into pieces. Blanche the corn husks.

In a saucepan, heat chicken broth; add saffron. Cover and remove from heat. Steep 30 minutes. Meanwhile, degrease bacon in microwave oven or heavy skillet.* Reserve 1 tablespoon bacon grease; discard the rest. Crumble bacon and set aside.

In a soup kettle with cover, heat bacon grease and oil. Add onion, celery, garlic, thyme, cilantro and oregano. Sauté until onion is translucent. Add potatoes and corn kernels, which are easier to remove if the husk is blanched first. (To remove kernels, take a sharp knife and drag it under them; they will fall off into a bowl. After removing kernels, snap one corn husk in half, and set aside). Sauté all at very low heat. Add the hot steeped broth. Add the reserved husk and cook10 minutes, then remove husk pieces to a colander; squeeze liquid from husks and discard. Continuing with the recipe, bring pot to a boil. Cook, covered, until potatoes are done,about 10 to 15 minutes.

Combine milk and cream. Dissolve cornstarch in the mixture. Add slowly to soup kettle, stirring. Once the milk is added to the recipe, avoid boiling the chowder; and stir carefully at intervals, okay? Cook until slightly thickened. (Don't forget the hot sauce!) Add salt and reserved bacon bits, prepared fish, and wine. Stir carefully, but well. Cover pot and cook 15 minutes at low heat. Stir in pimientos. Remove pot from heat, and allow to rest 10 to 15 minutes before serving. Sprinkle with almonds to add prestige and tradition.

Serves: 4 to 6.

* For instructions on how to degrease bacon, see Page 318.

Clarita's Gumbo
Sopa De Marisco

I wanted to prepare a "Gumbo" somewhat diferente. Here it is. It has been readily approved by my family, but of course, as with most families, Mom's cooking is always the best. The crabmeat and baby clams add a special touch.

1 pound medium-sized shrimp, cleaned and deveined
1 – 10 ounce can baby clams, undrained
1/2 pound crabmeat, chopped
2 tablespoons extra virgin olive oil
1 cup chopped onion
1 cup chopped red bell pepper
1 cup chopped celery
1 cup chopped carrots
1 pound okra, cut into 1/4-inch lengths
1 – 16 ounce can stewed tomatoes, chopped
3 garlic cloves, minced
2 tablespoons freshly minced thyme
2 tablespoons freshly minced tarragon
2 tablespoons freshly minced oregano
2 bay leaves, crushed
Juice of one lemon
1 tablespoon all-purpose flour
1 teaspoon toasted, crushed saffron*
6 cups hot defatted, low-sodium chicken broth
1 – 8 ounce bottle clam juice
1 tablespoon light soy sauce
1 teaspoon Louisiana hot sauce
1 teaspoon salt, or to taste
1/4 cup uncooked brown rice
1/4 cup very dry sherry

(continued...)

*For instructions on toasting saffron, see Page 322.

Place shrimp, clams and crabmeat in a large bowl and set aside to use later.

Heat olive oil in a large pot with cover. Add onion, pepper, celery and carrots. Stir with a wooden spoon to coat with oil. Add okra to the pot together with tomatoes, garlic, thyme, tarragon, oregano and bay leaves. Stir to mix well. Sprinkle lemon juice over all and stir again. Add flour and gently stir to facilitate cooking before adding any more liquids.

Add saffron to hot chicken broth. Pour into the pot, together with clam juice. Bring to a boil; then add the soy and hot sauce. Stir well. Add salt. When it boils again, add rice. Cover, lower heat. Cook 25 minutes, stirring occasionally.

Add reserved seafood and Tio Pepe sherry; stir carefully, and cook about 15 minutes longer. If the soup is too thick, add a little more broth, but not much, as gumbos are usually thick. Serve in deep soup bowls and enjoy!

Serves: 4 to 6.

...my cousin Lillian stopped at a quaint restaurant. She told me how the menu featured a Portuguese soup that intrigued her. She ordered the soup and enjoyed it so much that when she returned home, she tried duplicating it and came up with this terrific version...It is a winner in my book of recipes!

Portuguese Fish Medley Soup
Sopa Portuguesa

While traveling through New England, my cousin Lillian stopped at a quaint restaurant. She told me how the menu featured a Portuguese soup that intrigued her. She ordered the soup and enjoyed it immensely; so much so that when she returned home, she tried duplicating it, and came up with this terrific version that is simply delicious. It is a winner in my book of recipes!

When purchasing fish, ask at the market if they have purged mussels. If you choose, steam 12 mussels, and add 2 to each serving to lend a gourmet flair to an already glamorous soup. Steep saffron with the broth early in the day, well before starting recipe.

1 pound grouper, or any firm white fish

½ pound medium-sized shrimp, cleaned and deveined

½ pound sea scallops, halved

12 mussels, purged and steamed

2 tablespoons extra virgin olive oil

1 onion, finely minced

3 garlic cloves, minced

3 carrots, scraped and thinly sliced

2 celery ribs (inner ribs), sliced

2 tablespoons fresh minced thyme

2 bay leaves, crushed

1 – 16 ounce can stewed tomatoes, chopped

1 – 14½ ounce can defatted, low-sodium chicken broth*

1 teaspoon saffron, steeped in chicken broth*

Salt to taste

Hot sauce to taste

½ cup dry white wine

*For instructions on steeping saffron and making chicken broth, see Page 318, 322.

(continued...)

Carefully wash and prepare grouper or white fish, shrimp, scallops and mussels. (To prepare fish, cube grouper coarsely, and combine with scallops and shrimp.) Empty clams into a bowl.

In a 2-quart, heat-resistant casserole with cover, heat oil. Add onion, garlic, carrots, celery, thyme and bay leaves, and sauté a few minutes. Add tomatoes. Cook a couple of minutes longer. Add hot saffroned chicken broth, salt and hot sauce to taste. Stir to mix well, cover, and cook gently 30 minutes.

Now add the grouper, shrimp, scallops, and mussels to the casserole, together with white wine. Bring to a slow boil, cover, lower heat and cook another 15 minutes. Do not overcook fish. This soup may be ladled over yellow rice, or plain white rice.

Serves: 4 to 6.

Split Pea Soup
Sopa de Chicharos Verdes

Ay, que sopa tan rica! And to think you can eat heartily of this soup without feeling guilty about the fat, because sabes que? There's hardly any fat to worry about, and plenty of healthful fiber that makes a filling dish. Here we go...

1 – 14 ounce package split peas
1 quart defatted, low-sodium chicken broth*
2 carrots, scraped and thinly sliced
1 onion, finely chopped
1 bell pepper, finely chopped
3 garlic cloves, minced
1 potato, peeled and cubed

*For instructions about making broth, see Page 318.

Sprig of fresh parsley, finely chopped

1/2 teaspoon Spanish paprika

2 tablespoons fresh chopped oregano

2 tablespoons fresh chopped basil

2 bay leaves, crushed

4 tablespoons dry sherry

1 cup cubed very lean ham

Salt to taste

Hot sauce to taste

Remove all dirt and foreign particles from peas and wash carefully in a colander. In a large soup pot, bring broth to a boil. Add peas, carrots, onion, pepper, garlic, potato and parsley. Bring again to a boil, stirring to prevent peas from sticking. Now add paprika, oregano, basil, and bay leaves. Lower heat; cover and cook about an hour, stirring at intervals to avoid sticking.

When all vegetables – including the peas – are cooked, remove from heat and cool. Remove bay leaves. In an electric blender or food processor, purée the soup in batches. Return to soup pot, add sherry, minced ham, salt and hot sauce to taste. Bring to a boil, lower heat and cook another 15 or 20 minutes. Serve hot.

Serves: 4 to 6.

Vegetable Soup With Vermicelli
Sopa De Vegetales Con Fideos

I call this my "don't need anything else" soup:
Whichever vegetables are to your liking may be substituted for
those listed in the recipe. Accompanied by good crusty Italian bread or
French baguette, lightly brushed with olive oil and a dusting of Parm-
esan cheese, it is simply the greatest. And for dessert, maybe baked
apples with raisins and a sprinkle of vinito sherry. Olé!

2 tablespoons extra virgin olive oil

1 cup finely minced onion

1 cup finely minced bell pepper

1 cup thinly sliced carrots

1 cup fresh peeled, seeded and chopped tomatoes

1 cup chopped celery

2 garlic cloves, minced

1 cup shredded cabbage

1 cup thinly sliced yellow squash

6 new potatoes, cubed

1/4 cup finely chopped fresh parsley

2 bay leaves, crushed

2 teaspoons fresh minced basil

1 1/2 quarts defatted, low-sodium chicken broth*

Salt to taste

Hot sauce to taste

1/4 pound vermicelli, snapped in 2-inch lengths

1/4 cup grated Parmesan cheese

1 cup broccoli flowerettes, halved

In a large soup kettle or Dutch oven, add olive oil and heat.
Add onion, pepper, carrots, tomatoes and celery. With a wooden
spoon, stir gently to coat ingredients with oil. At low heat, stir-fry

for 3 to 4 minutes. Sprinkle with garlic; add cabbage, squash, potatoes, parsley, bay leaves and basil: You'll have a pot full of vegetables. Stir gently 2 or 3 minutes. Add broth. Bring to a boil, stirring gently. Add salt and hot sauce to taste.

Add vermicelli and cheese. Stir to mix well; cover, lower heat and cook 30 minutes, or until vegetables are cooked. Stir in broccoli. Cover and remove from heat. Allow to rest 10 to 15 minutes; the broccoli will cook until it is just crisp. If soup is too thick for your taste, add more chicken broth. However, remember the vegetables cook down, so give them a chance to cook about 5 minutes or so before adding additional broth.

Serves: 4 to 6.

Best Cream of Broccoli Soup
Crema de Brocoli

2 bunches of broccoli, coarsely chopped

2 tablespoons extra virgin olive oil

1 tablespoon butter or margarine

2 potatoes, peeled and cubed

1 leek (white part only), minced

1 teaspoon salt

2 tablespoons fresh minced tarragon

2 tablespoons fresh minced basil

4 cups defatted, low-sodium chicken broth*

1/2 cup low-fat evaporated milk

1 cup 1% milk

Hot sauce to taste

*For instructions about making broth, see Page 318.

To prepare broccoli, wash carefully, cut off flowerettes, and trim and peel the tough lower stalks; chop coarsely. Reserve a generous cupful of flowerettes for later use.

In a soup kettle with cover, heat oil and butter or margarine. Add chopped broccoli, potatoes, leek and salt. With a wooden spoon, stir-fry vegetables until well-coated with oil and butter.

(continued...)

Scatter tarragon and basil over all. Mix well and cook about 3 minutes, until fragrant.

Pour in broth; bring to a boil. Lower heat, cover and cook until vegetables are tender, 25 to 30 minutes. Cool. Combine both milks and hot sauce. Whisk to mix well. Set aside.

In an electric blender or food processor, pureé the soup in batches. Return to original cooking pot, and again place soup kettle on burner to heat. Add reserved broccoli flowerettes, and cook 2 minutes. Stir in milk and continue to heat, but do not boil. Let stand 10 minutes before serving. Broccoli flowerettes will be just crisp tender: Do not overcook! May be served with dollops of light sour cream.

Serves: 4 to 6.

Cream of Celery and Carrots Soup
Crema De Apio y Zanahorias

Vitamin C abounds in this recipe. Prepare it and serve to your family and friends and wait for the reaction. When the inquisition starts, apply my Mother's famous remark: Come y calla (eat and hush). I'm willing to bet they will go back for seconds...and only you will know the high nutritional value of this soup. .

1 tablespoon extra virgin olive oil

1 tablespoon margarine or butter

2 potatoes, peeled and cubed

4 cups scraped and thinly sliced carrots

2 cups thinly sliced celery (inner ribs)

1 teaspoon fresh minced basil

1 teaspoon fresh minced thyme

Salt to taste

Hot sauce to taste

*For instructions about making broth, see Page 318.

2 garlic cloves, minced
1½ cups peeled, seeded and chopped ripe tomatoes
5 cups defatted, low-sodium chicken broth*
1 cup skim or 1% milk
½ cup evaporated low-fat milk

In a Dutch oven or large soup pot, heat oil and butter or margarine. Add potatoes, carrots and celery. Stir with a wooden spoon until vegetables are well-saturated. Add basil and thyme (whenever possible, use fresh herbs), salt, hot sauce, garlic and tomatoes. Stir gently and cook at moderate heat 5 minutes. Pour in chicken broth. Bring to a boil. Lower

heat, cover and cook until vegetables are soft. Correct seasoning; add more if needed.

Remove pot from heat; cool. Pureé in batches in an electric blender or food processor. Return pureed soup to its original pot. Combine the two milks. Slowly add to soup, stirring continually. Reheat on simmer. Do not boil. If milk should curdle in soup, beat vigorously with hand beater and it will bind instantly. However, this should not happen if you follow directions...okay?

May be served hot or cold; but if you want to serve it cold, refrigerate overnight before adding the milk.

Serves: 4 to 6.

. . . .

Vitamin C abounds in this recipe. Prepare it and serve to your family and friends and wait for the reaction.

Cream of Mushroom Soup
Crema de Champiñones

*I find this soup to be very acceptable in the "cream soups"
category, even though it is not heavily laced with whipping cream and
rich sour cream. It makes an elegant luncheon dish or something you
might serve for a lazy Sunday brunch.*

You're going to keep this in your repertoire, I promise.

1 tablespoon extra virgin olive oil

1 onion, chopped

½ cup chopped celery ribs

2 tablespoons fresh minced oregano

2 tablespoons minced cilantro

¼ teaspoon nutmeg

¼ teaspoon cumin

1 Russet potato, peeled and cubed

1 teaspoon salt, or to taste

1 teaspoon hot sauce, or to taste

4 cups defatted, low-sodium chicken broth*

1 tablespoon butter or margarine

1 pound uniformly sliced mushrooms

1½ cups 1% milk plus ½ cup low-fat evaporated milk

1 tablespoon cornstarch

1 cup reduced-fat sour cream

Sprinkle of dry white wine

In a soup kettle or Dutch oven, heat oil. Add onion, celery,
oregano and cilantro. Sauté at low heat until onion is translucent
and all is fragrant. Add nutmeg and cumin. Stir well. Now add
potato, salt and hot sauce. Mix well, stirring gently 2 minutes. Pour
in chicken stock. Bring to a boil. Lower heat, cover and cook until
all vegetables are tender. Correct seasonings; cool.

*For instructions about making broth, see Page 318.

In an electric blender or food processor, pureé vegetables in batches and return to original soup kettle. Cover and place over lowest heat. In a heavy skillet, heat butter. Add mushrooms. Sauté gently until golden and most of liquid has evaporated. Pour into soup kettle with the pureed vegetables. Stir to mix well and cover pot.

Place cornstarch in a bowl. Combine 1% milk and evaporated milk. Add slowly to cornstarch, stirring to dissolve. Pour into soup kettle in a steady stream, stirring carefully. Increase heat source to low and cook, stirring until thickened. Serve with a dollop of light sour cream in each bowl.

Variation: If it's cream of chicken and mushroom soup that you would like, follow the recipe for cream of mushroom soup until you have sauteed the mushrooms; then, in the same skillet where mushrooms were cooked, add a tablespoon of butter. From chicken used to make the stock, shred breasts and brown deliciously at low heat in the butter. Add to soup kettle. Mix well. Now dissolve cornstarch in the milk and proceed with recipe.

Serves: 6.

The Original Vichysoisse
Sopa de Patatas-fria

It is a real pleasure to share my vichysoisse recipes with you. Now you have a choice: This recipe, chock full of fat and cholesterol, or the following one, low in both. Which to prepare? It all depends on you. Since this is a "special occasion" soup, it is permissible to indulge – once a year, maybe? For my son Manny's birthday, this great classic among soups is a must.

¼ pound butter or margarine
2 leeks (white part only), coarsely chopped
1 Spanish onion, coarsely chopped
6 boiling potatoes, peeled and cubed
Salt to taste

(continued...)

Hot sauce to taste
1/4 teaspoon nutmeg
5 cups defatted, low-sodium chicken broth*
1 cup 2% milk
2 cups "light" cream
1 cup whipping cream
Fresh chopped chives or toasted almonds for garnish

In a large soup kettle, melt butter or margarine. Add leeks (white part only), onion and potatoes. Sauté until onion is transparent, stirring to avoid sticking. Sprinkle salt to taste and a couple of good dashes of hot sauce. Add nutmeg. Sauté a minute or two longer. Stir in broth.

Bring to a boil, cover, lower heat and cook about 30 minutes. Remove pot from heat; cool. In an electric blender or food processor, blend in batches until very smooth and creamy. Return pureed soup to original cooking pot. Stir in the milk and light cream. Place over heat and bring to scalding stage (do not boil), stirring constantly. Lower heat, cover and cook 2 minutes. Remove from heat; cool. Pour into a soup tureen with cover for refrigeration overnight.

The next day, correct seasonings and slowly add whipping cream. Blend thoroughly. Return to refrigerator until ready to serve. Serve with a sprinkle of fresh chives or toasted almonds.

Serves: 6 to 8.

*For instructions about making broth, see Page 318.

An Affordable Vichysoisse
Sopa de Patates-Fria

It may not be as creamy as the original French version, but I assure you, it is very delicious, and the addition of toasted almonds adds the illusion of richness without high-fat consequences.

1 tablespoon extra virgin olive oil

2 tablespoons margarine, or 1 tablespoon butter

6 boiling potatoes, peeled and cubed

1 Spanish onion, chopped

2 leeks (white part only), chopped

1/4 cup toasted almonds

1/4 teaspoon nutmeg

Salt to taste

Hot sauce to taste

4 cups defatted, low-sodium chicken broth*

2 1/2 cups 1% milk

In a large soup kettle with cover, heat oil and margarine or butter. Add potatoes, onion and leeks (white part only). Stir and sauté until ingredients are well-coated with oil mixture. Add almonds and cook until golden. Sprinkle with nutmeg, salt and hot sauce. Add chicken broth. Mix carefully and bring to a boil. Lower heat, cover, cook until potatoes and vegetables are very tender, about 30 minutes. Add more salt and hot sauce if needed.

Remove pot from heat. Cool. In an electric blender or food processor, purée soup in batches. Return to original pot. Now, combine the two milks and stir into soup. Place pot on burner and heat slowly for about 10 minutes on simmer. Cool and refrigerate overnight.

The next day: Stir in the half of the milk and mix well. In adding the last 1/2 of milk, be careful to get the consistency you want. Pour half of the milk into the soup first, then add the rest if it is still too thin. Return to refrigerator until ready to serve.

Serves: 6 to 8.

*For instructions about making broth, see Page 318.

Spanish Salad Soup
Gazpacho

This great Andalusian soup is now an international favorite, featured on menus of fine restaurants throughout the world. Not only is it delightful to eat, it is almost fat-free as well. What a combination!

2 pounds, or 10 to 12, very ripe plum tomatoes,
    seeded and chopped
1 cucumber, peeled, seeded and coarsely chopped
1 tablespoon extra virgin olive oil
1 onion, chopped
1 green bell pepper, chopped
3 garlic cloves, minced
2 tablespoons fresh minced oregano
1 tablespoon fresh minced dillweed
2 or 3 dashes hot sauce
1 cup fresh toasted bread crumbs
¼ cup white wine or rice vinegar
4 cups defatted, low-sodium chicken broth*
1 teaspoon salt, or to taste
¼ teaspoon granulated sugar

Place tomatoes in a large mixing bowl. Cut 1 inch off each end of cucumber. Peel, then cut down its middle, lengthwise, and remove most seeds; chop coarsely and add to bowl.

Heat oil in skillet. Add onion, pepper, garlic, oregano, dillweed and hot sauce. Sauté until onion is soft and pepper translucent. Pour over vegetables in bowl. Scatter crumbs over all, and toss with two forks.

Add vinegar, 3 cups of the broth, salt and sugar. With wooden spoon, stir thoroughly. Correct seasoning; add more if needed. Reserve last cup of broth.

*For instructions about making broth, see Page 318.

In a blender or food processor, purée the soup in batches and pour into a soup tureen with cover for refrigeration; chill at least 3 or 4 hours, or overnight. If the soup is too thick, add gradually the last cup of broth from refrigerator, but keep in mind soup should be thickish. Serve in supremes over crushed ice.

Offer garlic-flavored croutons to sprinkle over each serving. It is customary to offer guests chopped, peeled and seeded cucumbers, tomatoes, onions and peppers – in separate bowls – to spoon into their soup. Frankly, I prefer croutons.

P.S.: PLEASE don't use tomato juice in recipe... Promise?

Serves: 6 to 8.

Collard Greens Soup
Verzada Asturiana

Ask a northern Spaniard (Asturiano) what he might like to take with him to heaven when it's time to go, and he will tell you a pot of Verzada, just is case there is none available up there; and that's the truth! It is indeed a hearty potaje; a no-fat version is impossible. However, I have come up with the next best solution, so that you and your family and friends can enjoy Verzada con gusto...without too much guilt.

2 quarts of water

1 ham bone

1 ham hock

1 pound beef short ribs

2 chorizos, degreased*

1 blood sausage Morzilla, degreased*

2 bay leaves, crushed

Salt to taste

Hot sauce to taste

*For meat degreasing instructions, see Page 318.

(continued...)

4 potatoes, peeled and coarsely cubed

1 bunch fresh collard greens or 2 packages frozen,
   finely chopped

2 tablespoons extra virgin olive oil, or bacon drippings

1 onion, finely chopped

1 green bell pepper, finely chopped

4 garlic cloves, pressed

1 teaspoon Spanish paprika

2 – 19 ounce cans cannellini beans

In a large soup kettle or Dutch oven with cover, bring water to a boil. Add ham bone, ham hock, short ribs, chorizos, sausage and bay leaves. Season with salt and hot sauce to taste. Again bring water to a boil. For 20 minutes at least, carefully skim off brown scum that surfaces as the meat cooks. Cover pot, lower heat (however, keep pot at a slow boil).

Cook approximately 30 minutes, or until meat is tender. Cool completely. Remove meat and sausage to a deep bowl. Remove all visible fat, cover, and refrigerate. Strain stock into a large bowl with cover. Refrigerate overnight.

The next day, remove the stock from the refrigerator and skim every trace of the blanket of fat that has surfaced during the night. Take out the bowl of meat; cube meat and slice chorizos; cut sausage into rings. Place all in a bowl and set aside.

Pour stock into soup kettle, and bring to a boil. Add potatoes and collard greens. (I prefer to use frozen collards because the vegetable is clean and well chopped). Lower heat and cover pot.

Meanwhile, heat olive oil or drippings in a large skillet. Add onion, pepper and garlic. Sauté until onion is limp. Add paprika. Stir quickly and pour over collard greens in soup kettle; bring again to a boil. Add beans and all of the reserved chopped meat. Stir well, cooking at low heat until potatoes and collard greens are cooked, about 30 or 45 minutes.

Serves: 6.

Vegetarian Potaje of String Beans
Potaje de Habichuelas Vegetariano

This is one of those dishes in which you may dump all its ingredients in a pot, cook leisurely and the result is a hearty potaje to satisfy the most finicky of appetites.

2 pounds fresh string beans, snapped in halves
2 tablespoons extra virgin olive oil
1½ cups minced onion
1 cup chopped green bell pepper
1 cup chopped red bell pepper
2 tomatoes, peeled, seeded, and finely chopped
¼ cup tomato sauce
4 new potatoes, peeled and cubed
2 cups baby carrots, scraped, but not sliced
4 garlic cloves, pressed
1 teaspoon Spanish paprika
1 – 19 ounce can garbanzo beans (chick peas), drained
2 cups defatted, low-sodium chicken broth
Salt to taste
Hot sauce to taste

Strip beans of strings and snap each in two. Wash and pat dry. Put them in a large soup kettle or Dutch oven. In a skillet, heat oil. Add onion and pepper. Sauté until translucent. Pour over beans in pot. Add tomatoes and the rest of the ingredients in order listed. Bring to a boil Stir well and correct seasonings, adding more if needed. Cover pot, lower heat and cook for one hour or until all vegetables are cooked.

A good suggestion: 2 cups of chopped Swiss chard added with the vegetables improves the taste.

Serves: 6.

Pebbles Tomato-Basil Soup
Sopa de Tomate Fresco

Pebbles are a unique group of restaurants in Central Florida. The concept has been created by my son Manny and his wonderful wife Gerry, after several years of research and total dedication.

Pebbles Restaurants have been voted repeatedly the favorite eating place by Floridians in Central Florida. Much of the success is due to the diligence of Tony Pace, our executive chef and good friend, whose talent in the culinary arts is unapproachable. Tony has worked, along with Manny and Gerry, tireless hours in menu planning for *Pebbles* and for other fine restaurants that we have opened recently, one of which is "Manuel's on the 28th" the recipient of many fine dining awards.

And so, here is a soup recipe from Tony's magical kitchen, which is requisimo...Enjoy!

2 tablespoons unsalted butter

2 tablespoons extra virgin olive oil

1 crushed garlic clove, unpeeled

¼ cup finely minced onion

5 tablespoons all-purpose flour

6 cups defatted chicken broth

4 medium size very ripe tomatoes, peeled, seeded and
    finely minced

¼ cup tomato sauce

1 teaspoon Spike

1 teaspoon Maggi seasoning

½ cup finely minced sweet basil

2 tablespoons minced cilatnro

¾ cup 2% milk

1/4 cup heavy cream

1 ounce cognac (or a dry sherry, such as Tio Pepe)

In a medium size Dutch oven or soup kettle with cover and non-stick interior, heat butter and oil. Add crushed garlic. Sauté until brown and discard. To pan, add onion; sauté until transparent. Add flour and cook, stirring until golden. Remove pan from heat. Slowly add chicken stock, stirring to dissolve possible flour lumps. Return pot to heat. Cook until thickened.

Add the tomatoes, tomato sauce and seasonings (spike and Maggi). Stir well and correct seasonings (salt and hot sauce) in accordance with taste and health tolerance. Bring to a slow boil. Cook 3 minutes, stirring. Cover soup kettle, lower heat to simmer and cook 20 minutes, stirring at intervals. Add the finely minced basil, cilantro and cognac (or sherry). Stir well; again check seasonings. Pour in the combined milk and cream. Mix well. Simmer 2 or 3 minutes (do not boil) and serve hot with home-made croutons.

Yield: 6 servings

Note: the original recipe calls for 1 cup of heavy cream, which undoubtedly gives the soup a thicker texture.

SALADS

Ensaladas

We are all interested in keeping fit and in consuming enough fiber and vitamins needed for good health. Salads can play a leading role. A good salad with a variety of fresh vegetables is an apt beginning for a fine dining experience. During the long hot summer months, a salad can be a complete, satisfying meal. Accompany your choice with a lightly buttered or oiled and toasted crusty bread. For dessert, choose a good selection of seasonal fruits served with a dollop of plain or vanilla yogurt. Scientists have also been discovering the many benefits of fiber, which salads offer in great quantity. The rich green and yellow vegetables and nuts are packed with vitamins and minerals, and are newly popular as main dishes among those trying to eat "light." Enjoy these light and healthy offerings!

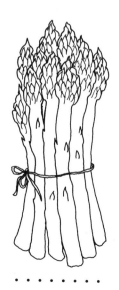

Recipes

Roasted Bell Pepper Salad

Mixed Greens Salad

Broccoli and Cauliflower Salad

Green Bean Salad

Asparagus Vinaigrette

Tomato, Onion and Cheese Salad

Spectacular Spinach Salad with Walnuts

Spicy Cucumber Salad

Watercress and Avocado Salad

Dignified Artichokes

Shrimp and Lobster Salad

Spanish Tuna Salad

Don Quixote Salad

Walnut Potato Salad

Enchanting Chicken Salad

Tropical Chicken Salad

Roasted Bell Pepper Salad
Ensalada de Ajíses

2 red bell peppers, cleaned and roasted
1 yellow bell pepper, cleaned and roasted
1 green bell pepper, cleaned and roasted
2 tablespoons extra virgin olive oil
2 or 3 garlic cloves, pressed
1/2 teaspoon white pepper
1/4 cup rice vinegar
1/4 teaspoon sugar
1 teaspoon salt
6 ounces Mozzarella cheese, thinly sliced
1 onion, sliced thinly in rings
2 tablespoons fresh minced tarragon
2 tablespoons fresh minced basil
2 tablespoons small capers
8 Kalamata olives, pitted and chopped
Bouquets of watercress or Italian parsley

Roast peppers until charred all over. Once charred, place peppers in a brown bag and allow to steam 10 to 15 minutes. Now, being careful to avoid burning your hand, take each pepper and cut in two lengthwise. Remove seeds and pith. Scrape off clinging stubborn blackened skin that does not come off, using a paring knife. Rinse under cold running water, then dry with paper towels. Cut into even strips about 1 1/2 inches wide, and set aside.

In a bowl, combine oil, pressed garlic, pepper, vinegar, sugar and salt; whisk to blend thoroughly. Keep at room temperature.

To assemble salad: In a pretty round salad platter, arrange the bell pepper strips, alternating artistically with cheese and onion rings. Cover with plastic wrap and refrigerate.

To the salad dressing in bowl, add tarragon and basil, capers and olives.

Mix gently. Allow salad dressing to marinate another 15 minutes, stirring now and then. Remove platter from refrigerator,

(continued...)

uncover and spoon dressing generously over the bell peppers, onion and cheese. Garnish with watercress or Italian parsley bouquets. Serve with *gusto*.

Serves: 4 to 6.

Mixed Greens Salad
Ensalada Mista De Verduras

When you mix these greens with a fat-free dressing, you have a delicious guilt-free feast. This is one of my family's favorites.

1 head romaine lettuce
1/2 head iceberg lettuce
1 bunch watercress, tough stems removed
2 cups spinach leaves
1 Belgian endive tulip
6 radishes, thinly sliced
Juice of one lemon
4 tablespoons red wine vinegar
3 tablespoons extra virgin olive oil
2 tablespoons fresh grated Parmesan cheese
2 garlic cloves, pressed
1/2 teaspoon salt
1/2 teaspoon white pepper
1/4 teaspoon granulated sugar

Wash greens thoroughly and blot or spin dry. (Radicchio, arugula, or Bibb lettuce can be used in this great salad if you wish). Tear into bite-sized pieces and place in a large container with cover. Separate Belgian endive leaves and cut into the bowl together with the radishes. Cover the container and refrigerate.

In a small bowl, combine lemon juice, vinegar, olive oil, cheese and garlic; whisk until well-blended. Add the salt, pepper and sugar and whisk vigorously again. Remove container from refrigerator, uncover and pour dressing over the greens. Toss to mix thoroughly without bruising vegetables. Wait 5 minutes, toss again, then serve in salad bowls.

Serves: 4 to 6.

Broccoli and Cauliflower Salad
Ensalada De Brocoli y Coliflor

When combined with the following dressing, broccoli and cauliflower could hardly taste better. It's a salad that you'll never tire of. Honest, it's that great! You may ask why I switched from wine vinegar to rice vinegar. Once you use rice vinegar, you'll love it as I do. It adds a subtle flavor to salads.

For the salad
La ensalada

1 cauliflower head, steamed and broken into flowerets
1 broccoli head, steamed and broken into flowerets
1 cup fresh sliced mushrooms
½ cup pitted and coarsely chopped Kalamata ripe olives
1 red bell pepper, seeded and pith removed, thinly sliced
1 onion, cut into thin rings
3 ounces feta cheese, crumbled

For the dressing
El Adobo

2 tablespoons olive oil
½ cup rice vinegar
1 teaspoon low-sodium soy sauce
2 tablespoons fresh lemon juice
2 garlic cloves, pressed
Salt and pepper to taste

In a steamer, cook cauliflower and broccoli about 3 minutes; remove and cool completely. Place steamed cauliflower and broccoli in a deep salad bowl. Add the mushrooms, olives and bell pepper. Toss gently. Add the onion rings and toss again. Scatter cheese over all and set aside.

(continued...)

Pour all salad dressing ingredients into a screw top jar. Shake to mix well. Now pour over the salad and with two forks, toss to mix thoroughly without bruising the vegetables. Refrigerate for at least an hour; toss every 15 minutes. Line a shallow salad bowl with crisp Bibb lettuce, and spoon the salad into the bowl.

Serves: 4 to 6.

Green Bean Salad
Ensalada De Habichuelas

For this salad you will need fresh green beans that snap smartly. When you combine green beans, albacore tuna and small new potatoes, you have a meal, and a satisfying one at that!

1 pound green beans, snapped in half

6 new potatoes, scraped and cut in half

2 6½ ounce cans albacore tuna, packed in water

1 onion, finely chopped

2 tablespoons extra virgin olive oil

Juice of one lemon or lime

2 tablespoons minced oregano

2 tablespoons minced sweet basil

3 tablespoons rice vinegar

Salt to taste

1 cup thinly sliced red onion rings

1 cup julienned green bell pepper

1 cup julienned red bell pepper

6 firm ripe cherry tomatoes, halved

In a vegetable steamer, place green beans and new potatoes. Cover and steam until potatoes are tender, 25 minutes. While vegetables cook, drain tuna and flake into a mixing bowl. Combine the next six ingredients and pour over the flaked tuna. Stir to mix well and set aside. Into large salad bowl, place cooked beans and potatoes.

Scatter tuna mixture over all, and toss lightly while still warm. Add salt if you like; add peppers and onion rings. Toss again. Place the halved cherry tomatoes over all. After placing the tomatoes here and there, do not toss; it would bruise the tomatoes, and you don't want that.

Serves: 4 to 6.

Asparagus Vinaigrette
Esparagos a la Vinagretta

The best asparagus in the world, in my opinion, is grown in Aranjuez, Spain. When I visit Spain, my usual diet for the duration of the trip is Esparagos de aranjuez y Merluza! These luscious white asparagus are now available in most specialty stores that handle Spanish imports. Esparagos a la Vinagretta is my favorite way to prepare this vegetable; the next one is a la mayonesa casera, both excellent recipes.

Vinaigrette
La vinagretta

2 tablespoons olive oil
3 garlic cloves, pressed
Juice of one lemon
1/2 cup wine or rice vinegar
1 teaspoon mustard
2 tablespoons fresh minced dillweed
2 tablespoons fresh minced tarragon
2 tablespoons onion, finely minced
2 tablespoons small capers
Salt and pepper to taste
2 tablespoons fresh minced parsley or 1 dried

(continued...)

In a mixing bowl, combine all vinaigrette ingredients up to and including salt and pepper; whisk to mix well; add the parsley and mix well; set aside to marinate.

2 pounds nice, thick asparagus (12 to 15 spears in each bunch)
Pimiento strips

Snap off the tough, hard end of the spears, and use only the tender upper part. In a vegetable steamer, place the asparagus and steam until tender, about 10 minutes; if you lack a steamer, use a large skillet filled with 1 or 2 inches of water, with cover. Add the asparagus, cover tightly and steam at low heat 10 minutes.

Remove asparagus to a lettuce-lined, pretty platter and separate into bunches of 5 and 6, tie with pimiento strips. Pour marinade over asparagus, saturating well. Cover with Saran Wrap and refrigerate for a few minutes.

Serves: 4 to 6.

Tomato, Onion and Cheese Salad
Ensalada De Tomate, Cebolla y Queso

In Central Florida we have the good fortune to have available all year scrumptious. Vine ripe tomatoes from Ruskin, Florida are some of the best. When they are in season, I take advantage by preparing spaghetti sauces and other great sauces that call for tomatoes, such as Creole and Catalana sauces in bulk. It saves time and there's always plenty of sauce on hand.

It is a little tedious to peel and seed tomatoes, but the result is so rewarding, it's worth the trouble. I peel and seed a large mountain of tomatoes, then place them in portioned freezer bags, so they are available later when I need them.

3 or 4 ripe tomatoes, as perfect as possible
1 block of Mozzarella cheese, thinly sliced
1 red onion, sliced into thin rings
¼ cup toasted pine nuts

. . . .

¼ cup fresh minced parsley

2 tablespoons wine vinegar

Juice of one lemon

2 tablespoons fresh, finely chopped basil or 1 tablespoon dried

2 tablespoons extra virgin olive oil

2 tablespoons small capers

Slice the tomatoes into ¹/₂ inch pieces, and place upon a pretty, shallow salad platter, alternating cheese and onion rings to form an artistic pattern. Scatter the nuts and parsley evenly over all.

Combine vinegar, lemon, basil, olive oil and capers in a small bowl, and whisk until well-blended. Pour over all, saturating the salad. Prepare salad 30 minutes before serving in order to allow ingredients to marinate with the dressing...okay? If you do not intend to serve immediately, cover with plastic wrap and refrigerate.

Serves: 4 to 6.

Spectacular Spinach Salad with Walnuts
Ensalada De Espinaca y Nueces

Here's spinach at its best! You may add other salad greens if you wish, but I prefer simply spectacular spinach.

1 large bunch of spinach, about 8 cups

1 orange, unpeeled and sliced thinly into rounds

3 slices Canadian bacon, grilled and cubed,
   or commercially pre-cooked

1 cup sliced mushrooms

½ cup coarsely chopped walnuts

1 onion, thinly sliced

(continued...)

3 tablespoons red wine vinegar

2 tablespoons extra virgin olive oil

1 teaspoon light soy sauce

1 teaspoon finely chopped fresh garlic

1/2 cup sesame seed crisp strips

Make sure spinach is young and invitingly green. Wash carefully to remove all dirt, and spin or blot dry; stem the spinach, and tear into a large salad bowl. Slice orange rounds in half, then into quarters. Remove seeds. Add to salad bowl together with the Canadian bacon, mushrooms, walnuts and onions. Toss gently.

Combine the next four ingredients in a small bowl. Whisk to mix well and pour over salad. Add the sesame seed strips and toss again. Let stand 10 minutes and toss again. Serve with pride.

Serves: 4 to 6.

Spicy Cucumber Salad
Ensalada De Pepinos

If you like cucumbers you're in for a treat! That is, if you like cucumbers. Add hot sauce to taste, or leave it out entirely. Whatever, you will enjoy the fresh, clean taste.

3 cucumbers, semi-peeled and thinly sliced

1 onion, finely chopped

1/4 cup fresh minced parsley

1/4 cup rice vinegar

1/2 teaspoon garlic salt

1/4 teaspoon granulated sugar

1 cup low-fat yogurt, drained overnight,* or low-fat sour cream

3 tablespoons low-fat mayonnaise

Dash of hot sauce

*For instructions on draining yogurt, see Page 322.

1 whole canned pimiento, chopped
2 tablespoons small capers
1 head Bibb lettuce
Curly endive or radicchio for garnish

Using a vegetable peeler, slice several sides of the cucumbers longitudinally end to end; slice and put cucumbers and onion in a large salad bowl and set aside.

In the container of a blender or food processor, combine parsley, vinegar, garlic salt, sugar, yogurt or sour cream, mayonnaise and hot sauce; blend 30 seconds to a smooth consistency. Remove to a bowl. Fold in pimiento and capers. Pour over cucumbers and onions. Toss gently and refrigerate, covered, an hour. Serve over Bibb lettuce arranged on individual salad plates, or in a pretty salad bowl lined with curly endive or radicchio.

Serves: 4 to 6.

Watercress and Avocado Salad
Berros y Aguacate

The combination of watercress and avocado, smooth and crunchy, is surprisingly good. This is my favorite salad. I bet it will become yours, too. This simple salad dressing goes well with most green salads and the recipe may be doubled and refrigerated to use as needed. However, remove the dressing from refrigerator at least an hour before using. Let it stand; then shake well.

For the dressing
El adobo

3 tablespoons extra virgin olive oil
1/4 cup rice vinegar
1 teaspoon garlic salt

In a small bowl, combine dressing ingredients, and whisk to blend well. Set aside and keep at room temperature. *(continued...)*

Salad ingredients
La ensalada

1 large, ripe avocado or 2 smaller ones, peeled,
    seeded and cut in chunks
2 bunches of watercress
1 head romaine lettuce (inner leaves only)
1 red onion, thinly sliced
1 tablespoon toasted sesame seeds

Cut avocado in half, remove seed, cut into wedges, peel and cut into chunks. Place in a large salad bowl. Remove long stems and other unappealing leaves of watercress and wash thoroughly. Place in salad spinner and spin dry, or blot dry with paper towels. Add to avocado in salad bowl. Do not toss at this time.

Of the romaine lettuce, use only the tender inner leaves. Wash and spin or blot dry. Tear into bite-size lengths. Add to salad bowl together with onion and sesame seeds.

Spoon salad dressing generously overall. With 2 forks, toss lightly to saturate with tangy dressing.

Serves: 4 to 6.

Dignified Artichokes
Alcachofas Con Dignidad

Serve these artichokes with pride. The dip alone will win for you numerous compliments from your friends and family...Ya veras. Allow time to drain yogurt overnight. Department stores and kitchen specialty stores stock attractive individual artichoke serving plates, which, by the way, make a lovely gift.

For the dip
1 cup non-fat plain yogurt, drained overnight,*
    or low-fat sour cream
1/2 cup low-fat mayonnaise
1 teaspoon Dijon mustard

*For instructions about draining yogurt, see Page 322.

. . . .

¹/₂ cup finely minced onion
1 teaspoon fresh lemon juice
1 teaspoon rice vinegar
1 tablespoon small capers
2 tablespoons fresh grated Parmesan cheese
2 tablespoons crumbled feta cheese
Dash of Louisiana hot sauce
1 tablespoon dry white Spanish sherry

For the artichokes
Alcachofas

4 or 6 artichokes, depending on size
Juice of half a lemon
2 teaspoons extra virgin olive oil

Combine all dip ingredients in a bowl; by hand, mix well; cover and chill. Wash artichokes under cold running water. Trim off stem ends so they will stand gracefully at attention when placed in a Dutch oven. Remove all unsightly leaves. Using kitchen scissors, trim off ¹/₄ inch from each leaf; then rub cut ends with a lemon wedge to prevent discoloration. With your fist, pound the top end of the artichoke against a cutting board: This opens the petals and allows the artichokes to cook evenly.

Now, place them in an upright position, stem side down, in a 4- or 5-quart pot or Dutch oven with cover. Do not submerge the chokes in water, but pour enough water into bottom of the pan until it reaches 1¹/₂ inches up the side. Squeeze lemon into water, and dribble oil over all. Bring the water to a boil, reduce heat, cover and cook about 20 minutes, or until leaves pull off easily. Remove cooked artichokes and turn them upside down to drain thoroughly.

Arrange upon serving platter, accompanied by the exotic dip. To eat, discard furry inside, remove petals, then dip away!

Serves: 4 to 6.

Shrimp and Lobster Salad
Ensalada De Langosta y Gambos

We can all certainly give ourselves permission to indulge in shellfish de vez en cuando at least once in a while. There is no doubt that lobsters are a delectable crustacean. When paired with shrimp, it's even more delectable. When preparing keep oils and fat to a minimum. The hazelnuts in this recipe add special verve.

1½ pounds medium-sized shrimp, cooked, peeled and deveined
3 – 4 or 5ounce lobster tails, cooked, shelled and cut into chunks
Juice of one lemon
2 finely chopped inner celery ribs
¼ cup sliced water chestnuts
2 tablespoons finely minced onions
½ red bell pepper, finely cut
½ cup toasted and chopped hazelnuts
½ cup non-fat plain yogurt, drained;* or low-fat sour cream
¼ cup low-fat mayonnaise
1 tablespoons fresh lemon juice
1 teaspoon extra virgin olive oil
1 teaspoon rice vinegar
1 teaspoon Dijon mustard
½ teaspoon Louisiana hot sauce
¼ teaspoon salt and white pepper
Bunch of watercress for garnish

In a medium-sized mixing bowl, place shellfish; sprinkle with lemon juice; set aside.

In another medium-sized bowl, combine celery, water chestnuts, onions, peppers and nuts; mix well and add to shrimp and lobster. In yet another medium-sized bowl, combine the rest of the ingredients, and beat with a whisk to mix well. Pour over the salad and with two forks, toss gently. Transfer to an attractive salad bowl, and garnish lavishly with watercress.

Serves: 4 to 6.

*For instruction how to drain, see Page 322.

Spanish Tuna Salad
Ensalada De Atun, Costa del Sol

Try this tuna salad for a delightful change. It enlivens a buffet table because it's colorful, but best of all, the curry, onion and basil flavors bring out the best of the tuna.

2 – 6¹/₂ ounce cans albacore tuna, packed in water

2 tablespoons olive oil

2 tablespoons rice vinegar

2 tablespoons minced onion

2 tablespoons minced basil

¹/₄ cup toasted pine nuts

¹/₄ teaspoon curry powder

¹/₂ teaspoon garlic salt

4 potatoes, boiled, peeled and cubed

1 tablespoon reduced-calorie Italian dressing

1 tablespoon lemon juice

1 cup early peas

¹/₂ cup sliced inner rib celery

¹/₂ cup sliced pimiento - stuffed olives

2 hard-boiled eggs, finely minced

¹/₂ cup low-fat mayonnaise

¹/₂ teaspoon dark brown mustard

¹/₄ cup buttermilk

1 tablespoon sherry

First, place tuna in a colander to drain for a few minutes. Now, turn into a bowl and separate into chunks with a fork.

In another bowl, combine olive oil, vinegar, onion, basil, nuts, curry powder and garlic salt; add to tuna, and mix lightly. Set aside. This may be prepared a day ahead, and allowed to marinate. Put potatoes in a 4- or 5-quart pot, and cover with water. Bring to a boil, cover and cook 25 minutes. Drain. When cool enough to handle, peel and cube. While warm, sprinkle with the dry salad mix and

(continued...)

lemon juice. Stir once gently. Allow to marinate one hour at least. Add tuna mix to potatoes, together with peas, celery, olives and eggs.

Mix mayonnaise, brown mustard, buttermilk and Amontillado Jerez Sherry. Pour over salad, and with two forks, toss lightly but thoroughly. Turn into a pretty salad bowl and garnish *a capricho* -- however you like.

Serves: 4 to 6.

Don Quixote Salad
Ensalada Don Quixote

Use a good crisp romaine for this romance-inducing salad. For added color add raddichio and a peppery arugula, both excellent choices. A combination of two or three makes a beautiful salad.

2 heads of romaine lettuce, tough stems removed

¼ cup raisins, soaked in 2 tablespoons light rum

¼ cup toasted and chopped walnuts

1 pickling cucumber, peeled and sliced

1 red onion, sliced thinly into rings

4 ounces feta cheese, crumbled

2 tablespoons extra olive oil

1 teaspoon finely chopped garlic

¼ cup rice vinegar

2 tablespoons fresh grated Parmesan cheese

Cherry tomatoes for garnish

Wash lettuce thoroughly, spin or blot dry, and tear into bite-sized pieces. If using romaine lettuce, use the tender leaves only; do not use the tough green outer leaves. Place in large bowl; add raisins and walnuts. Add cucumber, onion rings and feta cheese. Toss lightly.

Combine olive oil, garlic salt, vinegar and Parmesan cheese; mix well with a whisk. Pour over salad and with two forks, toss lightly but well. Transfer to a pretty salad bowl or divide among 6 salad plates. Garnish with the cherry tomatoes, whole or sliced in two.

Serves: 4 to 6.

Walnut Potato Salad
Ensalada de Patatas y Nueces

For a family outing or a Fourth of July celebration, this salad fits right in. It is a perfect accompaniment to any covered dish of the picnic category. The walnuts in particular make this salad outstanding.

5 large potatoes, boiled, peeled and cubed
2 tablespoons rice vinegar
2 tablespoons low-calorie dry Italian salad dressing
1 cup chopped inner ribs of celery
2 tablespoons finely minced onion
1/2 red bell pepper, cleaned and finely chopped
1/2 cup sliced pimiento-stuffed olives
2 tablespoons finely chopped parsley
2 hard-boiled eggs, finely minced
1/2 cup low-fat yogurt
3/4 cup low-fat mayonnaise
1 tablespoon extra virgin olive oil
1 tablespoon lemon juice
1/2 teaspoon prepared horseradish
1/2 teaspoon mustard
1/2 cup toasted walnuts
Pimiento strips and watercress bouquet for garnish

(continued...)

In a large 4- or 5-quart pot, place potatoes, cover with water and bring to a boil. Turn down to medium and cook briskly 20 minutes, or until potatoes are tender. Now, test potatoes (pierce only one) with a skewer. Drain water and allow to cool slightly.

When cool enough to handle (they should be warm), peel and cube. Place in a large mixing bowl. Sprinkle with vinegar and dust with dry dressing. Marinate about an hour, until potatoes are cool.

Combine celery, onion, pepper, olives, parsley and eggs; add to potatoes and toss carefully. In a separate medium-sized bowl, mix yogurt, mayonnaise, olive oil, lemon juice, horseradish and mustard; whisk and mix thoroughly. Pour over the potatoes, and with two forks, toss gently but well. Upon a shallow salad platter, pour half the potato salad. Sprinkle with half the walnuts. Spoon the remaining salad mixture over the walnuts, then sprinkle walnuts over all. Garnish *a capricho* with pimiento and watercress.

Serves: 6 to 8.

Enchanting Chicken Salad
Ensalada de Pollo, Encantadora

If you are looking for a chicken salad that is out of this world, you will enjoy this simple but simply delicious recipe. Artichokes, olives, celery and walnuts add a very special blend of flavors.

5 – 5 ounce chicken breasts, cooked, skinned, boned and cubed
1 teaspoon butter
1 tablespoon olive oil
1/2 cup low-fat plain yogurt or sour cream
1 cup low-fat mayonnaise
14-ounce can artichoke hearts, drained and finely chopped
1 tablespoon fresh lemon juice
1/4 cup sliced pimiento-stuffed olives
1/2 cup chopped hearts of celery
1/4 cup chopped walnuts

2 tablespoons fresh minced parsley

2 tablespoons fresh grated Parmesan cheese

Salt and pepper to taste

1 tablespoon dry sherry

Bibb lettuce leaves

Preheat oven to 350 degrees. Melt 1 teaspoon butter and 1 tablespoon olive oil, and brush chicken with it; put it in a 13x9x2-inch baking pan, covered. Bake 30 minutes. When chicken is cool, skin and bone it, and cut into cubes.

Place cubed chicken in a large mixing bowl. In another bowl, combine yogurt and mayonnaise; add artichokes. Sprinkle lemon juice over all. Now add the rest of ingredients in order given, except the lettuce, and mix well. Pour over chicken. With two forks, mix thoroughly. Cover and chill at least an hour. Transfer to a pretty salad bowl lined with leafy lettuce.

Serves: 6 to 8.

Tropical Chicken Salad
Ensalada de Pollo Tropical

The combination of chicken and tropical fruit is a staple of Caribbean cooking. Though in Florida, we are fortunate to have a good selection of fruit most of the year, elsewhere other seasonal fruit may be substituted for mango or papaya. Small green or purple seedless grapes are a fine substitute. Either way, you will have compliments left and right.

5 – 5 ounce chicken breasts, cooked, skinned, boned and cubed

Salt and pepper to taste

1 tablespoon butter or margarine

1 tablespoon extra virgin olive oil

Juice of one lemon or lime

1 teaspoon oregano

1/4 cup blond raisins, soaked in 2 tablespoons rum

(continued...)

1 cup unsweetened chunk pineapple, halved and well-drained
½ cup toasted hazelnuts or walnuts
1 cup diced ripe peeled mango
1 cup diced ripe peeled papaya
½ cup low-fat plain yogurt
½ cup low-fat mayonnaise
2 tablespoons low-fat sour cream
¼ teaspoon granulated sugar
1 can mandarin oranges, or other oranges for garnish
1 ripe avocado, peeled, seeded and sliced, for garnish
Juice of half a lemon or lime

First thing, and this can be done the day before, bake the chicken. For this recipe, five chicken breasts will give you enough. Preheat oven to 350 degrees F.

Salt and pepper chicken, and place in a shallow baking pan. Melt 1 tablespoon butter or margarine, and combine with 1 tablespoon olive oil, plus the juice of one lemon. Add to this ¼ teaspoon crushed dry oregano. Mix well and dribble over chicken. Cover and bake 30 minutes. Allow to cool, then dice. Cover and refrigerate until ready to use.

When you are ready to assemble the salad, in a large mixing bowl, combine chicken and raisins, pineapple and nuts; toss gently. Add mango and papaya, but do not toss yet. In a separate bowl, combine yogurt, mayonnaise, sour cream and sugar, and mix well. Pour over salad, and with two forks, toss lightly but thoroughly. Mango and papaya bruise easily, so be careful.

To garnish, use mandarin sections to outline the salad, or drape a ripe avocado, dipped in lemon juice and sliced, around its edges.

Serves: 4 to 6.

* *

The combination of chicken and tropical fruit is a staple of Caribbean cooking.

Hot Chicken Salad
Ensalada de Pollo, Caliente

This has been a favorite in my family for years. Lately, I've made just a few changes in the recipe, trimming butter and oil and adding fortifying herbs and spices. The addition of good dry sherry ties it altogether. The sherry is the hallmark of the Spanish cocina, or kitchen.

4 – 6 ounce chicken breasts
¼ cup lime or lemon juice
1 teaspoon finely chopped garlic
¼ cup dry sherry
1 shallot, minced
1 tablespoon butter or margarine
2 cups minced celery
1 cup fresh, thinly sliced mushrooms
½ cup toasted and chopped hazelnuts, divided
2 tablespoons olive oil
2 tablespoons flour
1 cup skim or 1% milk
½ cup defatted, low-sodium chicken broth
½ cup strained drippings
2 teaspoons low-sodium soy sauce
Pinch of nutmeg
2 tablespoons chopped cilantro
2 tablespoons fresh tarragon, or 1 tablespoon dried
2 tablespoons fresh basil, or 1 tablespoon dried
½ cup shredded part-skim Mozzarella cheese
Parsley bouquets for garnish

Preheat oven to 350 degrees F. Wash and trim chicken; place in a shallow baking pan measuring 13 x 9 x 2 inches. Sprinkle with lime juice and garlic salt; pour sherry around the chicken. Scatter shallots over all and dot with butter. Cover and bake 25 to 30 minutes.

(continued...)

Remove from oven and cool; when chicken is cool enough to handle, remove from pan and strain drippings. Cube the breasts into a large mixing bowl. Add celery, mushrooms and half of the hazelnuts. Toss gently and set aside.

Heat olive oil in a skillet. Add flour and cook, stirring until the flour turns a golden color. Remove skillet from heat. Combine milk, broth, drippings, soy sauce and nutmeg. Mix well. Slowly add to the skillet, stirring to smooth out any lumps. Return skillet to heat, and add cilantro, tarragon and basil; mix thoroughly. Cook at moderate heat until sauce thickens.

Transfer chicken mixture into the same pan in which it was baked. Pour sauce over all. Scatter remaining hazelnuts over casserole. Mix carefully.

Sprinkle cheese evenly over all. Bake 25 or 30 minutes, or until bubbly and cheese has melted. Remove from oven, and garnish with parsley bouquets.

Serves: 4 to 6.

FISH AND SHELLFISH

Pescados Y Mariscos

Today's trend towards healthful and nutritious eating habits has resulted in a tremendous increase in the consumption of seafood.

Seafood may very well be considered "fast food," simply because it cooks quickly and easily. The additional benefit of protein, vitamins and minerals makes it a welcome addition to any meal. A few species – mackerel, sturgeon, and bluefish, for instance, and some varieties of salmon are high in fat. Yet, most fish are surprisingly low in fat compared to beef and other meats.

In this chapter, you will see that my favorite choice for many of these recipes are firm white fishes of the low-fat species, such as scrod, orange roughy, red snapper, grouper and flounder, to name a few. Pompano is categorized as a moderately fat fish, but in my opinion, it is one of the very best tasting in the world. Mahi-mahi (dolphin) falls gracefully into this category, as does trout and most varieties of salmon.

No matter what species, fish cooks quickly always so avoid over cooking! Poaching, sautéing and baking are methods for cooking that retain moisture and enhance flavor.

Remember that fish and shellfish are extremely perishable, so allow them to remain in your refrigerator no longer than 24 hours. A good rule of thumb is to buy it, cook it, then serve it!

If you will be baking whole fish, keep in mind that fish requires expert scaling. At your seafood market, there is always the friendly fishmonger to help you. He is well-equipped with the necessary utensils and will do a good job.

It is much more convenient for this objectionable chore to be done there than in your kitchen!

If fillets or steaks are what you prefer, choose the whole fish, and ask the fishmonger to skin, bone and fillet it as you wish. Remember to ask for the trimmings (head, tail, bones) to make a good rich stock at home. If you don't have one of your own, the first recipe in this selection is my favorite.

The freshness of seafood is of utmost importance. Check for eyes that look alive and bulging; gills should boast a healthy pink color, and feel firm to the touch. There should be a clean – not fishy – smell. Your selection should make you feel that, for sure, it was the catch of the day.

Just a word about frozen fish. With today's modern technology of processing and blast-freezing fish right on the boat, the moment they are caught quality and freshness are usually preserved. Therefore, using frozen fish is not forbidden, yet fresh – as with most products – is always better.

Dive in to these easy-to-prepare seafood preparations – I know you will enjoy these treasures of the sea!

Recipes

Fish Stock

Herbed Lemon Trout with Champagne

Fillet of Grouper with Hot Honey Sauce

Poached Salmon in Green Sauce

Baked Salmon Patties

Red Snapper in Red Sauce

Baked Red Snapper

Beautifully Baked Halibut

Fillet of Flounder, San Isidro

Broiled Pompano with Sherried Sauce

Fillet of Pompano and Brown Rice

Fillet of Fish Picasso

Parslied Fish Steaks al Vino

Baked Fillet of Fish with Tomatoes

Seafood Shells

Creole Jambalaya

Festive Seafood Paella

Poor Man's Paella

Seafood Stew

Tuna Rice Casserole

Clarita's Tuna Nicoise

Mussels and Clams Vinaigrette

Mussels Paradise

Cherrystone Clams with Garbanzos

Salt Cod in Viscaya Salsa

Codfish with Herbs

A good fish stock is a necessary ingredient when preparing some of the dishes to follow. Clam broth or powdered versions are available in the supermarket if you are not able to make your own.

Fish Stock
Fumet de Pescado

2 pounds head, tail and fish trimmings

1 quart water

1 .5-gram container imported saffron threads,
    toasted and crushed*

1 onion, cut in two

1 sprig of basil

1 sprig of parsley

1 sprig of thyme

1 whole ripe tomato

1 bay leaf

2 garlic cloves, crushed

1 carrot, cut in thirds

2 cups dry white wine

Salt and hot sauce to taste

Rinse fish trimmings thoroughly. Place in a large, 2^1/$_2$ quart stock pot. Cover with water. Bring to a brisk boil. Skim several times. Add saffron, plus remaining ingredients. Reduce heat to low and cook covered 30 minutes, skimming if necessary until foam disappears. Strain stock through a fine sieve lined with cheesecloth layers.

Discard trimmings and vegetables. Once stock is thoroughly cool, use what you need in recipe. The rest may be frozen in containers for later use.

Serves: 4 to 6.

* For instructions on how to toast saffron, see Page 322.

Herbed Lemon Trout with Champagne

Trucha Asada al Champagne

This fish entree, so elegantly presented, is easily the highlight of a well-planned special occasion dinner. It is sure to please your most discriminating friends and relatives as well. Not only is it colorful but the crunchy texture and flavor blend with the wine to make it a night to remember. Use a dry "cava," a Spanish sparkling wine for the best results.

3 whole trout, less than a pound, boned and scaled,
   or pompano as a substitute
3 tablespoons extra virgin olive oil
Juice of one lemon
Salt and white pepper to taste
1/2 cup fresh minced cilantro
1/2 cup fresh minced tarragon
Olive oil spray
3 tablespoons fresh rosemary
3 garlic cloves, pressed
1 red bell pepper, roasted*
1 yellow bell pepper, roasted*
1/4 cup Champagne or sparkling wine, divided
1/4 cup pine nuts, chopped and toasted

Preheat broiler.
Brush trout with olive oil, reserving any that remains. Squeeze lemon juice over fish. Season prudently with salt and white pepper. Into the cavity of each trout, place 2 tablespoons fresh minced cilantro and tarragon and 1 tablespoon minced rosemary.
Slice squeezed lemon into 3 rings; place one in each cavity. Press openings to close.
*For instructions on roasting peppers, see Page 321.

(continued...)

Spray a broiler pan with olive oil. Place trout on broiler pan. Broil 4 minutes on each side, 5 inches from heat source. In the meantime, prepare a shallow baking pan that will cradle the trout comfortably. In a bowl, mix remaining cilantro, tarragon and rosemary with pressed garlic and the reserved olive oil. Mix well and scatter over baking pan. Place bell pepper strips artistically over herbs.

Change oven selector from broil to bake setting at 350 degrees F. Place broiled trout atop the vegetables; sprinkle with half of the champagne. Scatter the pine nuts over fish. Bake 15 minutes, uncovered; sprinkle rest of champagne. Remove from oven. Remove herbs and lemon from trout cavities and discard. Serve hot.

Serves: 4 to 6.

Fillet of Grouper with Hot Honey Sauce

Fillete de Pescado Cantabrico

Any fish fillet of a firm white texture may be substituted for grouper, a popular coastal fish. The sauce that accompanies this fish entree is a delightful meld of sour and sweet flavors, soft and crunchy textures. Chicken fillets are equally delicious with this sauce.

6 – 6 ounce fillets of fresh grouper, thinly sliced

2 tablespoons lemon or lime juice

½ cup all-purpose flour

½ teaspoon salt

1 teaspoon white pepper

1 teaspoon finely chopped garlic

2 tablespoons extra virgin olive oil

Olive oil spray

Place fish in a shallow glass or ceramic heat-resistant pan. Sprinkle with lemon juice. Set aside.

Combine flour, salt, pepper and garlic salt. Spread seasoned flour into a flat plate. Remove fish from pan onto paper towels. Pat dry. Brush fillets ever so lightly with 1 tablespoon of olive oil; reserve the rest. Coat each fillet with flour mixture; shake off excess. Spray a large non-stick skillet with olive oil spray. Add reserved oil and heat.

Add fish, and cook until done, about 8 minutes on each side.Clean original oven pan with paper towels. Place cooked fish in pan and place pan, covered, in oven warmer while preparing sauce.

Hot Honey Sauce
Salsa de Miel Calentica

³/₄ cup honey

3 tablespoons rice vinegar

¹/₂ cup light brown sugar

1 teaspoon hot sauce (more if you like)

2 tablespoons dry sherry

1 tablespoon cornstarch

¹/₂ cup water

¹/₂ red bell pepper, julienned

¹/₂ yellow bell pepper, julienned

Sprinkle of fresh minced dillweed

In a saucepan, combine honey and vinegar, brown sugar, hot sauce and sherry. Add cornstarch to water and stir to dissolve. Add slowly to ingredients in pan. Cook, stirring until mixture thickens. Remove from heat. Add bell pepper. Cover and set aside. The hot sauce will blanche the peppers until they are just crunchy.

Remove fish from warmer. Spoon some of the sauce over fish, then sprinkle fish generously with dillweed. Pour remaining sauce in a sauceboat and make room for it in the center of the platter.

Serves: 4 to 6.

Poached Salmon in Green Sauce
Salmon en Salsa Verde

In my opinion, one of the best ways to prepare salmon is poached. Served with a good sauce on the side, it makes an excellent company entree. The truth of the matter is that salmon does not require a lot of pampering during cooking. It is a hearty, nutritious dish that cooks quickly without fuss, with the added benefit of a distinct flavor all of its own. The addition of papaya and avocado gives the entree a real touch of elegance.

Ask the fishmonger to cut serving sizes of salmon steaks (not fillets) just less than an inch thick. This entree is just as good the day after it is first served, reheated in the microwave.

6 – 6 ounce salmon steaks
Juice of a one lemon
$1/4$ cup dry white wine
1 bay leaf, crushed
Salt and white pepper
$1 1/2$ cups water
$1/4$ cup 1% milk
$1/2$ cup low-fat plain yogurt
1 cup low-fat mayonnaise
1 tablespoon lemon juice
$1/4$ cup finely minced Italian parsley
2 tablespoons fresh minced green onion
2 tablespoons minced cilantro
2 tablespoons minced fresh basil
3 garlic cloves, minced
Salt
Lettuce leaves and slices of avocado and papaya
Sprinkle of lemon juice

In a large skillet with cover, place salmon steaks. Sprinkle with lemon juice and wine. Add bay leaf. Dust fish with salt and white pepper. Pour in 1½ cups of water. Bring to a boil. Cook briskly 1 minute. Reduce heat to low. Cover skillet and poach gently for 15 or 20 minutes, or until fish flakes easily.

While fish poaches, prepare sauce.

In a deep bowl, combine milk and next 9 ingredients, ending with salt. Beat with wire whisk until blended. Pour mixture into a blender container, and blend scarcely 10 seconds. Transfer to a bowl with cover. Check seasonings. Add more if needed. Refrigerate while fish cooks.

Prepare a pretty platter, and line with crisp lettuce. Place fish artistically over lettuce. Make room in center to accommodate sauce. Just before serving, garnish by placing salmon with alternate slices of avocado and papaya slices. Sprinkle with lemon juice to avoid discoloration.

Serves: 4 to 6.

Baked Salmon Patties
Torticas de Salmon

These salmon patties have always been a hit with my family and friends. The mixture also lends itself to a mouth-watering croquette. These patties are baked, not fried, and are deliciosos. Served with a baked potato and arroz cilantro rounds up an excelente meal.

Salsa

½ cup low-fat mayonnaise

½ cup low-fat plain yogurt*

2 tablespoons lemon juice

2 garlic cloves, pressed

2 tablespoons finely minced green onions or scallions

8 pimiento-stuffed olives, finely chopped

* You may wish to remove some of the whey from the yogurt. If so, increase yogurt to 1 cup, line a colander with double cheesecloth and place over bowl or plate; pour in yogurt, and refrigerate overnight. You should have ½ cup of yogurt for the recipe the next morning.

(continued…)

½ teaspoon hot sauce, or to taste

½ teaspoon salt, or to taste

1 tablespoon finely minced parsley or cilantro

In a bowl, combine all ingredients in order listed. Mix gently but thoroughly. Cover and refrigerate for one hour or longer.

Patties

1½ pounds leftover salmon, or a 15½ ounce can and
    a 7½ ounce can pink salmon

1 cup finely crumbled day-old bread

½ cup evaporated skim milk

1 teaspoon extra virgin olive oil

½ cup chopped green onions

¼ cup finely minced mushrooms

2 tablespoons dry vermouth

1 tablespoon lemon or lime juice

Salt and hot sauce to taste

1 tablespoon minced fresh dill

1 egg plus 1 egg white, well-beaten

1 cup seasoned dried bread crumbs

Olive oil spray

Preheat oven to 325 degrees F.

Drain salmon well, remove dark skin and bones; flake finely into a deep bowl. Combine bread and milk. When bread has absorbed milk, add to flaked salmon. In a small skillet, heat oil. Add onion and mushrooms. Sauté at low heat, until almost dry, 3 minutes. Add to salmon in bowl, together with vermouth, lemon juice, salt, hot sauce and dillweed. Add egg. With 2 forks, mix thoroughly but lightly. Form 10 to 12 patties.

Spread seasoned breadcrumbs in a shallow plate. Coat patties on both sides. Pat to make breading adhere. Shake off excess. Spray a cookie sheet well with olive oil. Place prepared patties on cookie sheet, and bake 20 to 25 minutes, until golden; remove from oven. Transfer patties to a pretty serving platter. Make room in center for the yummy sauce. Adorn platter with fresh herb leaves, such as parsley, basil or thyme.

Serves: 4 to 6.

Red Snapper in Red Sauce
Pargo en Salsa Colorada

One of the most incredibly delicious fish caught off of the Gulf Coast of Florida is red snapper which, in my opinion, is comparable to the famous Merluza, which resides off the coast of Spain. The meat of the fish is firm, yet juicy and pearly white. It rates high in nutrients, and adapts well to most fish recipes. Filleted or cut into steaks, it remains firm. It is the proud centerpiece of a very enticing meal.

6 – 5 ounce fillets red snapper
1 tablespoon extra virgin olive oil
Salt and white pepper to taste
Juice of a one lemon
1 tablespoon butter, or margarine
1 onion, peeled and chopped
4 garlic cloves
2 tablespoons fresh minced basil
2 tablespoons fresh minced thyme
2 tablespoons minced cilantro
1 tablespoon fresh minced oregano
$1/2$ teaspoon fennel seeds
$1/2$ teaspoon nutmeg
3 cups fresh tomatoes, peeled, seeded and chopped
$1/4$ cup dry white wine
2 tablespoons rice vinegar
$1/4$ cup fresh grated Mozzarella cheese
$1/4$ cup minced parsley

(continued...)

Preheat oven to 325 degrees F.

Place fillets in a shallow baking pan. then brush fish with the oil. Dust with salt and white pepper. Squeeze lemon juice over all. Set aside. In a skillet, melt butter. Add onion. Sauté until translucent. Add garlic, basil, thyme, cilantro, oregano, fennel and nutmeg. Sauté until fragrant, stirring with wooden spoon. Add tomatoes, wine and vinegar. Mix well. Cook no longer than 3 minutes. Remove from heat and cool slightly.

Pour mixture into an electric blender container or food processor. Pureé until smooth. Return blended mixture to skillet and heat thoroughly, adding a little water if needed. Pour over fish in casserole. Cover tightly with foil, crimping at edges. Bake 20 minutes. Uncover. Sprinkle with cheese. Return to oven. Bake uncovered until cheese melts, about 10 minutes. Remove from oven. Decorate with parsley and an extra sprinkle of wine. Serve hot.

Serves: 4 to 6.

Baked Red Snapper
Pargo Asado

Salsa, today's popular concoctions of tomatoes, onions, bell peppers, garlic, and herbs has become an integral part of the universal culinary language. It can be used very effectively to jazz up a variety of recipes. This red snapper, baked in a pool of well-seasoned salsa, is my family's favorite. In most Spanish homes, Pargo Asado reigns supreme on Christmas Eve. I prefer dried crushed oregano leaves for this recipe rather than fresh ones.

4 to 4$\frac{1}{2}$ pound whole red snapper, scaled, gutted and cleaned

1 tablespoon extra olive oil

1 lemon

2 tablespoons dry sherry

Salt and white pepper to taste

2 tablespoons extra virgin olive oil

1 onion, finely chopped

1 green bell pepper, finely chopped

2 tablespoons fresh minced basil

2 tablespoons minced cilantro

1 teaspoon dried oregano, crushed

3 to 4 garlic cloves, minced

3 cups fresh ripe plum tomatoes, peeled, seeded and chopped

1/4 cup plus 2 tablespoons dry white wine

2 tablespoons red or white wine vinegar

Parsley bouquets

At the fish market, ask the fishmonger to scale, gut and thoroughly clean fish. Leave head and tail on if you wish. Put fish in a shallow baking pan that will cradle it comfortably. Brush fish with olive oil. Cut lemon in half, crosswise, and slice a 1/4 inch round from it. Reserve for later. Squeeze the rest of the lemon over fish, then sprinkle with sherry. Dust prudently with salt and white pepper. Cover with foil and refrigerate for at least one hour. If you have room in the coldest part of your refrigerator, the fish can marinate overnight; however, dribble an extra tablespoon of olive oil over it, and cover securely with tin foil, okay?

When you are ready to prepare the fish, preheat the oven to 350 degrees F.

Using a large bowl, combine olive oil and next 9 ingredients in order listed, finishing with vinegar. Mix ingredients well. Cover bowl, and marinate at room temperature 30 minutes or so. Remove fish from refrigerator. Make 2 incisions on top of fish. Cut reserved lemon rounds in two, and stuff half lemon round into each incision. Lift fish slightly. Spoon half of the salsa mixture underneath. Pour remaining sauce over and around fish.

Bake, loosely covered with foil, 30 minutes, basting well at intervals. Remove foil. Bake uncovered another 30 or 40 minutes longer or until fish flakes easily. Remove from oven. Garnish with parsley bouquets and serve hot.

Serves: 4 to 6.

Beautifully Baked Halibut
Mero Asado con Gusto

Halibut compares favorably with Mero, a luscious and very famous fish with firm white flesh. It is caught off the coastal waters of Spain and is a very popular species. A constant debate continues among Spaniards about which of the two fish is the better, El Mero or La Merluza. The latter almost always ranks on top, but just barely. Both are both excellent fish and quite versatile, enough to permit almost any method of cooking. La Merluza is comparable to our Gulf Coast red snapper in texture, taste and appearance. It is available in some markets, but most often is frozen. For this recipe, halibut, red snapper, or any firm white fish will do just fine.

6 – 6 ounce fillets of halibut, uniformly sliced and less
    than an inch thick
Juice of one half lemon
Salt and white pepper
2 slices of bacon
1 tablespoon reserved bacon grease
1 tablespoon extra virgin olive oil
1 white onion, minced
1 cup chopped red bell pepper
1/4 cup slivered almonds
4 garlic cloves, minced
1/4 cup minced cilantro
2 firm ripe tomatoes, peeled and seeded
2 tablespoons dry sherry
1/2 cup sliced pimiento-stuffed olives

    Preheat oven to 375 degrees F. Spray with olive oil a 13 x 9 x 2 inch casserole and place fish in it. Squeeze lemon over fish, and dust with salt and white pepper.

    In a non-stick skillet, crisp bacon. Or, cook it in the microwave, which removes more of the fat. Remove to paper towels, crumble, and set aside. Discard grease from skillet, reserving 1 tablespoon. Add olive oil to skillet and heat. Sauté onions and peppers until translucent. Add almonds, garlic and cilantro. Cook, stirring, at low heat until almonds appear golden and all is fragrant, about 5 minutes. Add crumbled bacon and stir well.

Spoon mixture evenly over fish. Slice tomatoes onto a platter; carefully remove seeds. Place slices over vegetables, overlapping if necessary. Sprinkle with sherry and scatter olives over all. Dust with salt and white pepper.

Bake, uncovered, until fish is cooked, about 25 minutes.
Serves: 4 to 6.

Fillet of Flounder, San Isidro
Filete de Lenguado, San Isidro

A simple way with fillets of flounder. Cooks easily, deliciously and quickly. Ya veras.

6 – 6 ounce fillets of flounder, grouper, scrod or snapper
Juice of one lemon or lime
1/4 cup low-sodium soy sauce
Olive oil spray
2 tablespoons extra virgin olive oil
2 teaspoons butter or margarine
1 white onion, sliced in rings
1 cup thinly sliced fresh mushrooms, preferably button
    mushrooms
3 garlic cloves, minced
1 tablespoon freshly minced basil
1 tablespoon freshly minced thyme
1 tablespoon freshly minced oregano
2 tablespoons cider vinegar
2 tablespoons dry sherry
Dash of Spanish paprika
1/4 cup finely minced parsley

(continued...)

Preheat oven to 375 degrees F.

Place fillets in a shallow glass baking pan that will accommodate the fish comfortably. Combine lemon juice and soy sauce. Pour over fish. Cover. Marinate 30 minutes or so. Lift fillets to paper towels and pat dry. Strain marinade into small bowl; set aside for later use. Clean marinating pan and spray with olive oil.

In a large non-stick skillet, heat oil. Carefully sauté fish, about 4 minutes on each side. As fish cooks, using a wide spatula, remove fillets to prepared baking pan. Clean skillet. Add butter to skillet. When butter melts, add onion rings. At low heat, caramelize the onion, stirring with care; this will take about 3 minutes. With slotted spatula, remove onion rings from skillet. Spread evenly over fish. Cover and set aside.

To drippings in skillet, add mushrooms, garlic, basil, thyme and oregano. Sauté at low heat until mushrooms appear tender and all is fragrant. Combine vinegar, sherry (I recommend Tio Pepe), and reserved marinade; pour into skillet. Cook until liquid is slightly reduced. Spoon mixture evenly over fish. Bake, uncovered, 15 minutes. Fish should flake easily. Remove from oven. Sprinkle with Spanish paprika, then scatter with parsley. Serve *con gusto*.

Serves: 4 to 6.

Broiled Pompano with Sherried Sauce
Pompano a la Parrilla

Pompano is a fish in a class all its own. It is, without doubt, one of the finest and most sophisticated tasting of all fish. It lends itself beautifully to all methods of cooking. However, in order to capture the richness of the fish, baking or broiling are usually the best methods. Here is the broiled version that is in such demand in most fine restaurants.

3 whole pompano, less than a pound each
1 tablespoon extra virgin olive oil
Salt and white pepper to taste

Olive oil spray

2 tablespoons olive oil; or 1 tablespoon olive oil and
1 tablespoon clarified butter*

¼ cup lemon or lime juice

2 tablespoons dry sherry

½ teaspoon salt

2 tablespoons small capers

1 red bell pepper, roasted** and cut into uniform strips

Parsley for garnish

Ask your fishmonger to prepare the fish for broiling.
Preheat broiler unit.

At home, rinse fish well and pat dry. Brush lightly with oil and
dust prudently with salt and white pepper. Spray broiler pan with
olive oil. Place fishes side-by-side, without touching, on broiler pan.
Broil 5 inches from the heat source, 10 minutes or less per side, or
until fish flakes easily.

Remove pan from oven. Work diligently with each pompano.
Remove head and tail neatly to a bowl. Skin fish (the skin will peel
off easily). Carefully lift the fillets from each side of the fish,
leaving center spine cleared of meat. Add skin and center spine to
bowl.

Use a very sharp knife (this is important) to probe along the
edges of fillets to dislodge annoying small bones. Trimmings in
bowl may be discarded or used to prepare a good fish stock. As
fillets are cleaned of skin and bones, transfer to a heat-proof serving
platter. Cover and place in a heated oven warmer.

Combine in a screw-top jar the olive oil, lemon juice, sherry
and salt. Shake to dissolve salt. Pour into a saucepan and heat
gently without boiling. Remove platter from warmer. Spoon heated
sauce over each fillet. Sprinkle with capers, then arrange red bell
pepper strips randomly among the fillets. Scatter parsley over all.
Serve piping hot.

Serves: 4.

*For instructions about clarifying butter, see Page 317.
**For instructions about roasting peppers, see Page 321.

Fillet of Pompano and Brown Rice
Cacerola de Arroz y Pompano

Any firm white fish of your choice can take the place of pompano in this recipe. Also, brown or white long-grain rice may be substituted for the basmati brown rice. The basmati is both rich in taste and fiber.

6 – 5 ounce fillets of pompano, skinned and boned
Juice of one lemon
3 tablespoons dry white wine
1 teaspoon finely chopped fresh garlic
2 tablespoons extra virgin olive oil
1 cup minced onion
1/2 cup fresh minced red bell pepper
1/2 cup fresh minced green bell pepper
3 garlic cloves, minced
1/2 cup chopped water chestnuts
1/4 cup sliced pimiento-stuffed olives
2 tablespoons fresh minced tarragon
2 tablespoons minced cilantro
1 teaspoon salt
1 teaspoon hot sauce
2 cups brown basmati rice
3 3/4 cups defatted, low-sodium chicken broth
1/4 cup dry vermouth
2 tablespoons unbleached flour
2 tablespoons Parmesan
2 tablespoons extra virgin olive oil
2 tablespoons small capers
1 hard-boiled egg, finely minced
1 – 2 ounce jar pimientos, finely minced
1/4 cup finely minced Italian parsley
Spanish paprika to taste

Preheat oven to 325 degrees F.

In a pan with cover, put fish. Combine lemon juice, wine and garlic salt. Whisk until well-blended. Pour over fish. Refrigerate until needed.

In a heat-resistant, non-stick casserole measuring 12 x 3 inches with cover, heat olive oil. Add onion and bell peppers. Sauté until translucent. Add garlic, water chestnuts, olives, tarragon and cilantro. With a wooden spoon, stir well and cook at low heat until fragrant, 3 minutes or so. Add salt and hot sauce. Stir to mix.

Scatter rice over all, and cook until rice starts to pop, stirring constantly. Combine broth and vermouth. Pour over all. Mix carefully, but well. Bring to a slow boil. Cover, lower heat and cook over direct heat for 10 minutes. Stir again. Bake 20 minutes, until all liquid is absorbed and rice is al dente.

While rice cooks, remove fish from refrigerator. Pat dry. Combine flour and cheese. Dust fish lightly with mixture. Shake off excess. In a large non-stick skillet, heat oil. Sauté the fish until golden on each side. Place fish over rice in a decorative manner. Sprinkle capers over all. Return casserole to oven and cook 15 minutes, uncovered.

Remove casserole from oven. Combine egg and pimiento. As casserole comes out of the oven, spoon mixture over fish, then sprinkle parsley and paprika over all. Allow to rest 10 minutes before serving.

Serves: 4 to 6.

Fillet of Fish Picasso
Filete de Pescado Picasso

Here's a colorful fish entree as rich in color as any of Picasso's noted works. Any firm, white flesh fillet of fish can be prepared this way. Snapper, scrod, grouper or orange roughy are just a few good substitutes.

6 – 6 ounce fillets of white fish, such as grouper, snapper or sole
Juice of one lemon
3 tablespoons dry sherry
Olive oil spray

(continued...)

2 tablespoons extra virgin olive oil

1 onion, minced

2 garlic cloves, minced

2 tablespoons small capers

½ green pepper, roasted and cut in strips*

½ red pepper, roasted and cut in strips*

½ yellow pepper, roasted and cut in strips*

Salt and white pepper to taste

2 pounds assorted julienned fresh vegetables, such as carrots,
   zucchini, celery or string beans

Sprinkle of rice vinegar

Preheat oven to 375 degrees F.

Put fish in a shallow glass baking pan measuring 13 x 9 x 2 inches. Sprinkle with lemon juice and sherry. Cover, refrigerate and marinate 20 minutes or so. Remove fish from marinade to a large platter. Strain marinade and reserve. Clean marinating pan with paper towels. Spray pan with olive oil spray. Return fish to baking pan.

In a large skillet, heat oil. Add onion and garlic. Sauté until onion is translucent. Stir into the skillet the reserved marinade. Mix well. Spoon sauté over fish in baking pan. Scatter capers over all. Place in oven and bake 15 minutes. Remove from oven. Place strips of the roasted peppers artistically, as Picasso would, alternating colors. Dust with salt and white pepper. Return fish to oven and bake another 10 minutes, or until fish flakes easily.

In a vegetable steamer, cook julienned fresh vegetables. Transfer to a serving bowl. Sprinkle rice vinegar over hot vegetables. Toss carefully to mix. Serve with the fish for a most colorful and satisfying entree. *Buen provecho!*

Serves: 4 to 6.

*For instructions about how to roast peppers, see Page 321.

Parslied Fish Steaks al Vino
Pescado al Perejel con Vino

This recipe calls for fish steaks, as opposed to fillets; and in my opinion, red snapper steaks are best. It is a fish low in fat and firm in texture. It poaches beautifully and holds its shape well.

6 – 5 ounce red snapper fish steaks
Olive oil spray
3 potatoes, peeled and sliced into 1/2-inch rounds
$\frac{1}{2}$ cup minced Bermuda onion
$\frac{1}{2}$ cup julienned green bell pepper, divided
$\frac{1}{2}$ cup julienned red bell pepper, divided
3 garlic cloves, minced
2 tablespoons minced cilantro
2 tablespoons fresh minced thyme
$\frac{1}{2}$ teaspoon dried oregano
$\frac{1}{2}$ cup fresh minced parsley
Salt and white pepper to taste
2 bay leaves
$\frac{1}{4}$ cup extra virgin olive oil, divided
2 tablespoons all-purpose flour, divided
Salt and white pepper
$\frac{1}{2}$ cup dry white wine
Juice of one lemon

Wash steaks thoroughly. Spray with olive oil a large wide casserole, with cover. Layer potato slices to cover bottom of casserole, overlapping a few if necessary. Scatter onions over potatoes, followed by half of the peppers.

Combine garlic with cilantro, thyme, oregano and parsley. Sprinkle half of the mixture over onions. Dust all with salt and white pepper. Add the bay leaves. Now pour half the oil over all, and dust with half the flour.

Salt and pepper the steaks. Place snugly over vegetables. Dust with remaining flour. Scatter remaining bell peppers and parsley

(continued...)

mixture over fish. Pour wine around edge of casserole and add sufficient water until liquid emerges slightly at edge of casserole. Squeeze lemon juice over all, and dribble with remaining oil. Bring to a slow boil, cover, then lower heat. Cook over direct heat until potatoes are done, about 30 minutes.

Serves: 4 to 6.

Baked Fillet of Fish with Tomatoes
Pescado al Forno Entomatado

Often a recipe as simple as this one turns out to be a delight. You remember it because it's haunting flavors never quite disappear. This potato-fish combination is unique – one of so many different ways my mother prepared fish. It pleases me to be able to share with you her wealth of culinary knowledge. She had master chefs at her elbow including my father and my Uncle Pancho. I consider myself a very lucky lady to have had access to such expertise.

6 – 6 ounce fillets of firm white fish such as red snapper, orange roughy, sole or scrod

4 large potatoes

3 tablespoons extra virgin olive oil

Salt and white pepper

Olive oil spray

1 onion, minced

3 garlic cloves, minced or pressed

2 tablespoons fresh minced basil

2 tablespoons dry white wine

Salt and white pepper to taste

Juice of one lemon or lime

2 cups ripe plum tomatoes, peeled, seeded and chopped

1/2 teaspoon fennel seeds

1/2 teaspoon dried thyme

1 tablespoons small capers

Dash of Spanish paprika
Sprigs of fresh minced dill for garnish

Preheat oven to 350 degrees F.

Wash fillets. Peel potatoes. Slice thinly into rounds. Use a large non-stick heavy skillet with cover. Heat 2 tablespoons of the olive oil; reserve the rest. Layer potatoes in skillet. Dust with salt and pepper. Cover and simmer about 15 to 20 minutes, or until almost cooked. Do not brown. The potatoes should steam with the olive oil, so you must keep the heat low. If you have a problem with this, a few tablespoons of water added to the skillet will help; I find new, red-skinned potatoes cooperate very well in this endeavor.

Spray with olive oil a shallow, 2¹/₂ quart casserole. Carefully transfer potatoes to casserole, covering bottom with potato slices.

To the skillet add onions, garlic and basil. Cook at low heat until fragrant, 3 minutes. Be careful not to burn garlic! Add wine (an extra tablespoon won't hurt!). Mix well. Pour evenly over potatoes. Place fish fillets over ingredients. Dust with salt and white pepper. Squeeze lemon over fish.

Add remaining tablespoon of olive oil to skillet. Heat. Add tomatoes, fennel, thyme and capers. Cook, stirring, not more than 1 minute; just long enough to introduce ingredients to one another. Spoon mixture over fish in casserole. Place casserole in oven; bake 20 to 25 minutes, or until fish is cooked firmly. Five minutes before cooking time is up, sprinkle with Spanish paprika and dillweed.

Serves: 4 to 6.

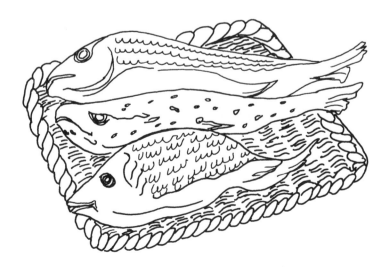

Seafood Shells
Cacerola de Marisco

This combination of seafood is best baked in individual shells or ramekins. They're perfect for presentation and the seafood combination cooks better, too. If these are not available a glass or ceramic, oblong casserole will do the trick. Follow the recipe closely and your image as a cocinera will go from buena to buenisima. I promise.

1/2 pound crabmeat, carefully picked through

1/2 pound small shrimp, cleaned and deveined

1 cup bay scallops

Juice of one lemon

2 tablespoons extra virgin olive or canola oil

1 onion, minced

1 cup chopped green bell pepper

1/2 cup thinly sliced celery

1/4 cup slivered, chopped almonds

2 or 3 garlic cloves, minced

1 – 2 ounce jar minced pimientos, well-drained

1 egg or 2 ounces egg-substitute

1/2 cup low-fat mayonnaise

1/2 cup skim or 1% milk

1/4 cup evaporated skim milk

1 teaspoon cornstarch

1/2 teaspoon Dijon mustard

1/2 teaspoon horseradish

2 tablespoons dry sherry

Dash of hot sauce

Dash of salt

2 tablespoons finely minced parsley

Olive oil spray

1/4 cup fresh grated Parmesan

Dash of Spanish paprika

Preheat oven to 325 degrees F.

In a large mixing bowl, combine cubed crabmeat, shrimp and scallops. Sprinkle with lemon juice. Set aside. In a large non-stick skillet, heat oil. Add drained seafood. Sauté only until shrimp turn pink. With slotted spoon, return to mixing bowl.

To drippings in skillet, add onion, green pepper and celery. Sauté gently until vegetables are translucent, about 3 minutes. Add almonds and garlic. Cook at low heat until almonds take on color, being careful not to burn garlic. Stir in pimientos. Pour mixture over seafood in bowl, but do not mix yet.

In a separate bowl, beat egg or egg-substitute slightly. Add mayonnaise, both milks and cornstarch. Beat with hand beater until well-blended. Add mustard, horseradish, sherry, salt and hot sauce. Blend in parsley. Pour over seafood in bowl. Toss with 2 forks until thoroughly mixed.

Spray shells or ramekins with olive oil. Spoon seafood mixture generously into shells. Sprinkle with the cheese.

Place shells upon a cookie sheet; bake in oven 15 minutes; sprinkle shells with Spanish paprika, and put back in oven 10 more minutes, or until bubbly and golden. Serve hot...outstanding!

Serves: 4 to 6.

Creole Jambalaya
Jambalaya Criolla

It does not take much to complete a hearty dinner with this recipe. A light soup of your choice, a crisp green salad, rounds of French baguettes brushed with olive oil, then dusted with grated Parmesan cheese, a flan for dessert and presto! Unlike many rice recipes, this produces a moist, tomato-rich feast. You will love this satisfying rice casserole. Ya veras.

1 pound, or 32 medium-sized shrimp, cleaned and deveined

2 slices lean bacon

1 tablespoon reserved bacon grease

2 tablespoons extra virgin olive oil

1 Spanish onion, minced

1/2 green bell pepper, seeded and coarsely chopped

(continued...)

½ red bell pepper, seeded and coarsely chopped

1 cup chopped celery

2 bay leaves, crushed

3 garlic cloves

2 tablespoons freshly minced basil

2 tablespoons freshley minced thyme

1 cup cubed lean ham

3 cups ripe tomatoes, peeled, seeded and chopped and drained

2 tablespoons tomato sauce

½ teaspoon Spanish paprika

1 teaspoon hot sauce, or to taste

Dash of salt

2 cups long-grain rice

4 cups defatted, low-sodium chicken broth

½ cup dry white wine

3 tablespoons parsley

Juice of one lemon

Preheat oven to 350 degrees F.

Clean and de-vein shrimp; set aside.

In a skillet or microwave oven, cook bacon until it is crisp. Remove to drain on paper towels. When cool, crumble and set aside. Discard bacon drippings, reserving 1 tablespoon.

In a 3-quart shallow heat-resistant casserole with cover, heat oil and bacon grease. Add onion, peppers and celery; sauté until onion is transparent. Add bay leaves, garlic, basil and thyme. Cook until fragrant, being careful to avoid burning the garlic. Add ham and reserved bacon. Stir and mix well. Cook 2 minutes or so. Add tomatoes, sauce, paprika, hot sauce and salt al gusto. Stir well with wooden spoon. Cook 3 minutes. Scatter rice evenly over all. Pour in broth and wine (I recommend Sauterne). Bring to a boil, stirring to keep rice from sticking. Cover, lower heat and cook 10 minutes over direct heat. Stir once or twice.

Add shrimp, and 1 tablespoon minced parsley. Squeeze lemon juice over all. Stir carefully. Cover and bake 20 minutes. Remove from oven. Liquids should be mostly absorbed by the rice. When you remove casserole from oven, check rice around its edge.

Sometimes you will find stubborn grains of rice that have not cooked properly; these need to be dealt with. Use a fork to carefully turn over in a folding motion the uncooked rice. Cover casserole tightly. The steam within will be sufficient for rice to finish cooking properly, *comprendes?* Scatter with remaining minced parsley. Cover tightly and allow jambalaya to rest 15 to 20 minutes before serving.

Serves: 4 to 6.

Festive Seafood Paella
Paella de Mariscos Festival

Paella, the exciting classic dish of Spain is today prepared in many ways throughout the Iberian Peninsula. While traveling through Spain, I sampled some of these dishes, and found them quite satisfying. Of course, most of these recipes are spin-offs from the one and only true Paella, which boasts a staggering potpourri of seafoods, meats and fowl. The following recipe is one to be cherished by a seafood-loving family. It is, indeed, a passport to heaven. Come along with me.

4¹/₄ cups defatted, low-sodium chicken broth or fish stock*
1 – .4-ounce container saffron, toasted**
1 red bell pepper, roasted**

In a saucepan with cover, bring broth or fish stock to a boil. Crumble in saffron. Cover, remove pan from heat, and allow to steep 30 minutes or so. While stock steeps, roast bell pepper. (Or, buy roasted peppers in a jar in your grocery). Cut in strips and set aside for garnish. Reserve one cup stock.

*For fish stock recipe, see Page 319.
**For instructions about toasting saffron and roasting peppers, see Page 321-322 .

(continued...)

Paella
La paella

1/2 pound medium shrimp, cleaned and deveined
1/2 pound sea scallops, halved
1/2 pound fillet of grouper, or other white fish like
     orange roughy or red snapper
1/4 pound lobster meat, cubed
12 mussels in shells, scrubbed and debearded***
Olive oil spray
1/4 cup extra virgin olive oil
1 1/2 cups minced onion
1 1/2 cups minced green bell pepper
5 garlic cloves, minced
2 ripe tomatoes, peeled, seeded and chopped
1/4 cup tomato sauce
2 bay leaves, crushed
2 cups rice
3 cups hot saffroned broth or fumet
1/4 cup dry white wine
Reserved 1 cup saffron stock
1 – 4 ounce can fillet of squids, drained of ink
1/2 cup frozen peas
1/4 cup fresh minced parsley
Dash wine
Roasted bell peppers for garnish

***For instructions how to debeard mussles, see Page 320.

Preheat oven to 325 degrees F.
Clean and prepare shrimp, scallops, grouper, lobster and mussels; set aside.
Spray with olive oil a 3 1/2 quart, round shallow casserole measuring 12 or 14 inches in diameter, or use a paella pan. In a

large, heavy skillet, heat all except 1 tablespoon of the oil; reserve last tablespoon. Add onions and pepper. Sauté until translucent. Add garlic, tomatoes, sauce and bay leaves. Stir to mix well; cook 3 minutes. Scatter rice evenly over all. (The rice commonly used is short-grain, or arborio, sold in Italian specialty stores; however, I prefer long-grain. It's your choice). Stir with wooden spoon to make certain rice is well-distributed.

Combine stock with the wine. Pour over rice. Mix well. Check seasonings; add more if needed. Bring mixture to a boil. Transfer to casserole. Place casserole over a large burner. Again bring to a brisk boil. Stir well. Cover and lower heat. Cook over direct heat 10 minutes. Stir once or twice to prevent sticking.

While rice cooks, combine seafood, except mussels, in deep bowl. When purchasing mussels, always ask for 2 or 3 extras, because you might have to discard unopened ones. Clean skillet with paper towels. Heat remaining oil in skillet. Add seafood to skillet and very gently sauté, 2 minutes. Add fish to casserole. Carefully mix with rice and other ingredients. Add anchovies. Pour in remaining hot saffroned stock. Stir and bring to a boil. Check seasonings.

Scatter peas over all. Carefully arrange mussels over rice in a decorative pattern. Cover casserole, and taking care not to burn yourself, bake 15 or 20 minutes or until rice is cooked and liquids are completely absorbed. Remove casserole from oven. Check mussels. Discard those that fail to open. Scatter parsley and wine over all, and garnish with strips of roasted bell pepper.

Serves: 6 to 8.

Paella, the exciting classic dish of Spain is today prepared in many ways throughout the Iberian Peninsula. This recipe is one to be cherished by a seafood-loving family. It is, indeed, a passport to heaven.

Poor-Man's Paella
Paella de Pobres

This rendition of the famous paella classic contains mostly vegetables, and is much more affordable than the original recipe. Use a paella pan with a cover, available in kitchen specialty stores, or a shallow, heat-proof pan measuring 14 x 3 inches. Such pans allow the rice to cook comfortably, with plenty of room for expansion.

1 cup small raw shrimp, cleaned and deveined

1 cup sea scallops, cubed

1 fillet of a firm white fish, such as grouper or red snapper, cut into 1½ inch pieces

4 cups defatted, low-sodium chicken stock

1 – .5 gram container saffron, toasted*

3 tablespoons extra virgin olive oil

4 boneless chicken thighs, fat removed and cut into serving pieces

1 onion, chopped

½ cup chopped red bell peppers

½ cup chopped green bell peppers

3 garlic cloves, minced

2 bay leaves, crushed

1 cup peeled, seeded and chopped plum tomatoes

¼ cup tomato sauce

¼ cup dry white wine

1 cup quartered baby artichokes

1 cup chick peas (garbanzos), or 1 can garbanzo beans

1 cup fresh snapped green beans

2 cups long-grain rice

Juice of one lemon

2 chorizos, degreased** and sliced into rounds

*For instructions on toasting saffron, see p. 322.

**For instructions on degreasing chorizos, see p. 318.

½ cup frozen green peas

1 – 2 ounce jar roasted red bell pepper, cut into strips

Sprinkle of wine

Parsley sprigs

Preheat oven to 325 degrees F.

Clean and prepare shrimp, scallops and fish; set aside.

In a saucepan, bring broth to a boil. Add crumbled saffron, cover, remove from heat, and steep 30 minutes. This may be done early in the day. Divide and reserve for later use.

In a large, heavy skillet, heat oil. Add chicken and brown well on all sides. With slotted spoon, remove to casserole. To drippings, add onions, peppers and garlic. Sauté until onion is translucent. Add bay leaves, tomatoes and tomato sauce. Cook, stirring 2 minutes.

Combine 2 cups of reserved chicken broth and wine. Pour into skillet and bring to a slow boil. Add this mixture to casserole.

Place casserole on a large burner. Add artichokes, chick peas and green beans. Stir *con cuidado*. Cook 1 minute.

Scatter rice evenly over all. Cook, stirring with care, 1 minute. Cover casserole and cook, 5 minutes. Add fish ingredients in order listed. Squeeze lemon juice over all. Pour in 1¾ cups of remaining chicken broth. Bring to a boil. Stir well. Cover and bake 15 minutes or until liquid is absorbed; uncover casserole. Place chorizo rounds over rice. Scatter the peas evenly. Cover and return to oven for 5 minutes.

Arrange roasted peppers in a pretty design across dish; sprinkle with wine and garnish with parsley bouquets.

Serves: 4 to 6.

Seafood Stew
Zarzuela de Pescado

An unforgettable fish potpourri that you will serve with pride! Cherrystone clams that you buy at the fish market have been purged, so what you have to do is give them a good scrubbing to eliminate possible sand stuck to shells. Make sure clams are closed tightly. Discard any that are not closed, so to allow for this, ask the fishmonger to throw in a few extra shells.

1 pound fillet of firm white fish, cut into 1 1/2 inch pieces
1/2 pound sea scallops, cut in half
1/2 pound shrimp, cleaned and deveined
1 – 4 ounce can squid, drained of oil and ink
18 small cherrystone clams in shells, scrubbed
1 tablespoon olive oil
1 onion, minced
3 garlic cloves, minced
2 tablespoons freshly minced basil
2 tablespoons freshly minced thyme
1 teaspoon crushed fennel seeds
1 cup sliced inner ribs celery
1/2 cup sliced pimiento-stuffed olives
3 very ripe tomatoes, peeled, seeded and chopped
1/4 cup tomato sauce
1 – 4 ounce jar minced pimientos, drained
2 bay leaves, crushed
4 cups saffroned fish stock*
1 1/2 pounds new potatoes, peeled and cubed
2 cups baby carrots, scraped
1/2 cup dry white wine
1/2 cup finely minced parsley
Juice of one lemon

*For information on saffron and fish stock, see pages 319, 322.

Clean, prepare and cut fish, scallops, shrimp, squid and clams; set aside.

In a medium-sized Dutch oven, heat the oil. Add onion and sauté until transparent. Add garlic, basil, thyme, fennel and celery. Cook at low heat until fragrant, about 3 minutes. Add olives, tomatoes and tomato sauce; cook 2 minutes, stirring to mix. Add pimiento, bay leaves and stock. (More may be added if you prefer a thinner consistency). Bring to a brisk boil. Add potatoes and carrots. Lower heat, cover and cook 20 minutes.

In large bowl, combine seafood: Fish, scallops and shrimp. Gently stir into Dutch oven. Cook until shrimp turn pink. Add chopped squid and clams. Cover and cook 10 minutes. Uncover, discard any unopened clams. Pour in the wine. Stir with care and cook uncovered 5 minutes at moderate heat. Sprinkle parsley and lemon juice over all. Cover, remove from heat and allow to rest 10 to 15 minutes before serving.

Serves: 4 to 6.

Tuna Rice Casserole
Cazerola de Atun

A very satisfying duo, tuna and rice. Readily accepted by most young people, and ready to eat within an hour. You may choose either water-packed tuna, or tuna in oil (which has many more calories and fat). Either one must be thoroughly drained before using.

3³/₄ cups defatted, low-sodium chicken broth
1 – 5 gram container of saffron threads, toasted,*
2 cans albacore tuna
2 tablespoons extra virgin olive oil
1 onion, minced
¹/₂ cup finely chopped red bell pepper
¹/₂ cup finely chopped green bell pepper
3 garlic cloves, minced
1 cup chopped celery
1 tablespoon fresh minced basil

(continued...)

*For instructions about how to toast saffron and steep broth, see Page 322.

1 tablespoon fresh minced thyme

Pinch of nutmeg

2 bay leaves

1 ripe tomato, peeled, seeded and chopped

2 tablespoons tomato sauce

Salt and hot sauce

2 cups long-grain rice

¼ cup dry white wine

½ cup frozen green peas

Pour chicken stock into a deep saucepan and bring to a boil. Add crumbled saffron. Cover. Remove from heat and allow to steep a minimum of 30 minutes. This may be done early in the day.

When the stock is ready, preheat oven to 350 degrees F. Drain tuna well, and cut into chunks. Do not flake. Set aside. In a large, non-stick heat-resistant casserole with cover, heat oil. Add onion, peppers, garlic and celery. Sauté until vegetables are transparent. Add basil, thyme, nutmeg, bay leaves, tomato and tomato sauce. Cook, stirring with a wooden spoon, 4 to 5 minutes. Add salt and hot sauce.

Scatter rice evenly over all. Stir to mix with sautéed ingredients, 2 minutes. Add reserved tuna. Combine hot saffroned broth with the wine (I recommend Sauterne). Pour this over all. Bring to a gentle boil. Stir carefully. Cover, lower heat and cook over direct heat 10 minutes. Stir carefully twice before covering casserole and baking 15 minutes, or until liquid has been totally absorbed. Remove from oven. Scatter peas over all. Cover and allow to rest 20 minutes before serving.

Serves: 4 to 6.

Clarita's Tuna Niçoise
Atun Nicoise Clarita

Paired tuna and fresh vegetables are indeed a great and satisfying entree, especially during summer, when light meals are so refreshing. Tuna Niçoise is technically a salad, but it can very well be served as an entree. The following recipe is the answer when you don' t know what to prepare for an impressive luncheon.

Dressing
Adobo

$1/4$ cup extra virgin olive oil

$1/4$ cup rice vinegar

Juice of one lemon

1 teaspoon salt

2 tablespoons fresh finely minced oregano

1 tablespoon fresh finely minced thyme

2 tablespoons fresh finely minced cilantro

3 garlic cloves, peeled or chopped

$1/2$ teaspoon hot sauce, or to taste

Into a screw-top jar, place all ingredients. Shake with energy until salt dissolves. Set aside, but do not refrigerate.

Salad
Ensalada

1 pound fresh baby string beans, washed and snapped,
   or 2 cans whole green beans, drained

2 pounds new potatoes, partly peeled and cut into quarters

2 – $6^{1}/2$ ounce cans albacore tuna, or $1^{1}/2$ pounds broiled
   fresh tuna

1 cup julienned red bell pepper

(continued...)

1 cup julienned green bell pepper

1 cup julienned yellow bell pepper

1 onion, thinly sliced into rings

½ cup sliced pimiento-stuffed Spanish Manzanilla olives

1½ cups artichoke hearts

3 hard-cooked eggs, thinly sliced

¼ cup toasted walnuts

1 – 4 ounce can anchovy fillets, drained

2 ripe tomatoes, thinly sliced

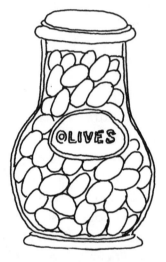

In a large vegetable steamer, place string beans and potatoes. Cover. Cook until potatoes are done. Remove from steamer. Transfer to a large mixing bowl. While vegetables are warm, saturate with 2 or 3 tablespoons of dressing. Cover and set aside.

If using fresh broiled tuna, cut into small pieces. If using canned albacore tuna, drain thoroughly and cut into small chunks. Place fish in bowl and set aside. Combine peppers, onion and olives in a large, roomy bowl. Toss lightly. Cut 5 artichokes in quarters, and add to vegetables in bowl. Add this to the string beans and potatoes, followed by the tuna. Mix gently but well. Saturate all with dressing. Transfer to a large shallow plate, distributing ingredients evenly and attractively. If you don't want to include the eggs, simply eliminate the yolks and julienne the egg whites. Scatter over all; scatter walnuts over all, then anchovy.

Outline platter with the tomato slices, and serve *enseguida* (right away).

Serves: 4 to 6.

Mussels and Clams Vinaigrette
Mejillones y Almejas Vinagreta

When purchasing shellfish at the fish market, remember that mussels and clams are usually purged. However, mussels are not debearded, since they die soon after beards are removed. Therefore, debeard the mussels and scrub both shellfish energetically to eliminate any possible grains of sand that may be stuck to shells.

2$\frac{1}{2}$ dozen small cherrystone clams in shells, purged and debearded*

2$\frac{1}{2}$ dozen small mussels in shells, purged and debearded*

1 cup dry white wine

1 teaspoon salt

2 bay leaves, crushed

$\frac{1}{2}$ cup water

3 tablespoons extra virgin olive oil

1 onion, finely chopped

1 red bell pepper, julienned in 1$\frac{1}{2}$ inch lengths

3 garlic cloves, minced

2 tablespoons fresh finely minced basil

2 tablespoons fresh finely minced thyme

2 tablespoons fresh finely minced oregano

Juice of 2 lemons

3 tablespoons rice vinegar

$\frac{1}{2}$ teaspoons Dijon mustard

$\frac{1}{2}$ cup reserved cooking stock

$\frac{1}{4}$ cup dry white wine

2 tablespoons small capers

$\frac{1}{4}$ cup fresh finely minced parsley

*For instructions how to clean and debeard shellfish, see Page 320.

(continued...)

Preheat oven to 300 degrees F.

Place shellfish in a deep saucepan with cover. Add wine, salt, bay leaves and water. Bring to a boil; cover. Cook at moderate heat 10 minutes or so, until shells open. With a slotted spoon, remove shells to a glass or ceramic shallow casserole with cover, open side up. Discard shells that remain closed. Cover and keep warm. Reduce liquid to 3/4 cup by cooking briskly. Strain into a small bowl.

In a heavy skillet, heat oil. Add onion, pepper, garlic, basil, thyme and oregano. Sauté at low heat until onion is soft and mixture is fragrant, about 3 minutes.

In a deep bowl, combine lemon juice, vinegar, mustard, stock and wine. Whisk to mix well. Add to sauté in skillet. Check seasonings; add more if needed. Cook slowly stirring 2 minutes. Spoon sauce over shellfish in casserole, saturating well. Sprinkle with capers and parsley. Cover and bake 10 to 15 minutes, until sauce and seafood are blended.

Serves: 6.

Mussels Paradiso
Mejillones at Paraiso

If you go to Brussels, of course you must have mussels. The concierge at the Windsor Hotel in Brussels, where I was staying, recommended that I go to "restaurant row," a famous street within walking distance from the hotel. Restaurants line both sides of the street, and most were excellent; every one featured a special kind of mussels on the menu.

We chose a quaint, diminutive restaurant. Mussels au gratin, laden with quality cheese were the best I have ever tasted. The following recipe is a nutritious version of the dish. For the main course, you can safely figure 12 mussels per person, or 6 for an appetizer. I chose the main course, and I ate every one of them!

4 dozen mussels, purged and debearded*

1 cup water

1/2 cup dry white wine

*For instructions on how to clean and debeard clams, see Page 320.

Juice of one lemon or lime

2 bay leaves, crushed

1 tablespoon butter plus 2 tablespoons olive oil

1 onion, finely minced

2 garlic cloves

2 tablespoons unbleached flour

1 cup 1% milk

1 cup reserved mussel stock

$\frac{1}{2}$ cup skimmed evaporated milk

1 tablespoon low-fat mayonnaise

$\frac{1}{4}$ teaspoon nutmeg

$\frac{1}{4}$ teaspoon cumin

$\frac{1}{2}$ teaspoon ginger

1 teaspoon Dijon mustard

$\frac{1}{2}$ cup grated Gruyere or Parmesan cheese, divided

Salt and hot sauce to taste

Fresh dill sprigs

Preheat oven to 350 degrees F.

Scrub mussels carefully, and put in a large pot with cover. Add water, wine, lemon and bay leaves; bring to a boil. Cover and cook briskly 10 minutes or until mussels open. Discard those that fail to open. With slotted spoon, remove mussels, still in their shells, to a large bowl. Strain cooking liquid, or stock, through a double layer of cheesecloth, and reserve for later use.

In a large, nonstick skillet, heat butter and oil. Add onion and garlic. Sauté until onion is soft. Stir in flour. Keep stirring with a wooden spoon until flour takes on a golden, delicate color. Remove skillet from heat.

Combine milk, one cup of mussel stock, mayonnaise, nutmeg, cumin, ginger and mustard. With hand beater, beat until smooth. Add the liquid mixture to the roux (flour mixture in skillet) very slowly, continue beating constantly with a whisk to dissolve all lumps.

Return skillet to heat. Cook at low heat until sauce thickens and aroma is heavenly. If you find the sauce thicker than you like, stir in 2 or 3 tablespoons of mussel stock. Sprinkle into sauce half of the cheese. Cook until dissolved. Add salt and hot sauce con

(continued...)

cuidado, but go easy because the cheese is salty. Continue cooking and stirring until sauce reaches su punto.

Preheat broiler. In a large oven-proof shallow casserole, place mussels, open side up; saturate with sauce. Scatter remaining cheese over all. Place casserole beneath broiler for 2 minutes, or until cheese melts into sauce. Sprinkle dillweed over all.

Serves: 4 diners, 12 mussels each; or 6 diners, 8 mussels each.

Cherrystone Clams with Garbanzos
Almejas con Garbanzos

This combination of beans and clams works better than you might think. If you do not like garbanzos (I can't imagine anybody not liking Spain's national bean), then substitute 2 cans of drained cannellini beans. Both work well in this recipe. Clams that are bought at fish markets are cleaned and treated; consequently, you need only to scrub them well again.

4 dozen cherrystone clams in their shells, cleaned and treated*

1 cup defatted, low-sodium chicken broth

Pinch of Spanish saffron

2 tablespoons extra virgin olive oil

1 onion, minced

1 red bell pepper, minced

4 garlic cloves, finely minced

2 bay leaves, crushed

1/4 cup freshly minced basil

1/4 cup fresh minced parsley

2 tablespoons tomato sauce

1/2 cup dry white wine

*For instructions about how to clean and debeard clams, see Page 320.

Salt and hot sauce to taste

2 cups garbanzo beans (cooked, canned are fine)

6 or 8 thin rounds of French baguette bread

Extra virgin olive oil

1-2 tablespoons finely chopped garlic

Clean and debeard clams and set aside.

In a small saucepan, bring broth to a boil. Crumble in the saffron. Cover, remove from heat and steep for about 30 minutes. In a large, deep skillet with a dome cover, heat olive oil. Add onions and pepper. Sauté until both are soft. Add garlic, bay leaves, basil and parsley. Cook slowly until fragrant. Stir in the tomato sauce, wine and reserved saffroned broth. Stir well and check seasoning; salt and hot sauce may be added at this point.

Add garbanzo beans and with a wooden spoon, stir to mix. Cook about 10 minutes. Place cleaned clams atop the other ingredients; bring to a nice boil. Cover and cook at moderate heat 10 minutes (or slightly less) until clams open. Discard those which fail to open.

Toast bread rounds and brush with olive oil; sprinkle with garlic. Place upright around edges of skillet in a scallop design. Dip from the skillet into shallow soup or spaghetti bowls.

Serves: 6 to 8.

Clams that are bought at fish markets are cleaned and treated; consequently, you need only to scrub them well again.

Salt Cod in Vizcaya Salsa
Bacalao en Salsa Vizcaya

This salt cod recipe is one of many that originated in the Spanish kitchen. There are various ways to prepare salted cod in my first book, Clarita's Cocina.

Salt cod is now available in one pound wooden boxes. On the West Coast of Florida, for instance, import shops like Castellano & Pizzo and Cacciatore & Sons stock boxed salt cod and sell more than you would imagine. Check under Latin American, Spanish, Hispanic or West Indian your local yellow pages if you have trouble locating this specialty. Keep in mind that salt cod must be soaked at least 24 hours before it is cooked to remove the excess salt, so allow plenty of time to do this recipe.

2 – 1 pound boxes salt cod
Water for soaking and cooking
Juice of one lemon or lime
2 tablespoons extra virgin olive oil
1 onion, chopped
1 green bell pepper, chopped
4 garlic cloves, minced
1 tablespoon freshly minced basil
1 tablespoon freshly minced thyme
1 tablespoon freshly minced oregano
2 bay leaves, crushed
3 ripe tomatoes, peeled, seeded and chopped
4 tablespoons tomato sauce
1 – 4 ounce jar minced pimientos, undrained
1/2 cup dry sherry
1 cup water
1/4 teaspoon granulated sugar
1 teaspoon hot sauce, or to taste
Olive oil spray

3 potatoes, peeled and sliced into ½ inch rounds
1 thin loaf French bread, cut into ½ inch rounds
2 tablespoons extra virgin olive oil
1 teaspoon chopped garlic
¼ cup fresh, finely minced dillweed or parsley

Preheat oven to 325 degrees F.

Remove salt cod from wooden boxes. Place in a roomy glass or ceramic pot with a lid. Cover with water; do not use salt cod cooking water – it would be too salty. Refrigerate and allow to soak 24 hours; change water at least 3 times during soaking process.

After desalting fish, place in a pan; add water to cover and bring to a boil. Cover and cook at moderate heat until fish flakes easily, 10 or 15 minutes. Drain and cool. Remove dark skin and bones. Flake into a deep bowl. Sprinkle with lemon juice. Cover and set aside.

In a large non-stick skillet with cover, heat oil. Add onion and pepper. Sauté gently until transparent. Add garlic, basil, thyme and oregano, and bay leaves. Cook 3 minutes, until fragrant. Add tomatoes and tomato sauce. Cook, stirring, another 3 minutes. Add pimientos, sherry (I recommend Tio Pepe), water, sugar and hot sauce. Stir well with a wooden spoon until sauce comes to a gentle boil, about 3 minutes. Cover, lower heat and cook 20 minutes or until sauce thickens.

Spray with olive oil a large, wide glass or ceramic casserole that is heat-resistant and has a cover. Line bottom with potato rounds, overlapping if necessary. Spoon one-quarter of the sauce over the potatoes. Scatter flaked cod over potatoes. Pour remaining three-fourths over all. Cover and bake in oven 45 minutes or until potatoes test done.

While cod bakes, prepare bread rounds. Allow 2 rounds per diner. Combine oil and garlic. With a bakery brush, coat each round lightly with mixture. Place bread on a cookie sheet in a single layer. Slide cookie sheet into the upper rack of oven for about 5 to 10 minutes, or until toasted. Remove from oven and cool at room temperature until crisp.

Remove casserole from oven. Place toasted bread rounds in an upright position, around edge of casserole. Now sprinkle with dill or parsley. Serve hot over steamed white rice.

Serves: 4 to 6.

Codfish with Herbs
Bacalao con Cilantro

Salt cod is popular in Spain because it is inexpensive, as well as flavorful. Many Spaniards refer to bacalao as comeda de pobres, poor-man's food. Each region has its own unique way of preparing the salted codfish.

Codfish comes ready cut in uniform squares. How grateful my mother would have been for this convenience!

2 pounds dried cod *(bacalao)*
2 egg whites
¼ cup unbleached flour
2 or 3 tablespoons extra virgin olive oil
1 onion, minced
1 cup finely chopped green bell peppers
3 garlic cloves, minced or pressed
½ cup finely minced cilantro
½ cup fresh, finely minced fresh parsley
2 bay leaves, crushed
1 teaspoon hot sauce, or to taste
1 cup dry white wine
Rice or mashed potatoes for 4-6

Remove codfish from box. Place in a wide bowl and soak 24 hours, changing water at least twice. Carefully remove dark skin and bones, then dip into egg-whites which have been beaten slightly in a medium size bowl. Lightly dust with flour; shake off excess.

Heat oil in large, non-stick skillet. Add bacalao and brown lightly on both sides. (Treat with utmost care so fish will not come apart.) Transfer fish to a 2-quart casserole with cover. To drippings in skillet, add onion, peppers and garlic. Sauté until translucent.

Add cilantro and parsley, bay leaves and hot sauce. Sauté over low heat until fragrant, about 2 minutes. Add wine to skillet; bring to a boil, stirring constantly. Pour mixture over *bacalao* in casserole. If needed, add a little water. Cover and cook, at low heat for 20 to 25 minutes being careful not to overcook.

Serve with rice or mashed potatoes.

Serves: 4 to 6.

POULTRY AND GAME

Pollo y Aves

Chicken, turkey, quail, and those dainty Cornish hens are all low in calories compared to other protein rich foods. Usually a small amount of fat added is enough to ensure excellent results.

Superb substitutes for fat and sodium are fresh herbs and spices. Wines, especially the good dry wines and sherries of Spain and California, are also marvelous for marinating and adding pep to any recipe.

Almost everybody enjoys chicken and game. So, when planning your next dinner menu, try one of these favorites on the following pages. In my opinion, they are also some of the fastest and easiest to prepare. *Es magnifico!*

And as for turkey, that luscious big bird should not be reserved only for special holidays! This year round treat that can be savored and served frequently in a potpourri of casseroles and entrees.

Here you will find recipes you can prepare and serve with pride; I know you will like them.

Recipes

Chicken "Castizo" with Mushrooms

Chicken in Sour Orange Sauce with Avocado

Honeyed Chicken Cutlets

Chicken Breast in Cranberry Sauce

Chicken with Capers, Number One

Chicken with Capers, Number Two

Marvelous Yellow Rice and Chicken

Chicken Valencia

Chicken in Rich Tomato Sauce

A Special Spanish Chicken Stew

Chicken Creole with Almond-Parsley Rice

Chicken in Cream Sauce

Chicken Stewed in Wine

Baked Chicken Breasts with Fresh Herbs and Vegetables

Baked Chicken Segovia

Delicious Chicken

Baked Chicken Vinaigrette

Cheesy Chicken Fillets

Chicken Breasts Veronique O La La!

The Cute Little Cornish Hen al Jerez

Marinated Cornish Hens

Stuffed Cornish Hens

Turkey Cutlets, al Vino

Poached Chicken and Broccoli Casserole

Chicken "El Botin"

Chicken Fricasee, Clarita's Way

Country Style Chicken Breasts

Chicken "Castizo" with Mushrooms
Pollo "Castizo" con Champiñones

A favorite chicken entree, with hardly any fuss y muy facil. Castizo is an endearing word that describes Madrilenos, those from Madrid with a sense of humor and friendly, bubbly manner. After a few tastes, you will bubble, too!

3¹/₂ or 4 pounds chicken, cut into 8 to 12 pieces
Juice of one lemon
¹/₂ teaspoon salt
¹/₂ teaspoon white pepper
2 strips lean bacon
1 tablespoon reserved bacon fat
1 tablespoon extra virgin olive oil
1¹/₂ cups fresh sliced mushrooms
¹/₂ cup pine nuts
1 onion, minced
3 garlic cloves, pressed or hand-minced
2 very ripe tomatoes, peeled, seeded and chopped
2 tablespoons tomato sauce
1 bay leaf, crushed
¹/₂ teaspoon basil, dried
¹/₂ teaspoon cumin
1 – 2 ounce jar minced pimientos, drained
¹/₄ cup Spanish dry sherry
¹/₂ cup defatted, low-sodium chicken broth
¹/₂ cup fresh minced Italian parsley

(continued...)

Preheat oven to 325 degrees F.

Trim all visible fat, wash and pat chicken dry; place chicken pieces in a large, non-metallic bowl. Squeeze lemon juice over chicken; dust with salt and white pepper. Marinate 30 minutes.

Meanwhile, in a large skillet, cook bacon until crisp. With slotted spoon, remove to a small mixing bowl. When cool, crumble. Strain bacon fat. Wipe skillet clean with paper towels. Return one tablespoon bacon fat to skillet. Add olive oil.

Lift chicken from lemon marinade. Blot dry. Heat oil and bacon fat. Cook chicken pieces about 5 minutes per side until they are browned. Set skillet aside and remove chicken to heat-resistant, glass or ceramic casserole dish measuring 12 x 3 inches, with cover.

Add mushrooms and pine nuts to skillet in which you cooked chicken. Sauté at low heat about 5 minutes, until both are delicately golden and most of liquid evaporates. With slotted spoon, remove to bowl that holds crumbled bacon.

Add onion and garlic to the same skillet. Sauté until translucent – be careful not to burn garlic. Add tomatoes, sauce, bay leaf, basil, cumin and pimientos. Stir to mix well and cook 2 minutes. Add sherry and broth. Bring to a boil, lower heat and cook 2 minutes. Taste; add salt and hot sauce al gusto. Just don't overdo it, okay? Stir well.

Scatter sauteed mushrooms, pine nuts and crumbled bacon over chicken in casserole. Carefully spoon sauté from skillet over all. Bring to a slow boil over direct heat, then place in oven for 20 minutes. Uncover, cook 10 minutes longer. Remove from oven. Sprinkle generously with parsley. Allow to rest 10 minutes before serving.

Serves: 4 to 6.

Chicken in Sour Orange Sauce with Avocado
Pollo con Naranja Agria y Aguacate

This is another of Tony Pace's, one of my favorite chef's creations. The orange sauce is prepared with sour oranges, an exotic citrus tree found in Florida and throughout the Caribbean. The fruit is inedible, but it makes a divine sauce or marinade. Sour oranges are found in most Hispanic markets and there is a bottled version but none is as good as the fresh. If you can not find sour orange, you can make a similar version by combining the juice of an orange with 2 teaspoons of lemon or lime juice.

1½ pounds chicken breast, boned and skinned;
   or 4 – 6 ounce boned breasts, trimmed and halved
¼ cup all-purpose flour
1 tablespoon grated Parmesan
½ teaspoon salt
½ teaspoon pepper
1 tablespoon extra virgin olive oil
1 tablespoon butter or margarine
3 garlic cloves, pressed
¼ cup dry white wine plus 2 tablespoons
3 tablespoons dry sherry
¼ cup defatted, low-sodium chicken broth
1 teaspoon arrowroot flour
Juice of a sour orange
1 tablespoon clarified butter*
1 – 12 ounce jar of roasted red bell peppers (Victoria)
1 ripe avocado, peeled and sliced
¼ cup fresh minced parsley or ⅛ cup dried
2 ripe plum tomatoes, peeled and seeded

Preheat oven to 325 degrees F.

Trim chicken of all visible fat, wash and pat dry. Between two sheets of waxed paper, gently pound chicken breasts until they are uniform, about a half-inch thick. In a shallow pie plate or pan, combine flour, cheese, salt and pepper; mix well, and dredge chicken; shake off excess flour.

In a heavy, non-stick large skillet, heat oil and butter. Brown chicken on both sides and transfer to a shallow ceramic or glass baking pan; bake 20 minutes. While chicken bakes, prepare sauce. In a deep mixing bowl, combine garlic, wine, sherry (I recommend

*For instructions on clarifying butter, see Page 317.

(continued…)

Tio Pepe brand), broth and arrowroot flour. Beat with whisk until smooth and flour is completely dissolved.

Place sauteing skillet over low heat. Slowly pour liquid mixture into skillet, stirring with wooden spoon to dislodge particles sticking to skillet. Correct seasoning. Pour in orange juice and butter. Cook 20 minutes, stirring at intervals until smooth and slightly thickened. Remove chicken from oven.

Cut roasted bell pepper into strips tapering to fit chicken breasts. Place a strip over each chicken breast and a slice of avocado over the bell pepper. (I recommend the dark California avocado).

Do not add avocado until you are ready to serve, as it will discolor and ruin the visual appeal of the entree.

Strain the sauce in the skillet into a bowl. Ladle on and around chicken breasts. Pour remaining sauce into a sauceboat. Believe, me, the sauce will not last *mi un minuta!* Scatter parsley over all. Place little rounds of plum tomatoes around chicken for a most impressive entree.

Serves: 4 to 6.

Honeyed Chicken Cutlets
Chuletas de Pollo a la Miel

It's sweet, yet spicy. This chicken recipe, for sure is es algo diferente. Served with brown rice and a medley of stir-fried or steamed vegetables, it will delight your family and friends. And it may add another jewel to your crown as the world's greatest cocinera. If you prefer a milder version to the hot jalapeno peppers, use half a can, or omit them entirely.

Para gustos se hicieron colores!

2¹/₂ pounds chicken breasts, boned and skinned,
    cut into 6-ounce cutlets
Spicy hot sauce to taste
1 cup honey
¹/₄ cup rice vinegar

1 teaspoon cinnamon

Dash of freshly grated nutmeg

1 – 4 ounce can jalapeno peppers, undrained

1/2 cup water

1/4 cup firmly-packed light brown sugar

1 tablespoon cornstarch, diluted in 1/4 cup water

1 red bell pepper, julienned

1 tablespoon extra virgin olive oil

1 cup unbleached flour, or may use all-purpose

1 teaspoon chopped fresh garlic

1/2 teaspoon white pepper

Olive oil spray

Preheat oven to 325 degrees F.

Trim, wash and pat dry the chicken; set aside while you prepare the sauce: In a quart-sized pot with a cover, place the next 8 ingredients, beginning with hot sauce and ending with brown sugar. Stir to mix well. Bring to a slow boil; then turn down and cook 5 minutes at medium heat.

Slowly add diluted cornstarch, stirring briskly. Continue to cook until thickened and clear, then about 2 minutes longer. Remove from heat. Add bell peppers – the heat from the sauce will blanch them.

Now turn to the chicken cutlets: Wash carefully, pat dry, and spread on waxed paper; flatten with a mallet until they are of uniform thickness, about 1/4 inch. Brush each cutlet with olive oil. Combine flour, garlic and white pepper. Dredge the olive oil-coated cutlets in seasoned flour; shake off excess.

Spray a 12-inch, non-stick skillet with olive oil, turn heat to medium-low, and add chicken. Do not crowd. If skillet does not accommodate all the chicken at one time, then cook in batches of 3, but clean skillet with paper towels and condition again with spray for each batch. Cook cutlets about 5 minutes per side. As the chicken browns, transfer to a shallow glass or ceramic oven pan measuring 13 x 9 x 2 inches.

Brush chicken generously with sauce, and bake, uncovered, in oven 20 minutes or so. Pour leftover sauce in gravy boat and pass to diners.

Serves: 4 to 6.

Chicken Breast in Cranberry Sauce
Pollo con Salsa de Arandanos

This is an unusual and very attractive chicken recipe that pairs tart and sweet ingredients along with crunchy and soft. The dish looks and tastes wonderful, is an easy yet elegant choice for dinner guests. Serve with baked potatoes or my Potatoes Cynthia, and a simply prepared vegetable, and you will be acclaimed "the best cook ever!" In this recipe, I use chicken breasts, but any part of the chicken, depending on your preference, may be used successfully.

2 pounds chicken breasts; or 6 pieces,
    about 5 ounces each, boned and skinned
1/2 cup unbleached flour
1/2 teaspoon curry powder
1/2 teaspoon cumin
1/2 teaspoon salt
2 tablespoons canola or olive oil
Olive oil spray
1 onion, peeled and thinly sliced
1 teaspoon orange zest
1/2 cup thinly sliced inner celery rib
1/4 cup fresh, thinly sliced mushrooms
1 cup whole canned cranberry sauce
2 tablespoons orange marmalade
1/4 cup white rum
1/4 cup chopped pecans

Preheat oven to 325 degrees F.

Remove all visible fat; wash and pat chicken dry. Place chicken pieces between two sheets of waxed paper and pound delicately with a meat mallet to a thin, uniform size, about a half-inch thick. Combine flour with curry powder, cumin and salt; mix well. Dredge chicken breasts lightly in flour mixture.

In a large, non-stick skillet, heat oil. Add chicken, 3 pieces at a time, and brown 3 minutes on each side. With olive oil, spray a glass or ceramic oven pan measuring 13 x 9 x 2 inches. As chicken browns, remove to oven pan. When all the chicken has been browned and placed in oven pan, add to the drippings onion, orange peel, celery and mushrooms. At low heat, sauté 5 minutes.

Now add cranberries, marmalade and Bacardi Rum; stir to mix well and heat thoroughly 2 minutes.Spoon sauce over each fillet. Cover pan with foil, crimp edges tightly, and bake about 20 minutes. Remove from oven, sprinkle with pecans and serve con orguello – with pride.

Serves: 4 to 6.

Chicken with Capers, Number One
Pollo con Alcaparira, Numero Uno

Capers, the bud of a Mediterranean plant that is pickled and used in cooking, are an integral ingredient of Spanish cuisine. They add a note of distinction and good taste to recipes. I also use my favorite cast iron utensils to make this dish: In my opinion, the best utensils for roasting and stewing. I inherited a set of three, and have used them extensively. The dark metal absorbs and conducts heat evenly, a great factor in browning. I hope you'll find a place in your kitchen for these utensils, along with the more modern versions coated with enamel. A terrific recipe...enjoy!

2¹/₂ or 3 pounds chicken breast or thighs,
    boned and skinned, about 8 to 10 pieces
Olive oil spray
4 tablespoons all-purpose flour
1 – .4 ounce envelope dry Italian dressing
¹/₂ teaspoon white pepper
2 tablespoons extra virgin olive oil
1 tablespoon butter or margarine
1 onion, minced

· ·

½ cup small capers

½ cup defatted, low-sodium chicken broth

½ teaspoon hot sauce

1 tablespoon balsamic or rice vinegar

2 tablespoons dry vermouth

1/4 cup grated fontina or Mozzarella cheese

Preheat oven to 325 degrees F.

Trim chicken of all visible fat, wash and pat dry. With a meat mallet, pound lightly between pieces of waxed paper to assure uniform thickness. Combine flour, dry dressing and pepper. Mix well. Dredge chicken pieces in the seasoned flour; shake off excess.

In a large non-stick skillet, heat oil and butter; add chicken. Brown nicely on both sides, about 5 minutes per side. When chicken is cooked, transfer to a rectangular shallow glass or ceramic baking pan measuring 13 x 9 x 2 inches.

To drippings in skillet, add onion. Sauté slowly until limp. Add capers and cook 2 minutes. Combine broth, hot sauce, vinegar and dry vermouth. Add to skillet. Stir to mix well, and bring to a boil. Pour over chicken, stirring so capers are evenly mixed. Bake 20 minutes.

Uncover, sprinkle with cheese and bake 10 minutes longer.
Serves: 4 to 6.

Chicken with Capers, Number Two
Pollo Con Alcaparras, Numero Dos

Perhaps you're seeking something quick to make for a luncheon, or for dinner after a hurried day? Then, this is it. This same method of preparation may be applied effectively to fish fillets.

4 pounds chicken , boned and skinned, cut into 6 breasts,
    or light and dark meat

⅔ cup white wine, or mild dry sherry

Juice of half a lemon or lime

$1/2$ teaspoon Dijon mustard

2 tablespoons fresh minced basil

2 tablespoons fresh minced oregano

$1/2$ teaspoon salt

2 tablespoons extra virgin olive oil

$1/4$ cup small capers

Preheat oven to 325 degrees F.

Wash chicken and pat dry; place in glass or ceramic baking pan measuring 13 x 9 x 2 inches. Combine wine, lemon, mustard, basil, oregano and salt, and pour into a screw-top jar. Shake to form an emulsion. Pour over the chicken, and marinate for about an hour.

Remove chicken from marinade, reserving marinade in a glass measuring cup. Set aside.

In a large, non-stick skillet, heat oil. Brown chicken on both sides, about 5 minutes per side. Return chicken as it browns to baking pan. To the skillet, add the marinade. Heat and pour over chicken. Scatter capers over all. Bake 15 to 20 minutes; if you use dark meat (drumsticks and thighs), allow an additional 10 minutes baking time.

Serves: 4 to 6.

Marvelous Yellow Rice and Chicken
Arroz con Pollo Maravilloso

Here's a simple arroz con pollo that you will find very delicious and algo diferente. A good, defatted chicken broth is essential to give this meal its distinctive flavor. With its bright yellow rice and tender chicken, and the bright reds and greens of the vegetables, this is also a dish children will love.

(continued...)

2¹/₂ pound fryer, cut into 8 pieces
2³/₄ cups hot defatted, low-sodium chicken broth
1 – .5 gram container imported saffron threads, toasted*
3 tablespoons extra virgin olive oil
1 white onion, minced
1 green bell pepper, finely-chopped
¹/₂ cup minced, roasted red bell pepper**
3 garlic cloves, pressed
1 ripe tomato, peeled, seeded and chopped
2 bay leaves
2 tablespoons tomato sauce
2 tablespoons lemon juice
¹/₄ cup dry white wine
1¹/₂ cups long-grain rice
Dash of salt
Hot sauce to taste
1 – 14¹/₂ oz. can artichoke hearts, drained, each cut in half
¹/₂ cup frozen peas
6 to 8 roasted red bell pepper strips
Fresh minced parsley for garnish

Preheat oven to 325 degrees F.

Trim all visible fat and most of the chicken skin; wash and pat dry. Combine broth and saffron in saucepan, bring to a boil; add saffron. Cover, and remove from heat; set aside to steep 30 minutes. In a large, non-stick oven-proof skillet with glass dome, heat oil. Add chicken pieces. Sauté at low heat, until golden, about 5 minutes. Remove to bowl and keep warm.

To the drippings, add onion, peppers and garlic. Sauté at low heat until vegetables are translucent. Add tomato, bay leaves and sauce. Stir to mix well. Cook 5 minutes. At this point, add the reserved chicken pieces. Mix carefully with sauteed ingredients.

*For instructions on toasting saffron and steeping saffroned broth, see Page 322.
**For instructions on roasting bell peppers, see Page 321.

Combine lemon juice with broth and wine. Pour over ingredients. Stir well. Scatter rice over all evenly, but carefully. Bring to a boil. Correct seasonings, adding salt and hot sauce to taste. Stir to assure proper distribution of rice and rest of ingredients.

Cover skillet. Reduce heat to low; cook 10 minutes over direct heat, stirring once to prevent sticking. Uncover skillet. Place artichokes evenly over all. Cover and bake 20 minutes. Remove skillet from oven. Uncover, scatter peas over all. Place pepper strips a capricho over ingredients. Cover and allow to rest 20 minutes before serving. (The heat of the skillet will be sufficient for the peas to be *al punto*. OK? Parsley bouquets will enhance this great entree. Children love it!

Serves: 4 to 6.

Chicken Valencia
Pollo Valenciano

Another "chicken and rice" recipe that will be appreciated by family and friends, and an excellent covered dish to take with you to that all-important party where the cooks like to outdo one another.
This one, my friends, is a winner!

2¹/₂ to 3 pounds chicken breasts and thighs,
    boned and skinned, about 12 pieces
Salt and white pepper
3 tablespoons olive oil
1 cup minced Spanish onion
¹/₂ cup thinly sliced celery
3 garlic cloves, minced
¹/₂ cup minced red bell peppers
¹/₂ cup minced green bell peppers
2 bay leaves
2 ripe plum tomatoes, peeled, seeded and chopped
¹/₂ cup cubed lean cooked ham

(continued...)

1 cup whole kernel corn
2 cups long-grain rice
3½ cups saffroned, defatted low-sodium chicken broth*
¼ cup dry sherry
½ cup sliced pimiento-stuffed olives
¼ cup fresh minced parsley

Trim all visible fat from chicken, wash and pat dry, and dust lightly with salt and white pepper. In a heat-proof casserole with cover measuring 12 x 3 inches, heat oil; add chicken and brown well, about 3 minutes per side. With slotted spoon, remove to bowl and set aside.

To drippings in skillet, add onions, celery, garlic, peppers and bay leaf. Reduce heat to low and sauté until onion and peppers are translucent. Add tomatoes, ham and corn. Mix carefully but well. Return reserved chicken to skillet; incorporate well with ingredients.

Sprinkle rice over all; cook 1 minute. Combine broth and sherry. Add to skillet. Mix and bring to a boil. Scatter olives over all. Correct seasonings; add more if needed. Reduce heat to low, cover and cook 5 minutes. Uncover. Stir well once. Cover and place in oven for 20 minutes or until rice absorbs liquids.

Remove from oven. Let rest 3 minutes. Sprinkle parsley over all, and with 2 forks, toss lightly. Again, cover. Place a kitchen towel over skillet cover and let rest 15 minutes before serving.

P.S. Why not sprinkle the casserole with ¼ cup dry sherry as it comes out of the oven? A shocker, believe me!!!

Serves: 4 to 6.

*For information how to prepare saffroned broth, see Page 322

Chicken in Rich Tomato Sauce
Pollo Entomatado

This recipe hails from Barcelona, Spain, a flamboyant and delicious recipe. A heat-proof casserole with cover, measuring 12 x 3 inches, accommodates the chicken comfortably. A good, tight cover is also essential.

3¹/₂ to 4 pounds chicken, cut into 10 pieces

2 tablespoons olive oil

1 Spanish or Vidalia onion, chopped

3 garlic cloves, minced

2 bay leaves

¹/₂ teaspoon cumin

2 tablespoons fresh minced oregano or
    1 tablespoon dried, crushed

2 tablespoons fresh minced tarragon or
    1 tablespoon dried, crushed

1 cup chopped celery

2 chorizos, degreased, casings removed and meat crumbled *

2 ripe tomatoes, peeled, seeded, and chopped

1 – 8 ounce can tomato sauce

¹/₄ cup sliced ripe olives

¹/₄ cup green pimiento-stuffed olives

¹/₂ cup dry white wine

¹/₂ cup defatted, low-sodium chicken broth,
    homemade or canned

Hot sauce

Salt

1 – 2 ounce jar minced pimientos, undrained

¹/₂ cup grated Gruyere or fontina cheese

*For instructions about degreasing meat, see Page 318.

(continued...)

Sprinkle of fresh minced parsley or dillweed
French baguette
1 tablespoon olive oil
Sprinkle of Parmesan cheese
Small jar of white asparagus

Preheat oven to 325 degrees F.

Trim chicken of all visible fat; wash and pat dry. Heat oil in heat-proof casserole. Add chicken pieces and brown carefully; about 4 minutes per side. When chicken browns, transfer to a platter and keep warm.

To the same pan, add onions to drippings and sauté until translucent. Add garlic, bay leaves, cumin, oregano and tarragon and celery. Mix well. Scatter chorizos over ingredients. Cook 1 minute. Add chopped tomatoes, tomato sauce and olives. Pour in wine (I recommend Sauterne) and chicken broth. Stir and mix well. Bring mixture to a boil. Add 1 generous teaspoon of hot sauce and salt to taste. Stir in pimientos. Mix thoroughly.

Cover casserole. Reduce heat to low and cook 20 minutes, stirring once to avoid sticking.

Return reserved chicken pieces to casserole. Saturate thoroughly with sauce. Bake in oven, covered, 20 to 25 minutes. Remove, uncover and scatter cheese evenly over chicken. Return to oven and bake, uncovered, an additional 10 minutes, or until nice and bubbly. Remove casserole from oven and sprinkle with minced dillweed or fresh parsley.

Note: For a fancy presentation, cut $1/2$ inch rounds of bread from a loaf of French baguette (about 10 to 12 rounds). Brush with olive oil and dust with Parmesan. Arrange in single layer on cookie sheet and bake for 15 minutes in oven set at 300 degrees F. Remove and cool completely before placing in an upright position around the edge of casserole. Drain a jar of white asparagus, and place stalks at an angle over the ingredients. Listen to the "oohs" and "ahhs" of your guests.

Serves: 4 to 6.

A Special Spanish Chicken Stew
Pollo en Caldereta

A delectable, nutritious, eye-appealing stew, unusual because of the orange and ripe olives it features. It was 1982 when my husband, Manuel, and I were traveling through Spain with friends. We stopped in all the paradores, or paradors – inns – along with way. The inns are found throughout Spain, and are operated by the Spanish Ministry of Tourism. There is a fixed price in lodging, which includes meals.

The inns must meet high standards imposed by the government or forfeit the right to operate; they are usually old castles that have been comfortably and elegantly refurbished for the enjoyment of the weary traveler, and the excitement of the expectant tourist. The paradores all boast superb cuisine, wine cellars resplendent with great Spanish wines and famous sherries.

It was near Valencia, en la costa de Azahar where we stopped for the night at an impressive, quaint inn. A restful inn, to say the least, with excellent cuisine and wine cellar. It was there I was first introduced to Pollo en Caldereta, an exquisitely prepared chicken entree, which was el plato del dia (specialty of the day). Here it is, as I remember it. I hope you enjoy this recipe as much as I did compiling it para ti.

2¹/₂ pounds of chicken, cut into 12 pieces
2 chorizos, degreased*
1 cup hot defatted, low-sodium chicken broth
Pinch of toasted saffron*
1 tablespoon olive oil
1 tablespoon butter
1 onion, minced
2 ripe tomatoes, peeled, seeded and chopped
2 garlic cloves, pressed or hand-minced
2 bay leaves
2 sprigs fresh thyme, minced

*For more about degreasing meat, see Page 318.
**For information about toasting saffron, see Page 322.

(continued...)

· ·

2 springs fresh basil, minced

2 sprigs fresh tarragon, minced

3 Russet potatoes, peeled and cut in chunks

1 sweet potato, peeled, cut in chunks

Salt and pepper

1 orange, sliced crosswise into rings

1/2 cup sliced ripe olives, cut to resemble truffles

1/2 cup good dry white wine

Salt

Hot sauce

1/4 cup fresh minced Italian parsley

Clean chicken carefully and remove all visible fat.

Spanish chorizos are high in fat; they should be degreased before using. A microwave does a good job. Pierce sausage at intervals; cook chorizo slowly over low heat about 3 or 4 minutes. When sausage is cool enough to handle, remove casing and crumble. Set aside. Place hot broth in saucepan. Crumble toasted saffron into broth. Cover and steep until ready to use.

Use a heat-proof casserole measuring 14 x 21/2 inches, with a cover. Heat oil and butter. Brown chicken in 2 batches, 5 minutes on each side. Transfer to bowl. Keep warm.

To drippings, add onions, tomatoes, garlic, bay leaves, thyme, basil and tarragon. Cook until fragrant and onion is translucent. Return chicken to casserole, then add potatoes and sweet potato, placing them among chicken pieces. Add salt and pepper to taste.

Slice orange into rings crosswise, and cut the rings again in half. Place over ingredients, peeling side up in decorative manner. Scatter olives and chorizo over all.

Combine wine and reserved saffroned broth, and pour over all. Bring to a boil. Add salt and hot sauce to taste. Cover and cook at low heat 30 minutes; check pan to assure all ingredients are cooking properly. Add more chicken broth if necessary, but it should not be soupy. Scatter with parsley, cook another 15 minutes and serve proudly.

Enjoy!

Serves: 4 to 6.

Chicken Creole
with Almond-Parsley Rice
Pollo Criolla con Almendras y Arroz

A spicy dish with an unusual medley of chicken, ham and tomato flavors, and you use only one dish! Herbs and spices come through beautifully to give this recipe a top rating of 10. A Caribbean recipe to say the least. Serve over almond-parsley rice for a festive entree. Give it a try!

2 pounds chicken breasts, about 5 –
    6 ounce fillets, boned, skinned and cubed

2 tablespoons olive oil

1 cup lean cubed ham

1 white onion, finely chopped

4 garlic cloves, minced

2 tablespoons fresh minced oregano or
    1 tablespoon dried, crushed

3 tablespoons fresh minced basil

2 ripe peeled, seeded and finely chopped tomatoes

1 – 8 ounce can tomato sauce

1 carrot, thinly sliced

1 cup dry white wine

¼ cup water

1 – 2 ounce jar minced pimientos, undrained

1 teaspoon salt

½ teaspoon granulated sugar

1 teaspoon hot sauce

½ cup frozen peas

(continued…)

Trim chicken of all visible fat, wash and pat dry. In a small Dutch oven or 2-quart casserole with cover, heat the oil. Add the chicken and ham. Sauté until chicken is golden. Remove with slotted spoon to a bowl; keep warm. To drippings left in Dutch oven, add onion, garlic, oregano and basil. Sauté stirring, until fragrant and onion is limp. Add tomatoes, tomato sauce, carrot, wine and water. Bring to a boil. With a skimmer, remove acid foam that surfaces.

Add pimientos, salt, sugar and hot sauce. Again bring to a boil. Add the chicken and ham, stir to mix well. Cover and cook at low heat 30 to 45 minutes.

Scatter peas over all. Stir carefully but well. Cook another 2 minutes. Remove from heat. Allow to rest 15 minutes before serving.

Serves: 4 to 6.

Almond-Parsley Rice
Arroz con Perejil

1 teaspoon butter
1/2 cup toasted almonds
1 teaspoon salt
1 1/2 cups long grain rice
1/2 cup minced fresh parsley

In a small saucepan, put one teaspoon of butter and heat at medium until it bubbles; add almonds, and sauté until golden, only a minute or two, watching carefully to avoid burning. Set aside. Fill a four-quart pan 3/4 full with water, add salt; bring to a boil. Add rice and cook briskly 15 minutes, uncovered, not longer. Remove from heat and strain rice. Transfer to a colorful serving dish. Scatter almonds and parsley over hot rice and with 2 forks, toss lightly. Allow to stand 15 minutes before serving.

Chicken in Cream Sauce
Pollo a la Crema

This creamy sauce is heavenly, and a little richer than good dieters might expect. However, I have reduced considerably the cream and butter in the original recipe.

The chicken cooks so tender, bathed in smooth sauce, with the crunch of water chestnuts and the flavor of herbs and cheese to give it an unusual sprightliness. Use chicken pieces your family likes best. In my family, no hay problema: We all like white meat, so I use breasts almost exclusively. Occasionally, when I have company for dinner, I'll slip in thighs and drumsticks to please my guests.

3 to 3½ pounds chicken breasts and thighs

1 celery rib

½ onion

½ bell pepper

2 bay leaves

1 ripe tomato

Sprig fresh parsley

Salt

1½ cups defatted, low-sodium chicken stock

¼ cup dry white wine

¼ cup half-and-half

1 teaspoon hot sauce, plus salt to taste

2 tablespoons olive oil

2 tablespoons unbleached flour

1 teaspoon butter

1 onion, minced

2 tablespoons fresh minced basil

2 tablespoons fresh minced thyme

¼ cup chopped water chestnuts

(continued...)

2 garlic cloves, pressed
1 tablespoon fresh minced parsley
1 – 2 ounce jar drained, minced pimientos
½ cup grated fontina or Gruyere cheese

To make broth from scratch, trim, wash and dry chicken, and place in a medium Dutch oven with cover, along with the next 6 ingredients, ending with parsley. Add salt al gusto, then fill pot ¾ full of water. Bring to a boil. Using a skimmer, skim off fat for about 10 minutes. Lower heat, cover and cook about 30 minutes. This should be done early in the day or the day before you plan to serve to allow time to defat chicken broth.

Cool chicken in broth. Remove to a bowl. Skin and debone, removing all traces of fat. Cut into chunks, cover and refrigerate. Strain broth into a pot with cover and refrigerate. Discard cooked vegetables. Refrigerate fully 2 or 3 hours.

Preheat oven to 325 degrees F.

One hour before serving, remove broth from refrigerator. With a good skimmer, remove all traces of fat. Remove chicken from refrigerator. Transfer to a 2½ quart casserole. Measure 1½ cups of broth into a deep bowl. Add wine and half-and-half. With hand whisk, beat until well-blended. Add lemon juice, hot sauce and salt to taste. Stir and mix well.

In a large skillet, heat olive oil. Add flour and cook to form a roux (flour should be golden, but not browned). Remove from heat. Slowly add liquid mixture, beating vigorously to avoid flour lumps. Return skillet to heat. Cook until thickened. Set aside.

In another skillet, heat butter. Add onion. Sauté until translucent. Add basil, thyme, water chestnuts, garlic and parsley. With wooden spoon, mix well and cook at low heat until fragrant, about 5 minutes. Add sauté to white sauce. Mix well. Sprinkle pimientos over all and incorporate into sauce.

Pour sauce over chicken in casserole. Cover and bake 20 minutes. Sprinkle cheese over all and bake, uncovered, 10 minutes, or until cheese melts slightly.

Serves: 4 to 6.

Chicken Stewed in Wine
Pollo Estofado al Vino

Always a winner! It never fails, believe me. A cast-iron Dutch oven with a clear glass cover should adorn your kitchen. It is sheer delight to prepare this recipe, and many others, in such a pot. However, you may have a favorite Dutch oven that will do just fine...so no hagas caso.

3¹/₂ pounds chicken, cut into 10 pieces

.5-gram package of saffron threads, toasted*

1¹/₂ cups defatted, low-sodium chicken stock

2 tablespoons olive oil

12 new potatoes, scrubbed

2 cups tiny baby carrots, scraped (do not cut)

1 celery rib, cut in half

¹/₂ peeled onion

¹/₂ bell pepper

1 ripe tomato

2 bay leaves

3 garlic cloves, pressed

Salt

Hot sauce

2 tablespoons tomato sauce

1 cup dry white wine

Trim all visible fat, and wash and pat chicken dry. Toast saffron. In a saucepan, heat chicken broth. Add the saffron, remove from heat, cover and steep. In a Dutch oven, heat oil; brown chicken pieces, 3 minutes on each side. Arrange potatoes and carrots evenly around the chicken.

Add celery, onions, pepper, tomato and bay leaves. Press garlic cloves over all, and add salt and hot sauce to taste. Combine tomato sauce and wine. Pour carefully over ingredients followed by the

*For instructions on toasting saffron and making broth, see Page 322.

(continued...)

chicken broth that has steeped with the saffron. Bring to a slow boil, turn heat down to low, cover and cook about 35 minutes.

Remove what is left of onion, pepper, tomatoes and celery. Cover and cook another 10 minutes, or until vegetables are done.

Serves: 4 to 6.

Baked Chicken Breasts with Fresh Herbs and Vegetables
Pechugas de Pollo al Horno
con Vegetales Frescos

The secret of this delectable recipe is that it cooks slowly and leisurely with wholesome ingredients. The finished product is without question an entree to be proud of. See for yourself.

2 or 2½ pounds of chicken breasts, about 6 ounces each,
    cut in halves
Salt and pepper
Olive oil spray
1 onion, sliced in rings
½ green bell pepper, thinly sliced
½ red bell pepper, thinly sliced
3 garlic cloves, pressed
2 tablespoons fresh minced tarragon
2 tablespoons fresh minced basil
2 tablespoons fresh minced oregano
2 bay leaves, crushed
2 tablespoons extra virgin olive oil
6 new potatoes, peeled and halved
12 baby carrots
Juice of one lemon

¹/₂ cup dry white wine
Salt and pepper
Dash of wine

Preheat oven to 325 degrees F.

Remove all visible fat from chicken, wash and pat dry. Sprinkle with salt and white pepper. Set aside. If you wish to cook 6 pieces of chicken instead of 4, you do not need to add extra ingredients, other than potatoes and carrots.

Spray olive oil in an oven-proof, 12 x 3-inch round glass or porcelain casserole with cover; it should comfortably cradle the chicken and its accompaniments. Salt and pepper chicken. Cover bottom of pan with half of onion and pepper rings. Press garlic cloves over rings. Combine tarragon, basil and oregano, and sprinkle half the mixture over vegetables. Add bay leaves.

In a 12-inch, non-stick skillet, heat oil. Brown chicken breasts lightly, 5 minutes per side. As chicken browns, place over ingredients in casserole dish, skin side up. Scatter remaining herb mixture and onion and pepper rings evenly over chicken.

Place potatoes with carrots around chicken. Combine lemon juice and wine. Pour over chicken. Cover. Bake 1 hour without checking. Remove cover, baste and sprinkle lightly with salt and white pepper. Bake another 30 minutes, uncovered, basting every 10 minutes. Remove from oven. Let rest a few minutes before serving.

If you're having company, you may wish to dress it up by transferring to a pretty, heat-resistant platter; but do so carefully, as the ingredients will be tender. Place chicken down center of platter, then adorn with vegetables. Ten minutes before serving, sprinkle with a little extra wine, and place in oven warmer.

Serves: 4 to 6.

The secret of this delectable recipe is that it cooks slowly and leisurely with wholesome ingredients.

Baked Chicken Segovia
Pollo al Horno, Segovia

This recipe produces a moist, succulent bird with a rich gravy that is paradoxically nearly fat-free. Though this is almost a one-pot meal, it is not a simple dish to make, so allow plenty of time to prepare. Still, the results are spectacular. Perfect for fancy dinner or Sunday with family.

4- or 5-pound roaster hen
2 unpeeled apples, cut into chunks
1 celery rib, sliced
1 onion, sliced
1 garlic clove, crushed
1 ounce high-quality cognac
Salt and white pepper to taste
1 tablespoon olive oil
Juice of one lemon
2 tablespoons minced cilantro
2 tablespoons fresh minced oregano
1/2 teaspoon ginger
1/2 teaspoon Spanish paprika
1/2 cup white Chardonnay wine
2 tablespoons low-sodium soy sauce
1 strip of bacon
1 pound new potatoes, partly peeled
1 pound baby carrots
1 sprig of fresh parsley
1 sprig of fresh dillweed, minced

Preheat oven to 325 degrees F.

Prepare roaster for baking by removing all visible fat, inside and out, and trimming excess skin. Wash and pat dry. In a small mixing bowl, combine apples, celery, onion and garlic; stuff the chicken with the mixture; set bowl aside. Truss and tie legs close to body with kitchen string; place in center of pan. Pour cognac over to flambé*, then sprinkle with salt and pepper to taste.

In the same bowl that held the stuffing, combine olive oil, lemon juice, cilantro, oregano, ginger, Spanish paprika, wine and soy sauce, and mix thoroughly. Place strip of bacon at an angle over breast. Saturate roaster with the oil-lemon juice mixture. Cover; bake in oven 1½ hours, or 20 to 25 minutes per pound, basting at intervals.

After an hour, remove bacon. Nestle potatoes and carrots around hen. Toss in the parsley sprig. Cook another 30 minutes, uncovered, or until vegetables are soft and hen is delightfully golden. Remove hen to cutting board; discard stuffing. Carve and arrange hen on a pretty platter. Surround with cooked vegetables. Sprinkle with dillweed and keep warm in the oven warmer. Allow juices to settle in pan. Skim fat with a spoon. Reheat and pour over chicken and vegetables.

*For flambé instructions, see Page 320.

Serves: 3 or 4.

Delicious Chicken
Pollo Sabroso

So simple, yet so sabroso. A fanciful dish with all the best goodies of Spanish cooking used in it; it produces a rich blend of flavors and textures that will wake the palates of your diners. Chicken parts of your choice may be used here. Do remove the visible fat, but do not debone.

3½ pounds chicken, cut into 8 to 12 pieces

Salt and pepper

2 tablespoons olive oil

Olive oil spray

1 red onion, cut in thin rings

3 or 4 garlic cloves, pressed or hand-minced

2 tablespoons fresh minced basil

2 tablespoons fresh minced oregano

(continued...)

½ cup pine nuts

¼ cup dry Spanish sherry

¼ cup defatted, low-sodium chicken broth

2 tablespoons lemon juice

¼ cup sliced ripe olives

1 cup frozen green peas

Preheat oven to 325 degrees F.

Trim chicken of all visible fat; wash and pat dry; dust with salt and white pepper. You may use up to 12 pieces without adding more accompanying ingredients. In a large, non-stick skillet, heat oil. Add chicken; brown nicely, 3 or 4 minutes per side. Spray a rectangular, 13 x 9 x 2-inch baking pan with olive oil. As chicken browns, transfer to pan.

To the drippings, add onion rings. Sauté until translucent, about 2 minutes. Press garlic over all. Add basil, oregano and pine nuts. Reduce heat to low and sauté mixture slowly and carefully for about 3 minutes. Spoon evenly over chicken.

Combine sherry, preferably Tio Pepe brand, chicken broth and lemon juice. Pour over chicken. Cover casserole with tin foil, crimping tightly at edges. Bake 30 minutes, or until chicken is tender. Remove foil.

Scatter olives and frozen peas over all. Return to oven for 10 minutes, uncovered. If using dark meat like drumsticks and thighs, pierce with skewer at thickest part to assure doneness. Liquid should run clear when pierced; if not, remove breasts and wings, cook dark meat an extra 10 minutes.

Serves: 4 to 6.

*A fanciful dish with all the best
goodies of Spanish cooking...*

Baked Chicken Vinaigrette
Pollo Asado Vinagretta

This is one of many recipes I remember with nostalgia: It was prepared by the loving hands of my wonderful mother so many, many years ago when I was growing up.

A delicious boiled chicken dish called La Olla was usually served on Sundays, like in most Spanish homes. However, on occasion, Mother surprised us with this unforgettable baked chicken; I confess I have tampered with her recipe to trim fat and sodium, so it is not the original version, but it is still fabulous. Use a good sherry like extra dry Tio Pepe.

2 to 2¹/₂ pounds chicken, about 8 pieces, quartered
Salt and pepper
Olive oil spray
2 tablespoons olive oil
3 garlic cloves, pressed
¹/₄ cup fresh minced oregano
1 teaspoon salt
¹/₂ teaspoon white pepper
¹/₂ cup rice vinegar
¹/₄ cup dry Spanish sherry
1 tablespoon soy sauce
1 tablespoon lemon juice
¹/₂ cup fresh minced dillweed or parsley
1 roasted red pepper*
1 roasted yellow bell pepper*

Preheat oven to 325 degrees F.

Remove all visible fat from chicken; wash and pat dry. Dust both sides lightly with salt and pepper. In a rectangular glass or ceramic baking pan measuring 13x 9x2 inches, spray olive oil and put chicken skin side down.

*For instructions about roasting peppers, see Page 321.

(continued...)

Cover pan with foil. Bake 30 minutes. While chicken cooks, place next 9 ingredients (use Amontillado or Tio Pepe sherry), in order given, beginning with olive oil and ending with dillweed or parsley, into screw-top jar. Shake with energy to create an emulsion.

Remove chicken from oven; turn pieces over gently. Saturate well with marinade. Return pan to oven, uncovered, and reduce heat to 300 degrees F. Bake another 45 minutes, thoroughly drenching chicken every 15 minutes with a baster until all marinade is used. Remove from oven.

Sprinkle with dillweed or parsley. Cut roasted peppers, which you can either char yourself, or buy in jars at groceries and specialty stores, in 2-inch strips and place over chicken, alternating in color. The colors of the Spanish flag! La Bandera Espanola, olé!

Serves: 6 to 8.

Cheesy Chicken Fillets
Pechugas de Pollo al Queso

One effective and simple way to enhance the taste of chicken is to marinate in teriyaki sauce and lemon juice. This recipe does just that. Teriyaki is a marinating sauce, available in bottles in the oriental section of most supermarkets. I was first introduced to this great sauce in – you guessed it – Madrid! The dish was called Cordero lechal a la Teriyaki, and the recipe is given later, in the meat chapter.

As for the other ingredients in this dish, you have probably concluded by now that I use lots of roasted red bell peppers in my recipes, simply because I like them. If you object to the peppers, consider them optional. Perhaps you've also noticed I'm not bashful about using olives in my cooking, either: They are muy Español! Served with skillet-browned new potatoes, a plain vegetable and a good tossed salad, this makes a great company meal.

2¹/₂ or 3 pounds of chicken breasts, 6-ounces each,
    boned and skinned
¹/₄ cup teriyaki sauce

Juice of one lemon

Salt and white pepper

Olive oil spray

2 tablespoons extra virgin olive oil

1 Spanish onion, sliced in rings

3 garlic cloves, minced or pressed

1/2 cup dry white wine

3 tablespoons small capers

6 thin slices lean ham

6 slices Swiss or fontina cheese

1 – 12 ounce jar roasted red bell peppers (Victoria)

Sprinkle of fresh minced basil, oregano or parsley

Preheat oven to 325 degrees F.

Trim chicken, and wash and pat dry; place in a 13 x 9 x 2-inch glass or ceramic baking pan. Combine teriyaki sauce and lemon juice. Pour over chicken. Dust lightly with salt and pepper. Cover. Refrigerate one hour or longer. When you are ready to cook the chicken, reserve marinade for later use. Clean the baking pan with paper towels, and spray with olive oil. Set aside.

In a non-stick large skillet, heat 1 tablespoon of the oil. Add onion rings, saute at low heat until transluscent and golden (this is called caramelizing). Spread onion rings to cover bottom of prepared oven pan.

Clean skillet with paper towels. Add remaining oil. Brown chicken in batches of 3. Cook each batch 3 minutes on each side. As chicken browns, place over onion rings in pan. Combine garlic, wine (I recommend Sauterne), capers and reserved marinade. Mix well. Pour into a small skillet. Cook briskly 2 minutes. Pour mixture over chicken breasts. Place one slice of ham over each breast. Bake, uncovered, 15 to 20 minutes.

Remove from oven. Drape one slice of cheese atop each chicken breast. Return to oven and bake another 10 minutes, or until cheese melts slightly. Place roasted bell pepper over each breast. Sprinkle with basil, oregano or parsley to deepen flavor and cover for a few minutes with foil before serving.

Serves: 4 to 6.

Chicken Breasts Veronique O La La!
Pechugas de Pollo Veronica

Veronique sauce is simply a good bechamel sauce to which white grapes are added, as well as a small amount of toasted almonds. I have come up with a "white" sauce that is lower in fat, but it's really good. It tastes sinful, but those of you watching your weight need not worry. I hope you like it!

2¹/₂ or 3 pounds of chicken breast, 6 ounces each, halved
Olive oil spray
1 teaspoon butter
¹/₄ cup chopped almonds
1 onion, finely minced
¹/₂ teaspoon fennel seeds, crushed
1 tablespoon butter
2 tablespoons olive oil
1 tablespoon unbleached flour
¹/₂ teaspoon salt
1 teaspoon hot sauce
1¹/₂ cups low-fat milk
¹/₂ cup skim evaporated milk
1 tablespoon lemon juice
2 tablespoons high-quality cognac
1 tablespoon fresh minced dillweed
1 cup seedless green grapes

Preheat oven to 300 degrees F.

Trim chicken breasts of all visible fat, and wash and pat dry. Coat a large, non-stick skillet with olive oil spray. Heat, cook chicken breasts in batches of 3. Brown on both sides, 3 minutes per side. Transfer chicken to 13 x 9 x 2-inch glass or ceramic oven pan sprayed with olive oil. Set aside skillet.

In a smaller skillet, heat butter. Sauté almonds, onion and fennel until golden, watching carefully to avoid burning. Set aside. In the same skillet in which you browned the chicken, add butter and oil. When hot, add flour, salt and hot sauce. Cook to form a roux.* Remove skillet from heat. Combine both milks. Slowly add liquid to roux, stirring briskly to avoid lumps. Cook at low heat until thickened slightly. Add reserved onion-mix, lemon juice and cognac. Cook 3 minutes longer. Add dillweed and grapes. Stir to mix well and cook another 3 or 4 minutes.

Pour sauce over the chicken. Bake, uncovered, 20 to 30 minutes, or until chicken is fully cooked, nice and bubbly.

Serves: 4 to 6.

*For instructions about cooking a roux, see Page 321.

The Cute Little Cornish Hen, al Jerez
Miniatura de Pollitos, al Jerez

Cornish hens cook to a tender goodness and usually, if prepared with care, are eye-appealing and go well with almost any vegetable. They're also a nice change from chicken, and can be substituted in many recipes that call for tender, small chicken (I call these pollitos). Yellow rice and chicken, for example, prepared with Cornish hens, results in an unusual and attractive casserole. Here is a recipe to cherish for family and special friends.

4 Cornish hens (1 or 1¹/₂ pounds each)

Salt and white pepper

1 onion, thinly sliced

4 garlic cloves, pressed or hand-minced

2 tablespoons olive oil

Juice of one lemon

¹/₄ cup dry Spanish sherry

¹/₂ cup defatted, low-sodium chicken broth

1 tablespoon soy sauce

1 teaspoon Spanish paprika

2 tablespoons fresh minced basil

2 tablespoons fresh minced oregano

(continued...)

½ teaspoon salt

½ teaspoon hot sauce

¼ cup ripe olives, sliced to resemble truffles

Minced parsley for garnish

Preheat oven to 350 degrees F.

Discard giblets and neck from hens. Remove excess fat, wash and pat dry. With sharp kitchen shears, split hens in half lengthwise (or ask yourbutcher to do it). Dust with salt and white pepper. Use a glass or ceramic rectangular baking pan measuring 13 x 9 x 2 inches or a round one, measuring 12 x 3 inches. Line with onion rings, and lay hens atop, cavity side up.

Combine next 11 ingredients, (I recommend Tio Pepe Sherry), ending with hot sauce. Pour into a screw-top jar. Shake to dissolve salt and form an emulsion. Spoon some of this mixture over hens and bake 30 minutes, partially covered. Remove from oven.

Using tongs, turn hens over carefully, skin side up. Saturate thoroughly with marinade mixture. Return pan to oven, reducing heat to 325 degrees F.

Bake, uncovered, 35 to 40 minutes, brushing generously with marinade every 10 minutes until all is used and pollitos are picture-perfect in color and tenderness. Scatter olives over hens and sprinkle with parsley.

Serve with parslied potatoes or brown rice and a vegetable of your choice.

Serves: 4 to 6.

Marinated Cornish Hens
Pollitos Adobados

The addition of hazelnuts gives these pollitos a classy appearance and a crunchy pizzazz. The Cornish game hen is a miniature chicken from 4 to 6 weeks old and usually weighing only 1½ or 2 pounds. One hen is usually enough per person because of the bird's relatively small ratio of meat to bone.

3 Cornish hens, 1½ to 2 pounds each; or 2 chicken fryers,
     2 to 2½ pounds each, cut into 12 pieces

. . . .

1 teaspoon butter

1/2 cup hazelnuts, husked and chopped

1/4 cup lemon juice

3 tablespoons water

3 garlic cloves, pressed

2 tablespoons olive oil

1 teaspoon salt

1/4 teaspoon granulated sugar

1 teaspoon hot sauce

2 tablespoons fresh minced basil

2 tablespoons fresh minced oregano

1 teaspoon Spanish paprika

1 teaspoon mustard

1/2 cup dry Spanish sherry

1 – 14 ounce can artichoke hearts, drained

1/2 cup minced Italian parsley

Carefully wash hens and trim of all visible fat. In a small skillet over low heat, melt butter. Add nuts and toast about one minute, being careful to avoid burning. Set aside. With very sharp kitchen shears, split hens lengthwise carefully; or, have butcher do it for you, as I do. In a glass or ceramic baking pan measuring 13 x 9 x 2 inches, place hens neatly, cavity side up.

Pour next 11 ingredients, ending with sherry, in order given into a screw-top jar. (I recommend Amontillado Sherry). Shake until salt is dissolved and liquid emulsifies. Spoon half of the emulsion over pollitos. Cover with tin foil and refrigerate 3 hours, turning once. Remove from refrigerator. Let hens rest at room temperature 20 minutes or so.

Preheat oven to 375 degrees F.

Remove hens to platter. Drain marinade and combine with remaining emulsion. With paper towels, clean casserole dish and spray with olive oil. Place hens, cavity side up, neatly in casserole. Saturate generously with marinade. Crimp tin foil over pan, seal tightly, and bake 30 minutes; turn hens, breast side up and spoon remaining marinade over all.

Quarter 6 good artichokes, and place evenly around hens. Reduce heat in oven to 325 degrees F. Bake 30 minutes longer, basting at intervals with pan juices. Remove casserole from oven. Scatter hazelnuts evenly over hens.

Return to oven and bake 10 minutes or until nicely browned. Sprinkle with parsley. Serve with baked potatoes and a vegetable.

Serves: 4 to 6.

Stuffed Cornish Hens
Pollitos Rellenos

An impressive company entree with an unusual stuffing featuring brown rice, walnuts and cannelli beans. It calls for basmati brown rice, produced in the Himalayan foothills, a long-grained, finely textured product with a perfumed scent induced by the aging process it undergoes to reduce moisture content. You can find it in health food and grocery stores.

6 – 1 pound Cornish hens
Dusting of salt
1 tablespoon butter
1 onion, minced
1/2 cup chopped celery
1/2 cup chopped red bell pepper
2 garlic cloves, minced
1 cup basmati brown rice
2 tablespoons lemon juice
2 tablespoons fresh minced chives
2 tablespoons fresh minced oregano
1/2 teaspoon fresh minced tarragon
1 teaspoon garlic salt
1 teaspoon hot sauce
2 cups defatted, low-sodium chicken broth
1 cup canned cannellini beans
1/4 cup chopped walnuts
Olive oil spray
1/4 cup dry sherry

2 tablespoons olive oil

1/2 teaspoon salt

1 cup baby carrots, steamed

1 cup snow peas, trimmed and steamed

Preheat oven to 425 degrees F.

Trim all visible fat, wash hens inside and out, and pat dry; dust lightly with salt. Set aside.

Use a 1 1/2 quart, heat-resistent saucepan with cover. At low heat melt butter; add onion, celery, bell pepper. Sauté until onion is translucent. Add garlic and rice. With wooden spoon, stir to mix well. Cook 2 minutes. Add lemon juice, chives, oregano, tarragon, garlic salt and hot sauce. Again, cook 2 minutes, stirring gently. Add broth. Bring to a boil, lower heat to medium-low, cover and cook 20 minutes. Add beans and walnuts. Toss carefully with 2 forks. Cover and cook 5 minutes longer. Let rest 5 minutes.

Spoon rice mixture into cavities of hens. Stuff loosely, as rice will cook more while the hens roast. Close cavities with wood picks and tie legs with kitchen string. Spray a large roasting pan with olive oil, and lay hens in it. Combine sherry, oil and salt, stirring to dissolve salt. Brush hens with mixture. Place in oven, and roast covered 30 minutes. Lower heat to 350 degrees F.

Scatter steamed carrots and snow peas around hens. Bake, uncovered, another 30 minutes, or until hens are browned and tender. Continue to brush with oil mixture until all is used. Transfer pollitos to serving platter and surround with cooked vegetables.

Serves: 4 to 6.

For the sauce
Salsa para los pollitos

1/4 cup degreased drippings from roasting pan

2 tablespoons flour

2 cups defatted, low-sodium chicken broth*

1 teaspoon low-sodium soy sauce

1 teaspoon Dijon mustard

1 teaspoon blond raisins, soaked 1 to 2 hours in
    2 tablespoons light rum

*For instruction about preparing broth, see Page 318.

(continued...)

Pour drippings into a medium non-stick skillet and heat. Stir in flour; stir and cook until flour takes on color and is bubbly. Remove skillet from heat. Combine broth, soy sauce and mustard. Blend well, then slowly add to skillet, beating vigorously to dissolve any flour lumps. Return to heat and cook until thickened. Add soaked raisins and rum. Mix well and cook 2 more minutes. Serve over hens.

Serves: 6 to 8.

Turkey Cutlets, al Vino
Chuletas de Pavo, al Vino

Turkey cutlets are now available in supermarkets, neatly packaged and ready for cooking. Preparing cutlets is so simple and muy sabrosas. A good mild dry Marsala wine makes this entree quite outstanding both in taste and eye appeal.

2 pounds turkey breast, boned and skinned, and cut into 6,
    5-ounce cutlets
¼ cup unbleached flour
1 teaspoon garlic salt
1 teaspoon white pepper
Olive oil spray
2 tablespoons olive oil
1 tablespoon butter
½ cup minced onion
1½ cups thinly sliced mushrooms
2 tablespoons small capers
1 cup dry Marsala wine
½ cup defatted, low-sodium chicken broth*
¼ cup chopped walnuts
¼ cup fresh chopped chives

*For instructions about preparing broth, see Page 318.

• •

Preheat oven to 325 degrees F.

Trim, wash and pat cutlets dry. Between 2 sheets of waxed paper, gently pound turkey cutlets with a meat mallet until they are a uniform, half-inch thick or less. Combine flour, garlic salt and pepper; mix well. Dredge cutlets lightly with flour mixture; shake off excess.

Spray a large, non-stick skillet with olive oil. Add 1 tablespoon olive oil to skillet and place over low heat. Brown turkey in batches of 3, cooking 3 minutes per side. As they brown, transfer to a round casserole dish with cover measuring 12 x 3 inches, which has been coated with olive oil spray.

Clean skillet with paper towels. Add remaining olive oil and butter. When butter is melted, add onion; sauté at low heat until translucent. Add mushrooms. Cook 3 to 4 minutes. With slotted spoon, remove from skillet and scatter evenly over cutlets in casserole. Sprinkle capers over all.

To the skillet, add wine and broth. Stir with wooden spoon to dissolve brown bits in drippings. Cook at low heat for about 4 minutes to reduce liquids a little. Pour over cutlets. Sprinkle with walnuts. Bake 20 minutes, covered, then 10 minutes uncovered, basting a couple of times as it cooks. Remove from oven and finally, sprinkle with chives. Allow to rest, covered, a few minutes before serving. This will give the chives a chance to "activate."

Serves: 4 to 6.

Poached Chicken and Broccoli Casserole
Cacerola de Brocoli y Pollo

This recipe shows off a combination of chicken, broccoli and toasted almonds that is a feast for eye and mouth. It makes a wonderful dish for a buffet table or fancy luncheon. Though many love nuts in a recipe like this one, if for some reason you don't enjoy almonds, leave them out. This will not affect the outcome of the recipe, asi es que, adelante! Translation: Go right ahead!

2½ pounds chicken, cut into 8 pieces

(continued...)

1 bay leaf

1 celery rib

Water

Salt

2 bunches fresh broccoli

2 tablespoons lemon juice

Sprinkle of garlic salt

Olive oil spray

1 teaspoon olive oil

1 onion, minced

2 tablespoons fresh minced oregano

2 tablespoons fresh minced basil

2 garlic cloves, pressed

1/4 cup chopped and toasted almonds

1 cup cubed lean ham

1 tablespoon olive oil

1 tablespoon, plus 1 teaspoon unbleached flour

1 cup skim or 1% milk

1/2 cup defatted, low-sodium chicken stock

3 tablespoons fat-free mayonnaise

1/2 teaspoon salt

1 teaspoon hot sauce

1/2 cup chopped roasted red peppers*

1/2 cup Swiss or other low-fat cheese

1/2 pound fresh asparagus

Sprinkle of Spanish paprika

Preheat oven to 300 degrees F.

Trim all visible fat from chicken; wash and pat dry. In a small Dutch oven, place chicken pieces, bay leaf, celery, water and salt. (Water should barely cover chicken); bring to a boil. Skim until all scum disappears. Lower heat, cover and poach until chicken is cooked, 25 or 30 minutes. Don't overcook.

*Buy in a jar at the supermarket, or roast yourself with instructions on Page 321.

. . . .

Carefully remove chicken from broth to a bowl with cover. Strain chicken broth into another bowl with cover. Pour ? cup of the broth over cooked chicken in first bowl to prevent poultry from drying out. Refrigerate both for at least 2 hours, or overnight.

Remove bowls from refrigerator. With a skimmer, remove all fat accumulated on surface of broth; measure $1/2$ cup of broth and set aside for later use; do not refrigerate again. Leftover broth should be frozen.

Remove visible leaves and tough parts of broccoli stems, wash and cut flowerets into uniform pieces; cut stems into $1/2$ inch pieces. Steam broccoli over boiling water, 3 or 4 minutes only. Immediately rinse under cold water to stop cooking process.

Transfer broccoli to a glass or ceramic baking pan measuring 13 x 9 x 2 inches. Sprinkle lemon juice over all (and here, while broccoli is warm, sprinkle with garlic salt, prudently, of course). Set aside.

Spray a large skillet with olive oil. At medium low heat, pour in olive oil. Add onion, oregano, basil, garlic and almond. Saute until onion is translucent and almonds take on a golden color, being careful not to burn garlic. Add cubed ham. Mix well and cook at low heat an additional 2 or 3 minutes. Pour into a bowl and set aside. Now you have 3 bowls!

Clean sauteeing skillet with paper towels. Add remaining tablespoon of olive oil. Heat; add flour and stir to mix well with a wooden spoon. Cook at low heat until flour takes on color and there is a nutty fragrance in your kitchen. The roux will be dry and crumbly. Remove skillet from heat, and combine milk, chicken stock, mayonnaise, salt and hot sauce to taste. Mix well until mayonnaise disappears. Add liquid slowly to roux, stirring continually, and with vigor, to avoid flour lumps. When smooth, return skillet to heat; cook stirring at low heat until thickened. Fold in peppers.

Remove chicken from bowl. Keep any extra stock for other uses. Scatter chicken pieces over broccoli and cover all with white sauce. Work sauce in with a spoon to penetrate all ingredients. Sprinkle cheese evenly over all.

Snap asparagus, using tender parts only. Place at an angle over the sauce.

Cover with aluminum foil and bake 30 minutes. Uncover. Sprinkle with paprika and return to oven for 10 more minutes, or until bubbly and ever so yummy – *Que rico!*

Serves: 6 to 8.

Chicken "El Botin"
Pollo "El Botin"

El Botin en La Calle de Los Cuchilleros is a fine restaurant, probably the finest in Madrid. Its owner, Antonio, is a good friend, so warm and convivial, as are most who live in Madrid, nicknamed Madrileños.

Specialties of the house are roasted piglet and baby lamb lechal. Both are excellent to eat, and as an added pleasure, they are presented to the diner in a most flamboyant way. Tourists might want to consider visiting the restaurant, located in one of the oldest neighborhoods. This part of Madrid is referred to as El Madrid Castízo, which refers to the wonderful exhuberance of its inhabitants.

2½ pounds of chicken breasts, skinned and boned,
    about 6 ounces each
2 tablespoons balsamic vinegar
3 garlic cloves, pressed
½ cup dry white wine
Salt and pepper
Olive oil spray
¼ cup flour
1 – .4-ounce envelope dry Hidden Valley salad dressing
1 tablespoon oil
1 cup fresh minced green onions
3 tablespoons fresh minced thyme
Salt
Hot sauce
½ cup pimiento-stuffed green olives
8 canned artichoke hearts, quartered
1 – 12 ounce jar roasted red bell peppers, cut in 2-inch strips

Preheat oven to 325 degrees F.

*For instructions on how to roast peppers, see Page 321.

. . . .

Trim chicken of all visible fat, wash and pat dry; pound gently with meat mallet between two sheets of waxed paper until the pieces are a uniform thickness of about ¹/₂ inch or less. Place in a large, oven-proof casserole measuring 13 x 9 x 2 inches. With fork, pierce chicken here and there to allow marinade to penetrate the meat.

Combine vinegar, garlic and ¹/₂ cup wine. Mix well, and pour over chicken. Dust lightly with salt and white pepper. Cover casserole, refrigerate for about 1 hour, turning once. Remove chicken from marinade; pat dry. Reserve marinade for later use. Clean casserole in which chicken marinated with paper towels, and spray with olive oil. Set aside.

In a mixing bowl or shallow plate, combine flour and dry salad dressing; dredge chicken pieces in mixture; shake off excess flour. In a large skillet over medium-low heat, heat oil. Brown chicken in 2 batches, 5 minutes each. Transfer to prepared casserole dish.

To drippings left in skillet, add green onions, thyme, salt and hot sauce to taste. With wooden spoon, stir to mix and cook until fragrant and onion is soft. Add reserved marinade and bring to a boil. Pour this mixture over chicken in casserole. Scatter sliced olives over all. Place quartered artichokes over all. Cover tightly. Place in preheated oven for 25 minutes. Uncover and bake an additional 10 minutes.

Serve with yellow rice recipe in Clarita's Cocina cookbook, but you may want to reduce oil it calls for! *Maravilloso!* Place strips of roasted red and yellow bell peppers, which you can either make yourself* or purchase in jars at groceries and specialty shops, atop dish.

Serves: 4 to 6.

Chicken Fricassee, Clarita's Way
Fricassee de Pollo, Estilo Clarita

Although there are countless chicken fricassee recipes in many cookbooks, I like to think this recipe is one of the best. It was my Uncle Pancho's, which he gave to my mother, Doña Clarita. She made some slight changes, as I have done. My version is almost guilt-free for weight-watchers, but it has not lost any of its sizzle. One way to trim even more calories: Sauté the mushrooms in a skillet coated only with olive oil spray, and scrimp on oil for sautéeing. All of this depends on your choice...just use fat prudently, okay?

(continued...)

3 to 3½ pounds of chicken, cut into 10 or 12 pieces
Olive oil spray
1 teaspoon olive oil
1 tablespoon wine vinegar
1 tablespoon lemon juice
1 teaspoon olive oil
1 cup chopped green onions
1 cup thinly sliced celery ribs
2 garlic cloves, minced
2 ripe plum tomatoes, peeled, seeded and chopped
3 tablespoons fresh minced basil
¼ teaspoon nutmeg
1 teaspoon Spanish paprika
Salt
Hot sauce
½ cup defatted, low-sodium beef stock
1 teaspoon butter
2 cups sliced mushrooms
1 cup defatted, low-sodium chicken broth*
½ cup evaporated skim milk
2 tablespoons cream
¼ cup dry vermouth
1 tablespoon olive oil
1 tablespoon plus 1 teaspoon unbleached flour
½ cup minced parsley
1 – 2 ounce jar roasted red bell pepper

*For instructions about how to prepare broth, see Page 318.
**For more on preparing a roux, see Page 321.
***For instructions on how to roast peppers, see Page 321.

Preheat oven to 300 degrees F.
Remove visible fat from chicken pieces, trim uniformly, wash and pat dry.

Spray a large, non-stick skillet with olive oil. Add oil and heat. Brown chicken in batches until cooked through and browned neatly, about 5 minutes per side. When chicken is done, transfer to a 3-quart casserole with cover, that has been conditioned with olive oil spray. Combine wine vinegar and lemon juice and brush over chicken. Cover and set aside.

Clean skillet with paper towels. Spray again with olive oil. Add olive oil and heat. Saute onions and celery until translucent. Add garlic, tomatoes, basil, nutmeg, paprika, salt and hot sauce. Stir well. Pour in beef stock. Cover and simmer 5 minutes. Remove from heat. Cool slightly.

In a small skillet, heat butter. Sauté mushrooms 5 minutes, or until they take on color. Set aside. In an electric blender container, purée the cooled onion-celery sauté. Pour into a bowl and set aside. In mixing bowl, combine broth, milk, cream and vermouth. Mix well.

To the large, cleaned sauté skillet, add the last tablespoon of olive oil. Heat. Mix in flour and cook to form roux. Remove skillet from heat. Should white sauce curdle or annoying flour lumps appear, use a hand beater or a wire whisk, and beat sauce vigorously to bind. Chances are, the sauce will not curdle again.

When cooking the roux,** the mixture will be crumbly and dry, and the flour will give off a nutty aroma; remove skillet from heat. Slowly add the liquid, stirring vigorously to prevent flour lumps. Return to heat. Stir with wooden spoon constantly until thickened. Add the puréed sauté and mix well.

Scatter mushrooms over chicken in casserole, then pour sauce over all. Cover and bake 20 minutes or until heated through. Sprinkle with parsley and garnish with roasted strips of red bell pepper, which you can make yourself*** or purchase in jars at groceries or specialty stores.

It's a long recipe, isn't it? But the outcome is beautiful...
Ya veras.
Serves: 4 to 6.

Country Style Chicken Breasts
Pechugas de Pollo Campesina

This simple and delicious casserole will be well-received by your family. The ingredients blend beautifully to create an unforgettable taste.

2¹/₂ pounds of chicken breast, boned and skinned,
    each breast halved and with tenderloin removed
Juice of half a lemon
2 slices bacon
1 tablespoon reserved bacon grease
1 tablespoon olive oil
1 onion, minced
1 red bell pepper, julienned
¹/₂ cup cubed lean ham
3 garlic cloves, minced
¹/₄ cup minced cilantro
3 tablespoons fresh minced oregano
1 bay leaf
¹/₂ teaspoon cumin
1 tablespoon balsamic or rice vinegar
3 cups (5 or 6) cubed red potatoes
¹/₂ cup frozen peas
1 small jar sliced mushrooms, undrained
1 cup dry white wine
¹/₂ cup defatted, low-sodium chicken stock*
Salt
Hot sauce

*For instructions about making stock, see Page 318.

Cut chicken breasts into strips, then cube the strips. Place in a bowl. Squeeze lemon juice over and dust lightly with salt; set aside.

In a large skillet, cook bacon and remove to drain on paper towels. Crumble when cool enough to handle. Discard all but 1 tablespoon of bacon grease from skillet.

Add olive oil and heat. Brown chicken cubes. With slotted spoon, remove to a heat-resistant casserole with cover.

To drippings, add onion, bell pepper, ham and garlic. Sauté at low heat until onion is translucent. Add cilantro, oregano, bay leaf and cumin. Stir carefully and cook 1 more minute. Add vinegar. Mix well, pour over chicken in casserole. Add potatoes, peas and mushrooms. Pour in the wine and chicken stock. Bring to a boil. Add salt and hot sauce. Sprinkle bacon bits over all. Cover casserole, cook at low heat about 25 minutes until vegetables are tender. Great over steamed rice.

Serves: 4 to 6.

MEATS

Carne

In our quest to provide healthful meals for our family and friends, we are fast gaining a new appreciation for old-fashioned, home-style cooking. It tastes so much better than commercially-produced food. Lowfat and free of harmful preservatives and additives – that's the way it should be.

I remember when I was a young girl, (not so long ago!), I would go grocery shopping with my mother to Demetrio's Market, the *supermercado* of West Tampa. Demetrio operated his business very effectively. At the back of the modest store was the spotless meat department where he excelled as an expert and informative *carnicero*, or butcher. My mother relied on his good judgment in choosing tender cuts of meat. Close inspection and the smell and feel of the meat was very important to her.

These type of independent meat markets, sadly, are slowly dying away, being replaced by glassed-in cubicles found in supermarkets. Though experienced, the feel is not the same as at Demetrio's.

In the past few years, many of us have begun to avoid red meat because of its high levels of cholesterol and fat. We consume sparingly. We purchase lean cuts of beef rather than prime cuts marbled with fat. But of course, on special occasions, a filet mignon or prime roast is a nice change. It satisfies the demanding "meat and potato" faction of your family. Here, ingenuity pays. Serve smaller portions, and glamorize with tastily-prepared fresh vegetables.

In the U.S. we are seeing a growing demand for veal, lamb and certain cuts of pork, so popular in Europe, especially in Spain. *El cordero lechal*, or milk-fed lamb, and *el cochinito lechal*, or piglets, are popular items and inspire much boasting among restaurateurs in Spain. Antonio's El Botin restaurant, in Madrid, is a good example, serving elegant renditions of these favorites. Should you find yourself there, take time to visit!

Go ahead and serve meat as a meal once in a while. Carefully choose the cut you want, and cook at the proper temperature. Use marinade; in addition to tenderizing, it enhances the taste of beef. Here is a selection of my most cherished meat recipes. I hope they "meat" with your approval!

Recipes

Piccadillo with Chick Peas and Pine Nuts

Eye of Round Pot Roast

Shredded Beef in Tomato Sauce

Stuffed Bell Peppers

Beef Burgundy with Cabbage

Beef Stew

London Broil

Lamb al Cognac

Baked Leg of Lamb

Marinated Lamb Chops with "Real" Mashed Potatoes

Oriental Country Style Ribs

Drunken Pork Chops

A Delicious Meat Loaf with Mushroom Sauce

Meat Loaf "Italiano"

Lilís Stuffed Potatoes

Tenderloin Roast with Fresh Thyme

Tenderloin Roast Simply Done

Veal Chops "Condessa"

Vienna Veal Cutlets and Concasse Sauce

Rolled Stuffed Flank Steak

Piccadillo with Chick Peas and Pine Nuts

Picadillo con Garbanzos y Pegnoli

Perhaps "exotic" is the word to use in describing this unusual Cuban dish. Picadillo is a combination of flavorful lean beef and a melange of wonderful herbs and spices. My addition of chick peas and pine nuts enhances an already very savory dish.

2 pounds lean ground round

1 tablespoon extra virgin olive oil

1 onion, minced

1 green bell pepper, cleaned, trimmed and chopped

1 red bell pepper, cleaned, trimmed and chopped

3 garlic cloves, peeled and minced

2 bay leaves, crushed

1 tablespoon oregano, dried

1 teaspoon nutmeg

1 ripe tomato, peeled, seeded and chopped

2 tablespoons tomato sauce

1/4 cup sliced pimiento-stuffed olives

1/4 cup chopped black olives

1 – 1/2 ounce jar of tiny capers, drained

1 cup defatted, low-sodium beef stock

1/2 cup dry red wine

3 tablespoons rice vinegar

2 chorizos, degreased, casing removed*

1 – 16 ounce can garbanzo beans (chick peas), drained

1 – 1 1/2 ounce jar minced pimientos, drained

1/4 cup chopped and toasted pine nuts

1/4 cup fresh, finely minced fresh parsley or cilantro

Dash of dry red wine

* For information on how to degrease sausages, see page 318.

In a large, non-stick skillet with cover, brown meat until the red color disappears. Drain meat thoroughly in colander. Return meat to skillet. Dribble oil over meat.

In a bowl, combine onions and next 6 ingredients, ending with nutmeg. Mix well and add to meat in skillet. Incorporate well with the meat. Cover and cook 3 to 5 minutes at low heat, or until onion is translucent. Check seasonings.

Add chopped tomato, sauce, olives and capers. Cook, stirring, 2 minutes. Combine stock, wine (I recommend Burgundy or a dry white wine) and vinegar. Pour over ingredients. Mix well. Cover and at low heat, cook 30 minutes, stirring occasionally. Liquids should be fully absorbed. Add crumbled chorizos, chick peas and pimientos; stir gently but well. Cover and cook 10 minutes.

Scatter toasted pine nuts over all, followed by parsley or cilantro; sprinkle with additional wine. Cover and cook 5 minutes. Serve over steam white rice – *sabroso!* Remove all visible fat that has surfaced before serving.

Serves: 4 to 6.

Eye of Round Pot Roast
Boliche Roast

This dish is made with a familiar cut of beef, popular in the kitchens of Latin families. It is usually accompanied by black beans and rice, definitely a Caribbean creation. In the Tampa Bay area, where there is a large Spanish-speaking population, boliche is indeed revered – so much so that in West Tampa, along a stretch of Columbus Drive particularly rich with Cuban restaurants, the locals refer to "Boliche Boulevard" – a nod to all the little restaurants that feature "boliche" on their menus. If you haven't dined there, it should be a must on your next trip to Tampa.

4 or 5 pounds boliche (beef eye of round roast)

4 tablespoons extra virgin olive oil

1 teaspoon dried oregano

1 teaspoon dried rosemary

4 garlic cloves, pressed

(continued...)

¼ cup dry red wine

3 tablespoons low-sodium soy sauce

Juice of one lemon

¼ teaspoon nutmeg

1 teaspoon salt

2 bay leaves

1 onion, minced

1 green bell pepper, seeded and chopped

1 celery rib, chopped

1 ripe tomato, peeled, seeded and chopped

¼ cup freshly minced cilantro

¼ cup high-quality cognac

½ cup defatted, low-sodium beef stock

1 pound new potatoes, peeled around middle

1 cup whole baby carrots

At the market, choose a boliche (eye of round), with the help of your butcher that is both lean and tender. At home, remove all connective tissues and visible fat.

In a large mortar or heavy porcelain bowl, combine 2 tablespoons oil, and reserve the rest; add oregano, rosemary and garlic. Mash with a pestle to a paste. Remove mixture to a mixing bowl. Stir in wine (I recommend Burgundy), soy sauce, lemon juice, nutmeg, salt and bay leaves.

Make gashes with a sharp knife at intervals all over the meat. Rub meat well with part of marinade introducing it well into the pierced meat. Line a roasting pan with tin foil, overlapping generously over side. Place roast in center. Pour remaining marinade over meat. Bring foil upward to form a tent that will seal meat and marinade securely. Refrigerate overnight. Turn meat once or twice while marinating.

The next day, preheat oven to 300 degrees F. Lift boliche from pan. Scrape off marinade and pour into a mixing bowl for later use. Heat reserved oil in roasting pan with cover. Sear meat well on all sides until nice and brown, about 15 or 20 minutes cooking time. Scatter onion, pepper, celery, tomato and cilantro around roast and sauté, stirring carefully with wooden spoon until onion is translucent and fragrant.

Combine reserved marinade with cognac and beef stock. Pour around meat. Bring liquids to a boil. Cover roasting pan, and bake 2 hours, or until meat is fork-tender. Remove roast to cutting board and allow to cool. Meanwhile, strain sauce in roasting pan through a colander, pressing on vegetables without forcing them through. Discard vegetables.

Slice cooled boliche thinly and return in its original form to the roasting pan. Pour strained sauce over boliche and add potatoes and carrots around meat. Return covered roasting pan to oven and increase heat to 325 degrees F. Bake for 30 more minutes, or until meat is very tender and vegetables are cooked. When removing roast from oven allow a rest period of 20 to 30 minutes; spoon off excess fat that surfaces.

Serves: 6 to 10.

Shredded Beef in Tomato Sauce
Ropa Vieja

This recipe's nickname is most peculiar: Ropa Vieja. It means: Old clothes. I know that sounds crazy, but it makes sense because the meat has a shredded appearance when it is done reminiscent of frayed clothing. This is a Cuban dish. It goes well with white rice, accompanied by a side dish of very ripe platanos (plantains), a cousin of the banana found in Latin markets.

This is a familiar entree found on menus of many restaurants of Latin origin and in the Caribbean. The succulent sauce that cooks with the beef has many facets. It is magnificently seasoned and may be used in any number of recipes that call for a good tomato sauce. Regardless of what it is called, Ropa Vieja is, in my book, one great recipe. For better results, cook meat one day ahead.

2¹/₂ pounds beef London broil

¹/₂ onion, peeled

1 ripe tomato

2 celery ribs, snapped in two

2 bay leaves, crushed

2 carrots, cut in two

1 teaspoon salt or to taste

(continued...)

Cut London broil across the grain in pieces, each piece about 2 inches wide. Remove all visible fat. In a Dutch oven, place cut meat and remaining ingredients in order listed. Pour in water to cover, ending 2 inches above ingredients. Bring to a brisk boil. Skim stock with a skimmer or large spoon: This assures a clear stock. Cover pot, lower heat to medium, and cook an hour until meat is tender.

Once meat is cooked, remove pot from burner, and allow meat to cool completely in stock. Remove meat to platter. Strain stock into a refrigerator jar or plastic container with cover, and chill 2 hours or overnight. Shred beef by hand into a deep bowl; cover and refrigerate 1-2 hours. Later, or the next day, defat stock. Reserve 1 cup to use in sauces. Freeze the rest for a good hearty soup.

Remove shredded beef from refrigerator and keep at room temperature while preparing sauce.

Sauce

1 tablespoon extra virgin olive oil

1 onion, finely chopped

1/2 green bell pepper, finely chopped

4 garlic cloves, minced

1/2 cup thinly sliced celery

2 tablespoons freshly minced oregano

2 tablespoons freshly minced cilantro

1 tablespoon freshly minced tarragon

1/4 teaspoon cumin

1/4 teaspoon nutmeg

1 teaspoon hot sauce

1 teaspoon salt, or to taste

3 cups ripe peeled, seeded and chopped tomatoes

1 – 8 ounce can tomato sauce

1 cup water

1 – 2 ounce jar minced pimientos, drained

1/2 cup defatted, low-sodium stock from meat

1/4 cup dry white wine

3 tablespoons wine vinegar

1/2 fresh or frozen cup frozen peas

In a large non-stick skillet, heat oil. Add onion, bell pepper, garlic and celery. Sauté with care to avoid burning garlic. When onion is translucent, add oregano, cilantro, tarragon, cumin, nutmeg, hot sauce, and salt. With wooden spoon, stir carefully and cook 3 minutes until fragrant.

Add tomatoes and sauce. Mix well and cook 2 minutes. Add water and pimiento; cook 1 minute; add stock, wine (Sauterne or any good white wine will do), and vinegar. Stir to mix well. Bring to a boil, then lower heat. Correct seasonings. Add more if needed. Cover and cook 30 minutes, stirring at intervals. Now add the shredded beef and introduce well to sauce. Cook another 20 minutes, stirring to avoid sticking. Add fresh or frozen peas just before removing pan from heat. Muy bueno! Serve over white steamed cilantro rice.

Serves: 4 to 6.

Stuffed Bell Peppers
Ajises Relleños

Pick peppers with care. Check closely for blemishes. Look for firm, straight and as near-perfect peppers as possible.

6 bell peppers, uniform in size
Olive oil spray
1 slice day-old bread, crust removed
1/4 cup skim evaporated milk
1/2 pound lean ground beef
1/2 pound lean ground veal
1/2 pound lean ground pork or cooked ham
2 chorizos, casing removed and degreased*
2 tablespoons extra virgin olive oil
1/2 cup finely minced green onions
1/4 cup toasted chopped almonds
2 tablespoons freshly minced cilantro

*For instructions about degreasing chorizos, see Page 318.

(continued...)

2 tablespoons freshly minced oregano

3 garlic cloves, pressed

3 tablespoons tomato sauce

Hot sauce to taste

Salt to taste

2 tablespoons Burgundy wine

2 tablespoons cognac

½ cup cooked long-grain white rice

2 tablespoons fresh grated Parmesan cheese

3 tablespoons seasoned bread crumbs

Preheat oven to 325 degrees F.

Wash peppers thoroughly, and put them, stem side up, in a 9 x 11 baking pan sprayed with olive oil. Cover with tin foil, and bake 10 minutes. Cool; cut across stem end of each pepper. Scoop out seeds and as much of the pith as possible without injuring the peppers. Set aside peppers and pan while preparing filling.

In a small bowl, crumble bread. Add milk. Set aside to soak.

In a large mixing bowl, place the three meats. Scatter degreased chorizos over. Mix with fork lightly. Heat a 12-inch, non-stick skillet, add meats in bowl. Cook until meat is no longer red; drain in colander. Return to same mixing bowl.

Wipe skillet clean. Add oil and heat. Add onions, almonds, cilantro, oregano and garlic. Sauté at low heat until fragrant, 2 minutes. Combine tomato sauce, seasonings (if needed), wine and cognac. Add to meat in bowl. Do not mix yet. Add cooked rice, reserved soaked bread, cheese and half the seasoned bread crumbs. Now with 2 forks, mix ever so lightly until ingredients harmonize with one another. Do not handle filling too much, okay?

Stuff each pepper with mixture loosely, but fill it to the very top. Pat the rest of the bread crumbs over each pepper to form a light crust. Place peppers in the same baking pan you used before. Pour Salsa Sauce, (recipe follows), around peppers. Bake, uncovered, approximately 25 to 30 minutes. Serve with steamed rice.

You may have leftover filling. It freezes well. Stuff zucchini or tender yellow squash with this filling; it is exceptionally good! First, you quickly parboil squash: Place squash in a 2-quart saucepan and cover; cook at low heat, stirring until squash is tender, about 15 minutes. Slice down center, scoop out seeds and stuff with leftover filling. Dust with grated cheese and bake 20 minutes at 350 degrees F., or until nicely bubbly and golden.

Serves: 4 to 6.

Sauce

1 tablespoon extra virgin olive oil
1 tablespoon finely minced onion
³/₄ cup tomato sauce
Pinch of nutmeg
¹/₄ teaspoon dried cumin
¹/₄ cup dry sherry
¹/₂ cup water, or defatted, low-sodium beef stock

Combine all ingredients in order listed; bring to a boil. Check seasonings. Cook, covered, 5 minutes at low heat; pour sauce around bell peppers already in baking pan, and bake as directed.

Beef Stew
Carne Estofada

This recipe is chock full of vegetables, and enhanced with the addition of fresh minced herbs. This is a very hearty and flavorful stew that's a perfect one-dish meal. I think you will like it!

1½ pounds lean beef stew meat, cut into 1½ inch cubes

2 tablespoons unbleached flour

½ teaspoon salt

½ teaspoon white pepper

2 tablespoons extra virgin olive oil

1 onion, minced

½ green bell pepper, chopped

½ red bell pepper, chopped

2 celery ribs, thinly sliced

2 tablespoons freshly minced cilantro

2 tablespoons freshly minced oregano

1 tomato, peeled, seeded and finely chopped

¼ cup tomato sauce

¼ teaspoon nutmeg

2 bay leaves, crushed

4 cups defatted, low-sodium beef stock

1 cup baby carrots, cut in two

1 cup fresh string beans, snapped into 1-inch lengths

1 cup fresh sliced mushrooms

4 new potatoes, cubed

½ cup dry white wine

2 tablespoons low-sodium sauce

1 teaspoon Worchestershire sauce

. . . .

Dust meat with mixture of flour and salt and pepper. In a large skillet, heat oil; add meat and brown quickly on all sides. With slotted spoon, remove meat to a 2-quart, deep casserole, heat-resistant and with a lid. To drippings in skillet, add onion, peppers, celery, cilantro and oregano. Sauté, stirring until all is fragrant. Add tomato, sauce, nutmeg, and bay leaves; cook 3 minutes. Pour in beef stock. Stir to mix and bring to a boil.

Pour over meat in casserole. Place casserole over a large burner. Bring to a boil. Cook briskly, stirring, for 2 minutes. Lower heat. Cover and cook until meat is fork tender, about 30 minutes. Check and stir every 15 minutes to avoid sticking. At this point, check seasonings. Add more if needed.

Add to casserole carrots, string beans, mushrooms and potatoes. In a separate bowl, combine wine (I suggest Sauterne), soy sauce and Worcestershire; stir well and pour into casserole. Bring to a boil; cook 1 minute. Lower heat, cover and cook until meat and vegetables are tender, about 20 minutes. Serve with noodles or over white rice.

Serves: 4 to 6.

Beef Burgundy with Cabbage
Carne Guisada Con Col

Here's a beef stew to keep the meat lovers in your family happy. Of course, if cabbage is frowned upon, substitute 2 cups stringbeans and 1-1 1/2 pounds of small, semi-peeled new potatoes 30 minutes before cooking time is over.

2 1/2 pounds very lean beef, cut for stewing into 1 1/2 inch pieces

3 slices lean bacon

1 tablespoon reserved bacon grease

1 tablespoon extra virgin olive oil

2 cups minced green onions

4 garlic cloves, minced

1 cup thinly sliced celery

(continued...)

1 tablespoon fresh minced thyme

1 tablespoon freshly minced cilantro

1 tablespoon freshly minced oregano

2 bay leaves, crushed

1 tablespoon balsamic or rice vinegar

1½ cups dry red wine

½ cup defatted, low-sodium beef stock

¼ cup light soy sauce

1 cup whole baby carrots

1 – 1 pound white cabbage, cut into wedges

Trim meat of all visible fat. Cook bacon in your microwave oven or in a heavy skillet; remove and degrease carefully. Discard all except 1 tablespoon grease; put bacon grease and oil into a Dutch oven. Add meat. Brown well. Add onions (use both white and green parts), garlic, celery, thyme, cilantro and oregano, and bay leaves. Sauté until fragrant, stirring, for about 3 minutes.

Add vinegar, wine (use Burgundy), stock and soy sauce. Bring to a boil. Taste for seasoning; add more if needed. Cover pan and lower heat. Cook slowly for 2 hours. After 1½ hours, check meat. If fork tender, scatter carrots over all. Place cabbage, cut side down, over meat; steam with stew a half hour more until tender.

Remove from heat. Allow to rest 10 to 15 minutes. Remove all fat that comes to surface. Serve with brown rice and a good crisp salad. *Maravilloso!*

Serves: 4 to 6.

London Broil

Carne a la Parrilla

This cut of beef is somewhat chewy. However, if marinated for a few hours before broiling and then cut across the grain in thin slices, you will enjoy a good, flavorsome piece of meat. The marinade will not only enhance the taste of the meat, but will also help to tenderize it.

2¹/₂ to 3 pounds London broil, scored by the butcher
on both sides
Juice of one lemon
¹/₂ cup dry red wine
¹/₄ cup light soy sauce
3 garlic cloves, pressed
1 sprig of fresh oregano
1 sprig of cilantro
2 tablespoons extra virgin olive oil
Olive oil spray
Salt and white pepper to taste
Sauteed mushrooms for garnish, sliced in halves

Remove connective tissue and all visible fat from meat. Place on work-board and cover with waxed paper; with a meat cleaver, pound gently. (This will aid in tenderizing). Place meat in large Dutch oven with cover.

Combine lemon juice and remaining ingredients in order listed. (I recommend Burgundy wine). Pour into a screw-top jar with a tight lid. Shake to mix well, then spoon over meat. Cover and refrigerate 4 hours or overnight, turning meat every few hours.

Remove meat from refrigerator an hour before broiling. Turn on broiler; lift meat from marinade. Spray rack on roasting pan with olive oil. Brush meat well with marinade. Place under broiler, about 4 inches from the heat. Broil 5 minutes on one side, turn, saturate with marinade and broil another 4 to 5 minutes. Do not cook beyond medium-rare, or the meat will be tough.

(continued...)

Remove meat to platter. Sprinkle immediately with salt and pepper. Create a foil tent and place over meat. Let rest 15 minutes before slicing thinly, against the grain. Serve with caramelized onion rings sautéed with mushrooms.

Serves: 4 to 6.

Caramelized Onion Rings With Mushrooms
Cebolla Sofrita con Champiñones

2 Bermuda or Vidalia onions, peeled and sliced into rings

1¹/₂ pounds mushrooms, coarsely chopped

¹/₄ teaspoon light brown sugar

¹/₂ teaspoon salt or to taste

1 tablespoon butter or extra virgin olive oil

¹/₄ cup dry Spanish sherry

Peel onions and slice into onion rings. Pare mushrooms of unsightly blemishes and wash carefully; avoid bruising; slice coarsely. Combine onion and mushrooms in a large bowl; sprinkle with sugar and salt.

In a large non-stick skillet, heat butter. When it starts to bubble, add onion and mushrooms. Now, with a wooden spoon, stir vegetables carefully and continually until onion looks transparent. Pour in the sherry. Cook and stir at low heat until onion is deliciously golden. Mushrooms will have released quite a bit of liquid. Cook until almost dry.

Turn onto serving platter and serve with the thinly-sliced London broil. If you can spare the calories, serve the meat with a modified Bearnaise Sauce.

Serves: 4 to 6.

. . . .

Lamb "al Cognac"
Cordero "al Cognac"

Lamb is the number one meat consumed by the average Spaniard of the Iberian Peninsula. In fact, there is a saying that goes: De la mar el mero...y de la tierra el cordero. So, consequently, the variety of lamb recipes in a Spanish kitchen is endless.

2 pounds lean lamb for stewing, cut into 1½ inch pieces
1 tablespoon unbleached flour
1 onion, chopped
1 red bell pepper, chopped
4 garlic cloves, minced
½ cup finely minced cilantro
2 bay leaves, crushed
2 lean bacon slices
1 tablespoon reserved bacon grease
1 tablespoon extra virgin olive oil
1 cup defatted, low-sodium beef stock
½ cup dry red wine
Salt and pepper to taste
1 teaspoon hot sauce
1 teaspoon butter, or extra virgin olive oil
1 cup thinly sliced button mushrooms
1 teaspoon Spanish paprika
1 cup fresh or frozen peas
2 tablespoons cognac
3 tablespoons light soy sauce

Ask your butcher to cut the lamb to your specifications. Make sure all visible fat is removed. At home, place lamb in a mixing bowl and dust with flour; set aside. (No salt yet, okay?) In another bowl, combine onion, pepper, garlic and cilantro; also set aside.

(continued...)

In a 12-inch skillet or microwave oven, cook bacon. Remove to paper towels and crumble when cool. Reserve 1 tablespoon bacon grease, and discard the rest.

In a Dutch oven, heat bacon grease and oil; add lamb. Stirring and watching, brown quickly on all sides until it is fully browned and red color disappears. With slotted spoon, remove to glass bowl. To drippings, add onion mix in second bowl. Stir carefully, scraping up brown particles and mixing well. When onion is soft, return meat and crumbled bacon to Dutch oven. Stir to mix well with the sautéed vegetables. Add stock and wine. Bring to a boil, mixing well. Add salt, pepper and hot sauce to taste. Lower heat, cover and cook until meat is tender, about 1 hour.

In the meantime, in a small skillet, heat butter; add mushrooms and sauté until golden; sprinkle with paprika. Stir quickly, and add to the meat. Scatter peas overall. Cover and cook 30 minutes more until meat is very tender.

For the "finale" carefully flame the cognac.* Pour over all. Stir once. Cover and allow to rest 20 minutes. Spoon off excess fat that surfaces. If for eye appeal you wish to enrich the color of the stew, add 3 tablespoons light soy sauce along with the liquids. Reheat slowly.

Serves: 4 to 6.

*For instructions about flaming a dish, see Page 320.

Baked Leg of Lamb
Cordero Asado

If it is a boneless leg of lamb that you plan to cook, leave the messy cutting job to a friendly butcher at the market; ask him to bone, trim and discard all visible fat. It is a great help when you can bring the lamb home already prepared for cooking, no es verdad?

4 or 4¹/₂ pounds boned leg of lamb
¹/₄ pound lean ham, thinly sliced
Salt and white pepper

2 garlic cloves, slivered

2 tablespoons plus 1 teaspoon extra virgin olive oil

Olive oil spray

1 onion, chopped

2 tablespoons fresh chopped rosemary

3 garlic cloves, chopped

1 cup tomato sauce

¼ cup dry sherry

½ cup defatted, low-sodium beef or chicken broth

2 tablespoons low-sodium soy sauce

1 teaspoon Dijon mustard

Preheat oven to 300 degrees F.

Unwrap lamb. Place ham slices down center of meat. Sprinkle with salt and white pepper. Roll meat, securing ham within. Tie with kitchen cord. Again, prudently sprinkle with salt and pepper.

With a sharp knife, make gashes at intervals on meat. Insert garlic slivers deep within. In a large heavy skillet, heat 1½ tablespoons of the oil, reserving the rest for later. When it is good and hot (but not smoking!), brown lamb well on all sides. Spray with olive oil a large, heavy roasting pan to be used in cooking.

To drippings, add onion, rosemary and garlic. Sauté at low heat until fragrant, about 2 minutes, being careful not to burn garlic. In a bowl, combine tomato sauce and remaining 4 ingredients, including reserved olive oil. Mix well. Add to sautéed onion mixture; cook 2 more minutes. Cool slightly.

Pour mixture into an electric blender container or food processor, and pureé until smooth. Return blended mixture to bowl; then spoon over and around lamb in pan. Cover tightly, and bake at least 3 hours, basting at 15 minute intervals. Meat should be cooked to incredible tenderness. If during cooking, roast needs more liquid, add small amounts of beef or chicken stock.

If you want a meal-in-a-pot, about 30 minutes before cooking time is up, add small new potatoes.

Serves: 6 to 8.

Marinated Lamb Chops with "Real" Mashed Potatoes

Chuletas de Cordero Adobadas con Patatas Majadas

My beautiful daughter, Carmen Maria, has such a refined palate that she quickly detects even minute changes in food preparation. She was barely 10 years old when my husband brought home a package of newly-introduced dried potato flakes. I followed package directions, except instead of milk, I added half-and-half; instead of 1 tablespoon of butter, I added 1/2 stick. I beat the mixture energetically until it was light and fluffy. I even threw away the box, so there was no earthly way she could know their true origin.

At dinner, I served a roast and the mashed potatoes, sure that Carmen would be fooled. She took one taste of the potatoes, and then another. She looked at me, and very sweetly asked, "Mom, are these potatoes real?" I could not believe that she would know the difference! I thought they were great! In the competitive hospitality business, we quickly learn the importance of taste in order to maintain the business. My Carmen learned about this at a very tender age...don't you think?

"Real" Mashed Potatoes
Patatas Majadas

2¹/₂ pounds potatoes, peeled and cubed

¹/₂ onion

2 garlic cloves, unpeeled and crushed

Salt to taste

1 bay leaf, crushed

5 tablespoons butter or margarine

2 tablespoons cream

¹/₄ cup skim ricotta cheese

¹/₂ cup light cream

1 tablespoon freshly minced parsley or dill

In a 4-quart pan, place potatoes, onion, garlic, salt and bay leaf; add water to cover. Bring to a boil, cover, reduce heat, and cook 15 to 20 minutes or until potatoes are tender.

Discard onion, garlic and bay leaf. Place hot potatoes in large wide mixing bowl. Mash thoroughly with an old-fashioned potato masher or large fork – not an electric hand beater. Add butter and cream. Beat until both disappear. Combine ricotta and cream. Mix well. Add gradually to potatoes, beating briskly to obtain fluffy mashed potatoes.

Return mashed potatoes to original cooking pot. If you find the potatoes too stiff, incorporate 1 tablespoon at a time of skim milk until it reaches the right consistency. Place pot over low heat for about 2 minutes, stirring continually. Spread in pretty dish with a sprinkle of parsley or dillweed.

The Marinade
El Adobo

¹/₄ cup low-sodium teriyaki sauce

2 tablespoons extra virgin olive oil

Juice of one lemon

Sprig of cilantro or oregano, minced

3 garlic cloves, pressed

¹/₄ teaspoon cumin

¹/₄ cup dry red wine

Preheat oven to 250 degrees F.

Combine all ingredients in bowl; mix well. (I recommend you use Burgundy wine). Pour into a screw-top glass jar, and shake gently to mix several times during day. Do not refrigerate. Do not add salt to marinade, since teriyaki sauce has salt in it. Teriyaki sauce can be found in the oriental section at your supermarket. Marinating pans are available in most kitchen specialty stores.

(continued...)

Lamb Chops
Chuletas de Cordero

12 lamb chops, 4 to 6 ounces each
Olive oil spray
1 red bell pepper, roasted, then cut in strips*
1 yellow bell pepper, roasted, then cut in strips
2 tablespoons freshly minced parsley for garnish

When purchasing lamb, make sure chops are of uniform size and thickness; just less than ³/₄ inch thick is ideal for this recipe. Ask the butcher to trim off a good portion of the extended bone of each chop for easier handling.

Trim all visible fat from chops. Place in a marinating pan of plastic, glass or stainless steel with a tight lid. The chops may overlap, which is okay. Pour marinade over lamb. Cover and refrigerate overnight or at least 3 to 4 hours. Every now and then, turn marinade pan over and shake gently. Remove lamb from refrigerator one hour before cooking.

Spray with olive oil a large, non-stick skillet with cover. Do not crowd meat. Brown quickly on both sides. Lower heat, spoon some marinade over each chop; cover skillet, cook 4 to 5 minutes. Turn chops and repeat procedure. Cook another 4 to 5 minutes, covered. When both sides are nicely browned, remove to a large heat-proof platter.

Drain juices in skillet to a small bowl. Clean skillet with paper towels. Repeat cooking method with remaining chops. Use all marinade. Remove second batch of ribs to join first batch in platter. Again drain any juices in skillet into the small bowl. Let juices rest, then defat by skimming fat off the top with a skimmer.

Arrange chops around the edge of the platter, leaving inside space for mashed potatoes. Alternate colors of bell pepper strips between chops; fill space left in center of platter with yummy potatoes, piled high; sprinkle all with parsley. Place platter in warm oven for 10 minutes before serving. Heat defatted juices in small bowl and spoon over the chops.

Serves: 4 to 6.

*For instructions about how to roast peppers, see Page 321.

Oriental Country Style Ribs
Costiller de Puerco Oriental

The late Ann McDuffie, food editor at The Tampa Tribune for many years, was a good friend. She was an expert on recipes and menu planning. When I told her my idea about putting my cherished recipes into a book, she was very enthused, and offered to help in any way she could.

Often she would call when a recipe that appeared in the newspaper seemed special, as this one was. "I know you will change it and undoubtedly improve it," was her comment. "Just let me know what you are doing with these ingredients." I followed the recipe and it turned out to be a winner.

So in her memory is this terrific recipe that appeared in her column so many years ago, with just a few changes. These ribs are indeed for a rare and special occasion. Just perfect for a 4th of July, Memorial Day, or a covered dish for a family gathering.

4 pounds country-style pork ribs
Olive oil spray
1 cup light brown sugar
2 tablespoons cornstarch
$1/2$ cup finely sliced celery ribs
$1/2$ teaspoon ginger
$1/2$ cup finely minced onion
2 tablespoons honey
$1/4$ cup light soy sauce
$1/2$ cup water
$1/2$ cup dry white wine
2 tablespoons rice vinegar
2 tablespoons shredded orange rind, zest removed
1 – 8 ounce can unsweetened crushed pineapple
Dash of salt
$1/2$ teaspoon hot sauce
$1/4$ cup shredded fresh coconut

(continued...)

Preheat oven to 350 degrees F.

When purchasing ribs, ask butcher to cut into serving pieces and remove as much as possible of the visible fat. Spray a shallow roasting pan with olive oil. Place ribs in it and cover pan with foil, crimping at edges; bake one hour.

In a medium-sized saucepan, combine sugar, cornstarch, celery and ginger. Stir in remaining 9 ingredients, ending with salt. Cook over low heat until thickened. Remove ribs to platter with a slotted spoon. Drain pan drippings and discard. Clean pan with paper towels.

Return ribs to pan. Brush with half of the hot sauce. Sprinkle with half of coconut. Turn ribs. Spoon remaining sauce over ribs and sprinkle with remaining coconut. Cover pan with foil and return to oven. Bake 30 minutes.

Uncover and continue baking until meat is deliciously tender and brown.

After ribs are cooked, allow to rest 30 minutes or so; spoon away excess grease that rises to the surface. Serve with any of the brown rice recipes found in the vegetable chapter of this book, or white rice, tossed with parsley and almonds.

Serves: 4 to 6.

Drunken Pork Chops
Costillas de Puerco Borrachas

Here the lowly pork chop takes on an air of importance; the combination of wine, cognac and fresh herbs and vegetables make for a lovely marriage. Use a quality cognac!

6 center cut pork chops, less than 1 inch thick

2 unpeeled garlic cloves, crushed

4 tablespoons olive or canola oil

2 baking potatoes, peeled and cut in thin rounds

Salt and pepper

$1/2$ pound fresh mushrooms, thinly sliced

1 onion, sliced in rings

$1/2$ green bell pepper, julienned

$1/2$ red bell pepper, julienned

¹/₂ cup minced cilantro

¹/₂ cup dry white wine

2 tablespoons high-quality cognac

2 tablespoons rice vinegar

¹/₄ cup water

Preheat oven to 350 degrees F.

Ask the butcher to trim extended chop bone, so it will not interfere with cooking. It will also be easier to handle. Trim all visible fat and membrane from chops. Rub each chop with crushed garlic.

In a large, 12-inch, nonstick skillet, heat 1 tablespoon oil, reserve the rest; add pork chops and sear on both sides. After searing, lower heat and brown meat well on both sides, about 5 or 6 minutes per side. Remove chops to platter and cover.

Choose a 3-quart, round, non-stick casserole measuring 13 x 3-1/2 inches, with cover. Grease bottom with 1 tablespoon of the reserved olive oil, and line bottom with potato slices; dust with salt and pepper. In a small bowl, combine mushrooms, onion, peppers and cilantro; cover potatoes with half of this mixture, and dribble with the last tablespoon of reserved olive oil. Nestle browned chops over vegetables. Dust meat with salt and white pepper. Cover pork chops with remaining vegetables.

Combine wine, cognac (I recommend Cardinal Mendoza), vinegar and water; pour into casserole around chops. Dribble with 1 more tablespoon of olive oil.

Cover casserole and cook at high heat until it starts to boil; then cook briskly 1 more minute. Bake, covered, one hour, or until chops and vegetables are tender.

Serves: 4 to 6.

. . . .

Here the lowly pork chop takes on an air of importance...wine, cognac and fresh herbs and vegetables make for a lovely marriage.

A Delicious Meat Loaf with Mushroom Sauce

Salpicón Delicioso

I pride myself on the meat loaf recipe that I devised for my first cookbook, Clarita's Cocina. So many readers who have prepared the meat loaf have taken precious time to write and tell me how great it is, which makes me feel so good.

1 pound lean ground top round beef
1/2 pound uncooked, ground turkey breast
1/4 pound lean ground ham
1 slice whole wheat bread, crust removed
1/2 cup evaporated skim milk
1 tablespoon olive oil
1 onion, minced
3 garlic cloves, minced
1/4 cup chopped water chestnuts
3 tablespoons tomato sauce
1 teaspoon salt
1 teaspoon hot sauce
1 egg, beaten
2 tablespoons fresh minced parsley
1 tablespoon fresh minced tarragon
1 tablespoon seasoned bread crumbs
2 egg whites, beaten to meringue consistency
1/2 cup cubed white cheddar or other flavorful cheese
Olive oil spray
2 slices bacon

Preheat oven to 325 degrees F.
Ask your butcher to grind beef, turkey and ham together.
In a large mixing bowl, place meat and mix well. In a small bowl, crumble bread, and pour milk over it; set aside to soak. In a

10-inch skillet, heat oil, then add onions, garlic, water chestnuts, tomato sauce, salt and hot sauce.

Cook 2 minutes, stirring, then pour over meat in bowl. Add egg, parsley, tarragon, reserved bread and bread crumbs. With two forks, mix lightly but thoroughly to blend all ingredients.

Beat egg whites until they form peaks, and in folding motion, incorporate into mixture until meringue disappears. Please, do not handle meat roughly.

Add cubed cheese. With fingers, poke cheese cubes into meat loaf.

Spray olive oil in a 13 x 9 x 2-inch glass or ceramic oven pan. Turn meat mixture into center of pan and shape into a meat loaf. Cut bacon strips in two and stretch each piece at an angle across the meat, tucking ends under.

Bake 30 minutes. You will see fat and scum released from the meat: With a kitchen spoon, remove it from pan, blotting with paper towels if necessary.

Pour prepared mushroom sauce (see following recipe) over all, ladling mushrooms on top of meat loaf. Bake another 30 minutes uncovered, basting at intervals. Remove pan from oven. Allow to stand 15 or 20 minutes before slicing.

Serves: 6 to 8.

Mushroom Sauce
La Salsa de Champiñon

1 teaspoon extra virgin olive oil or butter

1 cup fresh, sliced mushrooms

1/2 cup tomato sauce

1/2 cup defatted, low-sodium beef or chicken broth

1/2 cup dry red wine

In a deep skillet, melt the butter or heat the oil. Add the sliced mushrooms. Cook until golden and liquid begins to evaporate. Add tomato sauce, beef stock and wine (I recommend a full-bodied Burgundy). Cook 3 or 4 minutes at moderate heat. Pour over meat loaf, and bake another 30 minutes.

Meat Loaf "Italiano"
Salpicón "Italiano" Relleno con Queso

I introduced this recipe when I was appearing on a program with a cooking segment on Tampa's WTVT Channel 13. Requests from viewers for the recipe were overwhelming. For 22 years, I was associated with the television program; I will never forget the wonderful people I met while doing it...nostalgic memories!

1½ pounds lean beef ground round

1 slice day-old bread, crust removed

½ cup skim evaporated milk

2 tablespoons olive oil

1 onion, minced

2 tablespoons minced cilantro

1 tablespoon fresh minced oregano

3 garlic cloves, pressed

¼ cup chopped, toasted almonds

3 tablespoons tomato sauce

½ cup seasoned bread crumbs plus 2 extra tablespoons

1 egg, slightly beaten, or ¼ cup egg-substitute

Salt

Hot sauce

Preheat oven to 325 degrees F.

To assemble meat loaf: Place meat in large bowl. In a smaller bowl, soak the crumbled bread with the milk; set aside. In a large skillet, heat oil. Add onion, cilantro, oregano and garlic; sauté 2 minutes. Pour over meat in bowl, but do not mix yet.

To meat, add almonds, tomato sauce, bread crumbs, reserved soaked bread – milk and all – and egg. Season al gusto with salt and liquid hot sauce.

With 2 large forks, mix ingredients into the meat, lightly but thoroughly. The mixing has to be light. Remember, the less the meat is handled, the juicier the meat loaf.

Once all ingredients are properly introduced to the meat, set the bowl aside.

Cheese Filling
Relleno de Queso

1/2 cup low-fat ricotta cheese
1/4 cup grated, low-fat Mozzarella cheese
1/4 cup Parmesan cheese
1 egg; or 2 ounces (1/8 cup) egg-substitute
2 tablespoons fresh minced parsley
Salt and pepper to taste
Olive oil spray
2 lean bacon strips, cut in half and stretched
Handful of bread crumbs
1/4 cup dry wine
1/2 cup defatted, low-sodium beef stock
2 tablespoons tomato sauce or good ketchup

Combine ricotta with next 5 ingredients, ending with pepper; mix well and set aside. Spray with olive oil a glass, ceramic or stainless steel baking pan measuring 13 x 9 x 2 inches. Divide meat mixture in two portions; one portion should use 1/3 of the meat, the other 2/3. Place the larger portion in oven pan, and shape into a meat loaf. With the back of a spoon, form a deep canal down the center of the meat. Fill canal with cheese mixture. Cover cheese with the remaining 1/3 of the meat. Do this carefully.

With hands, shape into a meat loaf, sealing the filling within. Press to form a uniform loaf. Pat reserved bread crumbs over meat. Stretch bacon strips at an angle across meat. Secure with toothpicks (or tuck under). Bake 30 minutes, uncovered. Remove scum and grease, using paper towels if necessary.

Combine wine (I recommend Burgundy), stock, and tomato sauce or ketchup. Pour over meat loaf; return to oven, and continue baking another 30 minutes, basting once or twice. Delicioso! Allow to rest 30 minutes before slicing.

Serves: 4 to 6.

Lil's Stuffed Potatoes
Patatas Rellenas, Lilly

Here's a recipe from my cousin Lil, who is an excellent cook even if she doesn't think so. The filling that lurks within these potatoes and the way they are assembled is really una maravilla. Plan on preparing at least two per person – one will never do! They are that good!

1/2 pound lean beef ground round

1/2 pound uncooked ground turkey, white meat only

1 tablespoon olive oil

1 onion, finely minced

2 garlic cloves, pressed

2 tablespoons minced cilantro

2 tablespoons fresh minced parsley

1/2 teaspoon dried oregano, crushed

1/2 teaspoon fresh nutmeg

1/4 cup finely chopped red bell peppers

1/4 cup finely chopped green bell peppers

1/4 cup toasted chopped hazelnuts or pine nuts

1/2 cup sliced pimiento-stuffed olives

2 tablespoons small capers

1/4 cup tomato sauce

1/2 cup dry white wine

2 tablespoons rice vinegar

Pinch salt

Hot sauce

4 large Idaho potatoes, peeled and cubed

1 teaspoon salt

1 teaspoon fresh grated Parmesan cheese

2 eggs

Water

1 cup seasoned bread crumbs

3 tablespoons canola oil

Sprig of parsley
1 orange, sliced
1 lemon, sliced

In a mixing bowl place beef and turkey; mix to blend with a fork. In a large skillet, non-stick and with cover, brown meats until red disappears. Drain well in colander. Return to skillet; dribble with oil. Add onion and next 7 ingredients, ending with green bell peppers. Cook, stirring with wooden spoon, until onion appears translucent.

Add nuts, olives and capers; cook 3 minutes. Combine tomato sauce, wine and vinegar. Add to meat in skillet. Mix well. Cook 2 minutes; now add salt and hot sauce *al gusto*. Lower heat, cover skillet and cook 20 to 30 minutes, or until almost (not quite) dry. Set aside to cool.

Put potatoes in a 3-quart saucepan with a lid. Cover with water and add salt. Bring to a boil. Cook, covered, at reduced heat for 20 minutes, or until potatoes are tender. Drain and transfer to a wide mixing bowl. Sprinkle cheese over potatoes. With an old-fashioned potato masher or large fork, mash the potatoes, but good! Cool slightly.

To assemble: Scoop 2 tablespoons of mashed potatoes into your left hand. Knead a few seconds. With the back of a spoon, press potatoes to form indentation down center. Fill with 2 tablespoons of filling. Cover with another 2 tablespoons of mashed potatoes. Work with your hands to form a smooth oblong roll, about 2 inches long. Make sure filling is contained within the mashed potatoes. Repeat this until all ingredients are used.

Beat eggs with water in a deep plate until frothy. Spread bread crumbs in a shallow plate. Roll finished product first in crumbs, then in egg mixture, and again in crumbs. Gently shake off excess. Start with 3 tablespoons canola oil. Heat in a large non-stick skillet. Place stuffed potatoes in skillet. Do not crowd. If the skillet is a roomy one, you can do 6 potatoes in a batch. You will be surprised how very little oil it takes to brown these. As they brown, transfer to a large shallow platter, lined with paper towels.

You will not need more than 3 or 4 tablespoons of oil for browning with plenty leftover. This beats deep frying, where they would soak up lots of grease, *no es verdad?* Remove paper towels from platter. Garnish a capricho with parsley and slices of lemon and oranges banking the potatoes.

Yield: 12 potatoes.

Tenderloin Roast with Fresh Thyme
Solomillo Asado con Tomillo Fresca

Aunt "Jo" was the sister I never had. Whenever I prepare this recipe, I think of her and the fun times we had together. It uses the tenderloin – the most costly and tenderest piece of meat. Cooked properly, this recipe never fails, and I offer it to you in memory of Aunt Jo: This was her favorite.

4 to 5 pounds beef tenderloin

Olive oil spray

1 cup dry red wine

¼ cup low-sodium soy sauce

3 tablespoons extra virgin olive oil

3 sprigs fresh thyme, or 1 teaspoon dried thyme

1 teaspoon salt

1 teaspoon white pepper

3 tablespoons fresh minced Italian parsley or chives
   or 1½ tablespoons dried

1/4 cup melted butter, or margarine

Preheat broiler.

Remove tenderloin from refrigerator. Prepare a broiling rack and medium-sized roasting pan, with cover, that accommodates the roast comfortably. Spray rack with olive oil to prevent sticking. Remove all connective tissue and visible fat from meat. Set roast in pan.

In a small bowl, combine wine, soy sauce, olive oil, thyme, salt and pepper. Mix well with a wire whisk, and pour over meat. Cover and refrigerate overnight, turning meat every few hours. In the morning, turn meat as often as possible in the marinade. Remove pan from refrigeration one hour before broiling.

Place meat on rack in roasting pan. Broil 20 minutes per side, 5 inches from heat source, basting until all marinade is used. Use a meat thermometer to insure desired doneness: 130 degrees F. rare; 140 for medium; 160 for well-done. This roast is also fine for barbecuing on an outdoor grill.

Remove tenderloin to a pretty serving platter. Add parsley or chives to melted butter. Pour mixture over hot meat. Cover loosely with foil tent. Let meat rest 15 minutes before slicing. Serve with "Three Peppers Vinaigrette" (recipe follows), and baked potatoes.

Three Peppers Vinaigrette
Ajises Vinaigrette

1 green bell pepper, roasted*

1 red bell pepper, roasted*

1 yellow bell pepper, roasted*

1 red onion, thinly sliced into rings

1 tablespoon olive oil

2 tablespoons small capers

¼ cup rice vinegar

Cut roasted peppers in half. Remove seeds and pith. Cut into strips, julienne style. Combine with onion rings. In a large skillet, heat oil. Add peppers, onion rings and capers. Sauté 2 minutes. Pour in the vinegar. Mix well. Cook briskly another minute. Transfer mixture to a pretty serving platter and serve with the meat; or, spoon mixture around tenderloin to create a flamboyant and beautiful roast.

Serves: 4 to 6.

*For instructions on roasting peppers, see Page 321.

Tenderloin Roast Simply Done
Lomo de Carne Sencillo

A tenderloin, or filet of beef is a tender and tasty cut of meat that, although expensive, produces little waste and provides very good eating, de vez en cuando (once in a while). It is excellent without the helping hand of a marinade, but if you want to fancy it up – be my guest!

4 to 5 pounds beef tenderloin

3 tablespoons extra virgin olive oil

3 unpeeled garlic cloves, crushed

2 tablespoons low-sodium soy sauce

Olive oil spray

Salt and pepper to taste

Keep meat in refrigerator until you are ready to use. Meanwhile, in a small screw-top jar, combine olive oil, garlic and soy sauce; shake well; set aside for an hour. One hour before cooking, remove meat from refrigerator. Trim 2 inches from each end of tenderloin , and save for other uses – this will give the roast an even thickness. Trim all connective tissues and visible fat.

Preheat oven to 400 degrees F.

Brush meat well with the olive oil-garlic mixture. Spray with olive oil the roasting rack and pan, and put meat in the middle. Insert meat thermometer to assure desired doneness. Roast 20 minutes on one side; turn roast and repeat, 20 minutes more on the other side. Remove from oven to a serving platter.

Season immediately with salt and pepper on both sides. Cover loosely with a tent of foil and allow to rest 15 minutes to allow seasonings to penetrate. (Slicing will be easier.)

Accompany with your favorite potato and fresh garden vegetables.

Serves: 6 to 8.

Veal Chops "Condessa" with Raw Onion and Parsley

Costillas de Ternera con Mojo Crudo, "Condessa"

Mojo Crudo, familiar in most Spanish kitchens, is a mixture of raw onions and fresh minced parsley. It resides harmoniously with steaks, chops and grilled fish. A quick and tasty dinner that's good for family as well as well-heeled guests.

6 veal chops, 6 ounces each, less than 1 inch thick
2 unpeeled garlic cloves, crushed
Salt and pepper
2 tablespoons olive oil
¼ cup dry white wine
Juice of one lemon
2 Bermuda onions, finely minced
1 cup fresh minced parsley

Trim chops of all visible fat. Between sheets of waxed paper, pound slightly, if you wish, with a meat mallet. Remove garlic cloves from the pod, but do not peel. With the palm of your hand, crush them. The pulp of the garlic is thus contained within the peel, and is easier to rub over meat or fish.

Brush meat with the crushed garlic cloves. Dust chops lightly with salt and white pepper. Use a large, 12-inch, non-stick skillet with cover. Add olive oil with the remains of the garlic. When garlic browns, remove from skillet.

Add veal chops, browning quickly on both sides. Cover skillet and lower heat. Cook meat until done, about 10 minutes on each side. Remove chops to serving platter. De-glaze skillet with wine and lemon juice. Strain over the meat. Combine onion and parsley. Mix well. Spoon over each chop. Garnish platter *a capricho* – however, you like – and serve pronto!

Serves: 4 to 6.

Vienna Veal Cutlets and Concasse Sauce
Chuletes de Viena con Salsa Concasse

In purchasing veal for this or any other recipe, make sure the meat is milky white or slightly pink. This assures tenderness. Veal is not always easy to find, and that is because it is less popular in the U.S. than in Europe, where it is consumed in abundance.

It was in Vienna, Austria, where I feasted on veal cutlets and sachertort for one whole week. The veal's delicate taste was unforgettable. The following recipe is one that I have repeated many times at home, to the delight of my family.

6 veal cutlets, 6 ounces each
1 egg or 2 ounces egg-substitute
1 teaspoon Dijon mustard
1/2 cup unbleached flour
2 tablespoons fresh grated Parmesan cheese
2 tablespoons toasted, finely ground almonds
1/2 teaspoon baking powder
1 teaspoon salt
1 teaspoon white pepper
1 teaspoon Spanish paprika
2 tablespoons olive oil, or 1 tablespoon each olive oil and butter

Concasse Sauce
Salsa Concasse

1 onion, finely chopped
3 garlic cloves, minced
1/4 cup finely minced cilantro
2 tablespoons fresh, finely minced oregano
2 cups ripe, peeled and seeded tomatoes

2 tablespoons tomato sauce

½ cup dry wine

¼ cup defatted, low-sodium beef stock

Olive oil spray

½ cup grated Gruyere cheese

Preheat oven to 350 degrees F.

Prepare cutlets by removing any visible connective tissues and fat. (Veal, remember, is very low in fat.) With the flat side of a meat mallet, pound between 2 sheets of waxed paper until very thin and of uniform thickness.

In a wide bowl, combine egg or egg substitute and mustard; beat with wire whisk until blended. Combine flour and next 6 ingredients, ending with paprika. Spread mixture onto a flat surface platter or pie plate. Dip each cutlet into egg mixture, then in flour mixture; shake off excess coating, and place in single layer on a large flat platter.

In a large, non-stick skillet, heat oil; brown veal in batches of 3. Transfer to platter lined with paper towels. Using the same skillet in which meat was browned, add onion, garlic, cilantro and oregano. Turn heat down to low, and mix with wooden spoon, scraping up all particles stuck to skillet; cook 3 or 4 minutes. Add tomatoes and sauce. Cook briskly 1 minute, stirring. Pour in wine and stock; bring to a boil. Check seasonings. Add more if needed. Cover skillet and cook 5 minutes, ni un minuto mas, okay?

To assemble: Use a glass or ceramic baking pan measuring 13 x 9 x 2 inches. Spray pan with olive oil. Spoon concasse sauce into the pan. Place cutlets at an angle across the sauce. Sprinkle with cheese. Bake 20 to 25 minutes, or until bubbly. Now is this yummy or what!

Serves: 4 to 6.

It was in Vienna, Austria, where I feasted on veal cutlets and sacher tort for one whole week...

Rolled Stuffed Flank Steak
Rollo de Carne, Fiesta

A most colorful and fantastic way to prepare flank steak. A good marinade will contribute immensely to a superb outcome. You will love this!

2½ to 3 pounds beef flank steak
Dusting of pepper

For the marinade
Por el adobo

1/4 cup cognac
1/2 cup red wine
2 tablespoons low-sodium soy sauce
2 garlic cloves, pressed
1 tablespoon olive oil

For the omelette
Por la tortilla

1 cup minced spinach
2 tablespoons olive oil, divided
1 tablespoon butter
¼ cup finely chopped, slivered almonds
1 onion, finely minced
1 – 1 ounce jar of minced pimientos, drained
½ cup finely minced, cooked ham
3 tablespoons grated fontina or Gruyere cheese
2 eggs plus 1 egg white, or 6 ounces egg-substitute
Salt and white pepper

Reserved marinade
El adobo

1 cup defatted, low-sodium beef stock

1 – 8 ounce can tomato sauce

2 garlic cloves, pressed

Salt

Hot sauce, if needed

When purchasing meat, ask the butcher to score it on one side and to remove connective tissues and all visible fat. At home, dust meat generously with pepper, cover with waxed paper, then with a meat mallet, pound gently. Place meat in a pan, preferably glass with a cover, for refrigeration.

In a little mixing bowl, combine cognac, wine, soy sauce, garlic and olive oil. Mix well and pour over meat. Refrigerate overnight, or at least 4 hours before cooking. Turn at intervals. Remove meat from the refrigerator 1 hour before cooking. During that hour, prepare omelette.

In a saucepan, cook spinach until wilted, about 5 minutes. Drain well and set aside. In a large non-stick skillet, heat half the oil, reserving the rest, along with butter; add nuts and onion. Sauté 3 minutes, until both are golden. Add pimientos, ham and cheese. Stir carefully to mix. Add spinach. Mix well.

Beat eggs and egg white or egg-substitute until well-blended but not foamy. Scatter sautéed ingredients evenly over skillet surface. Pour eggs over all. Allow a light crust to form. Turn omelette uncooked side down. When completely set and cooked, turn into a round, flat platter. Omelette should be very thin.

Lift meat from marinade to a work board. Strain marinade into a measuring cup for later use. Lightly dust meat with salt. Place omelette on prepared meat.

Roll tightly, jelly-roll fashion, with the omelette securely contained within the steak. Tie roll with kitchen cord.

Heat remaining olive oil in same large skillet where omelette was cooked. Brown meat on all sides. Place in roasting pan with cover. Prepare a light sauce to accompany the meat as it cooks.

(continued...)

Preheat oven to 300 degrees F.

Combine ingredients for reserved marinade; pour into a saucepan and bring to a boil. Skim. Cover, lower heat and cook 5 minutes. Pour around meat roll. Cover pot and bake in oven $1^1/_2$ hours; add more liquid if needed. Cook until meat is very tender. Mashed potatoes are great with this entree!

Serves: 4 to 6.

PASTA

Pasta, an increasingly popular item in our daily menus, appears in various forms worldwide, and its versatility is endless. When I visited Spain in 1989, I was pleasantly surprised at the many ways pasta was prepared in my relatives' homes. Pasta has been popular in Spain for many years, and is an important part of many exciting entrees. "It is better," my cousin proclaimed, "than in Italia itself!" (Of course, this is Spanish boasting, and let me tell you, they really know how to boast!)

However, to prove a point, she instructed la cocinera to prepare a different pasta side dish every day in addition to the main course. What a feast! The manicotti made with crepes and the famous *platillo*, made with angel hair pasta, are two very old Spanish recipes. They were magnificent. I particularly remember the manicotti, baked in a rich bechamel sauce and lavishly adorned with walnuts. Both recipes are included in this chapter.

Of course in these recipes I rely heavily on herbs and spices to maintain fine flavors. Fat and sodium have been reduced to a minimum. Yet flavor remains. For instance, my basic meatless sauce, made mostly with fresh products, is *excelente* on its own or, if you prefer, you can add meat, fowl or fresh fish.

Enjoy these pasta dishes which I feel preserve the joy and *buen gusto* of good eating.

Buen provecho!

Recipes

Confetti Pasta

Eggplant with Chorizos and Tomatoes

Shrimp with Spaghetti

Manicotti in White Sauce

Pasta with Pine Nuts and Fresh Tomato

Angel Hair Pasta with Chicken and Chorizo

Angel Hair at Its Best

Spinach au Gratin with Angel Hair

Elegant Tomato Sauce

Spaghetti with Turkey Meatballs

Pasta Paella

. . . .

Confetti Pasta
Pasta Confetti

This recipe features a robust medley of vegetables and pasta, well-balanced nutritionally and flamboyant as only Spanish pasta can be. If you prefer, steam the vegetables over hot water, approximately 10 minutes, adding broccoli at the end stages to preserve its verdant color.

3/4 pound #8 spaghetti
2 tablespoons extra virgin olive oil
1 onion, minced
1/4 cup pine nuts
3/4 cup broccoli flowerets, cut small and uniformly
3/4 cup cauliflower, cut small and uniformly
1/2 cup thinly sliced baby carrots
1/2 cup snow peas, trimmed and cut in thirds
1/4 cup sliced pimiento-stuffed olives
1/4 cup sliced ripe olives
1/2 cup sliced fresh mushrooms
1/2 cup fresh asparagus, tender part only, cut small
1/2 cup chopped green bell pepper
1/2 cup chopped red bell pepper
3 tablespoons fresh minced basil
3 tablespoons fresh minced thyme
2 tablespoons rice vinegar
1/4 cup dry white wine
3 garlic cloves, minced
Salt and pepper
1 teaspoon salt
1 teaspoon olive oil
1/4 cup fresh grated Parmesan cheese
1/2 cup crumbled feta cheese
Minced dillweed or parsley for garnish

(continued…)

Measure pasta, set aside. In a large Dutch oven, heat oil. Add onion and nuts. Sauté until golden. Add next 12 ingredients in order listed, ending with thyme. Lower heat, and with wooden spoon, stir-fry 5 minutes. Add vinegar, wine and garlic. Mix well and continue to cook over low heat, stirring at intervals, another 5 minutes. Add salt and pepper al gusto and set aside.

Heat a 4- or 5-quart stockpot $3/4$ full of water until it boils. Add salt and olive oil; snap spaghetti in two, drop in, and cook 10 to 12 minutes. Drain, but reserve 1 cup of cooking water. Add cooked spaghetti to vegetables in pot. If needed, pour $1/2$ cup of cooking water over spaghetti mixture. Sprinkle with Parmesan cheese and toss with 2 long-handled kitchen forks to mix thoroughly.

Transfer to a pretty large serving platter. Scatter feta cheese over mixture, but do not toss again at this point. Sprinkle with dillweed or parsley. Allow to rest a few minutes before serving.

Serves: 6.

Eggplant with Chorizos and Tomatoes
Berenjena con Chorizos y Tomates

Eggplant is a versatile vegetable found year-round in produce markets. Its skin is dark purple. At its best, it should be a shiny deep purple in color, free of blemishes or dark bruises, and should feel firm and heavy to the touch. Big eggplants are not the best; those weighing 1 to 1½ pounds are tastiest.

This is a special recipe that I think you will like. Eggplant, chorizo and fresh tomatoes translates into a great combination. If you do not care for chorizo, you may substitute a sausage of your choice. Or, for that matter, consider sausage optional and forget it.

1 pound #9 spaghetti
2 eggplants, 1 to 1½ pounds each
Dusting of salt
Olive oil spray
3 tablespoons extra virgin olive oil, divided

. . . .

1 Spanish onion, minced

4 or 5 garlic cloves, minced

¼ cup fresh minced basil or 2 tablespoons dried

¼ cup minced cilantro

½ teaspoon crushed fennel seeds

½ teaspoon curry powder

5 ripe tomatoes, peeled, seeded and chopped

½ cup tomato sauce

Hot sauce to taste

Salt

1 – 14 ounce can defatted, low-sodium chicken or beef broth

2 chorízos, casing removed, degreased*

2 tablespoons dry sherry

1 teaspoon salt

1 tablespoon extra virgin olive oil

¼ cup grated Gruyere cheese

2 or 3 tablespoons fresh minced dillweed or parsley

Measure pasta; set aside. Preheat oven to 325 degrees F.

Semi-peel and cut eggplant crosswise into ½ inch rounds. In a deep bowl, dust generously with salt; cover and allow to rest 30 minutes. The eggplant will "bleed" water. When time is up, rinse, pat dry, and cut slices into cubes.

Spray a baking pan with olive oil. Arrange eggplant pieces closely together, and brush with half of the oil. Cover. Bake 20 minutes, or until soft but still a little firm. While eggplant bakes, prepare sauce.

In a large, 12-inch skillet with cover, heat remaining oil. Add onion, garlic, basil, cilantro, fennel and curry. Sauté at low heat until fragrant and onion is soft. Add tomatoes and tomato sauce. Stir to mix well. Bring to a slow boil. With a skimmer or big spoon, remove acid foam from surface. Add salt. Be generous with hot sauce and stingy with salt. Stir and mix well. Cook 2 minutes at low heat. Pour in broth. Mix throughly and bring to a boil; when it boils again, remove from heat. (The eggplant should be done).

*For instructions about how to degrease chorizos, see Page 318.

(continued...)

Now spray with olive oil a 2^1/$_2$ quart shallow casserole with a cover, and transfer eggplant into it. Pour contents of skillet over eggplant in casserole. Scatter chorizo and sherry (I recommend Tio Pepe) over all. Mix thoroughly, cover, lower heat and cook slowly for about 30 minutes, until all is tender.

While it cooks, fill a large pot with water; add salt and olive oil. Bring to a quick boil. Snap spaghetti in two; add to boiling water, stirring continually until you see pasta is not sticking together. Cook briskly, uncovered, for about 12 minutes. Pasta should be al dente. Drain. Reserve ^{1}/$_2$ cup cooking water. Pour pasta over sauce in casserole, and add reserved cooking water if ingredients appear too dry. Sprinkle with cheese. Toss thoroughly and scatter dillweed or parsley over all. Let rest 10 minutes before serving.

Serves: 6.

Shrimp with Spaghetti (and Class)
Gambas con Estilo

There is no fat at all in shrimp, but, of course, some of the ingredients add a few calories here and there. An occasional fling will satisfy the appetite without causing undue pangs of guilt, no es verdad?

1 pound #8 spaghetti or linguine

2 pounds shrimp, 16 to the count, cleaned and deveined

1 tablespoon extra virgin olive oil

1 onion, finely minced

2 inner celery ribs, chopped

^{1}/$_2$ cup sliced water chestnuts

2 bay leaves

4 garlic cloves, pressed or finely minced

^{1}/$_4$ cup sliced pimiento-stuffed Spanish olives

1 – 16 ounce can tomato sauce

. . . .

1 ripe tomato, peeled, seeded and chopped

1 tablespoon rice vinegar or balsamic

Louisiana hot sauce and salt to taste

$^1/_2$ cup dry sherry

$^1/_2$ cup chicken broth or clam juice

Pinch of salt

1 teaspoon extra virgin olive oil

$^1/_4$ cup fresh minced parsley

$^1/_4$ cup grated Parmesan cheese

Measure pasta. Wash carefully, clean and devein shrimp.

In large, non-stick skillet, heat oil. Add onion, celery, chestnuts and bay leaves. Sauté until onion is soft, 2 to 3 minutes. Add garlic and olives. Cook another 2 minutes, stirring with wooden spoon.

Combine tomato sauce, tomato and vinegar. Add to sauté mixture. Stir well to incorporate all ingredients. Add hot sauce and salt to taste. Pour in sherry and broth or clam juice. Bring to a boil, stirring carefully. Lower heat, cover and cook sauce 20 minutes only.

While sauce cooks, fill a 4- or 5-quart stock pot $^3/_4$ full of water, add a pinch of salt, and heat. When water boils, dribble oil in the water. Snap spaghetti in two and add; cook briskly not more than 12 minutes; reserve 1 cup of cooking water before draining well. Transfer pasta to a large mixing bowl; pour $^1/_2$ cup of cooking water over spaghetti to keep moist. (Do not discard remaining $^1/_2$ cup cooking water – you may need it later for leftovers – if you have any.)

Back to the sauce: Add shrimp, and cook 10 minutes, or until shrimp turns pink. Pour sauce over pasta in bowl, and with 2 long-handled kitchen forks, toss well. Add parsley and cheese; toss again thoroughly in a down-and-over motion. Pour spaghetti onto a pretty, heat-proof company platter. Place in a warm oven until ready to serve – just don't forget it because the shrimp will overcook. Not more than 10 minutes in the warmer now, okay?

Serves: 6.

Manicotti in White Sauce
Manicotti en Salsa Blanca

Divine crepes! This is the recipe as I remember it, prepared in my family's home in Madrid. However, the cheese used in the filling for the crepes, as I recall was requesón, comparable to farmer's cheese. If you'd like to try something other than white sauce with the manicotti, try a good concasse (tomato sauce). Have fun and try it both ways!

For the crepes
Para los crepes

1 cup all-purpose flour

1 cup 1% milk

$1/2$ cup water

$1/2$ teaspoon salt

$1/4$ teaspoon nutmeg

1 tablespoon butter plus 1 tablespoon olive oil

4 eggs, or 8 ounces egg-substitute

1 tablespoon cognac

Vegetable oil spray

Combine flour, milk, water, salt and nutmeg. With a whisk or hand beater, beat vigorously to create a smooth, thin batter. Blend in the butter and oil, whisking to incorporate into the batter. Stir in eggs and cognac. Refrigerate mixture 30 minutes. Stir at 10-minute intervals. To assemble crepes: Remove batter from refrigerator and mix well.

For best results in cooking, spray a non-stick, 10-inch skillet with vegetable oil, and heat cautiously at low temperature, so as not to burn the spray substance. Pour 3 tablespoons of batter into center of skillet; quickly rotate to coat the bottom of skillet evenly. Cook until bottom is set, about 2 minutes. With a Teflon spatula so you don't scratch the skillet's surface, flip and cook until golden specks appear. Repeat until all batter is used. Cover crepes with waxed paper and keep warm until ready to use.

Filling for Crepes
Relleno para Crepes

¹/₄ cup finely minced cooked ham
2 cups low-fat ricotta cheese
¹/₂ cup fresh grated Parmesan cheese
1 cup fresh grated low-fat Mozzarella cheese
2 tablespoons fresh, finely minced parsley
1 teaspoon fresh, finely minced dillweed
¹/₂ teaspoon salt
¹/₂ teaspoon white pepper
1 egg or 2 ounces egg-substitute
Vegetable oil spray

If using egg, beat well. Combine all ingredients except the last in order listed; mix well, but do not beat. Taste. Correct seasonings if needed. Allow to rest 10 minutes.

Remove crepes from warmer. Spray with vegetable oil a glass or ceramic oven pan measuring 13 x 9 x 2 inches. Place a generous tablespoon of filling (maybe a little more than 1 tablespoon) in the center of each crepe; flap over ends to enclose filling in crepes. As crepes are filled, place seam down in oven pans, side by side. Cover and set aside while preparing white sauce.

White Sauce
Salsa Blanca

2 tablespoons extra virgin olive oil plus 1 teaspoon butter
2 tablespoons all-purpose flour
2 cups skim milk
¹/₄ teaspoon nutmeg
¹/₂ teaspoon salt
¹/₄ cup fresh grated Parmesan cheese
¹/₄ cup chopped walnuts
1 – 2 ounce jar roasted red bell peppers, drained and cut in strips

(continued...)

Preheat oven to 325 degrees F.

In a non-stick, 12-inch skillet, heat oil and butter. Add flour. Cook, stirring until flour takes on color and imparts a nutty fragrance. Remove skillet from heat. Combine milk, nutmeg and salt. Slowly add to flour, stirring with a whisk very vigorously to dissolve lumps that may form. You must be sure there are no flour lumps before returning skillet to heat. Cook sauce over medium heat until smooth. Add Parmesan cheese and mix well.

Pour sauce over manicotti in oven pan. Scatter walnuts over all and place strips of pepper over each manicotti. Bake until bubbly, about 20 to 25 minutes.

Serves: 6 to 8.

Pasta with Pine Nuts and Fresh Tomato
Pasta con Pignoli y Tomate Fresco

This recipe is best when it is made with lovely fresh herbs still glistening from the garden, but if you find yourself in a pinch, use dried herbs. This recipe combines a potpourri of herbs, including basil, thyme and oregano. The combination is so satisfying that your family and friends will demand repeat performances (like once a week!).

³/₄ pound angel hair pasta

Dribble of extra virgin olive oil

1 teaspoon salt

3 tablespoons extra virgin olive oil

1 cup finely minced onion

3 garlic cloves, minced

¹/₂ cup pine nuts

2 tablespoons fresh, finely chopped basil

2 tablespoons fresh, finely chopped thyme

2 tablespoons fresh, finely chopped oregano

2 tablespoons rice vinegar

Salt

5 ripe tomatoes, peeled, seeded and coarsely chopped

$^1/_2$ teaspoon fennel seeds

$^1/_2$ teaspoon ginger

1 cup fresh grated Parmesan cheese, divided

1 cup fresh cooked peas, or frozen

Measure pasta and set aside. Fill a 4- or 5-quart pot $^3/_4$ full of water and add a dribble of olive oil and salt. Heat water while making sauce.

Meanwhile, in a 12-inch, non-stick skillet, heat oil on low, adding onion, garlic and pine nuts, and sautéing until onion is soft. Add basil, thyme and oregano; cook at low heat until fragrant, about 3 minutes. Add vinegar and salt al gusto. Stir and mix a minute longer. Add tomatoes, fennel and ginger to skillet; cook about 5 minutes, mashing tomatoes with the back of the spoon.

Now, when pasta water boils, snap pasta in half and cook 3 minutes, then drain, reserving 1 cup of the cooking water. Place pasta in a large mixing bowl. Pour $^1/_2$ cup of reserved cooking water over pasta, and add $^1/_2$ cup cheese. Toss with 2 kitchen forks.

Back to the skillet. Add peas; cook just one minute. Place this flamboyant mixture over pasta and sprinkle with remaining cheese. Toss with energy, but lightly, until well-mixed.

Muy rico!
Serves: 6.

Angel Hair Pasta with Chicken and Chorizo
Platillo de Pollo y Chorizo

A favorite in my home...and I bet it will be in yours also. And it is so good for you, too! Not to mention the lovely texture of the thin pasta combined with the haunting flavors of real saffron combined with chicken and chorizo.

³/₄ pound angel hair pasta

3¹/₂ pounds of chicken, cut into 12 pieces

1 chorizo, degreased*

Dusting of salt

.4-gram package saffron, toasted**

3 cups defatted, low-sodium chicken broth

2 tablespoons extra virgin olive oil

1 onion, chopped

¹/₂ cup chopped green bell pepper

¹/₂ cup chopped red bell pepper

¹/₂ cup fresh, thinly sliced mushrooms

3 garlic cloves, pressed

1 bay leaf, crushed

1 ripe tomato

3 tablespoons tomato sauce

1 teaspoon salt

1 teaspoon hot sauce

¹/₄ cup dry wine

1 – 2 ounce jar minced pimientos

¹/₄ cup chopped and pitted green olives

2 tablespoons minced parsley or dillweed, or 1 tablespoon dried

*For instructions about degreasing chorizo, see Page 318.
**For instructions about toasting saffron and preparing broth, see Page 322.

Preheat oven to 325 degrees F. Measure pasta and set aside. Wash and trim chicken, and remove all visible fat. Degrease chorizo and set aside. Dust chicken lightly with salt. Put toasted saffron in hot chicken broth and allow to steep before starting recipe; reserve for later use.

Now, in a 12 x 3-inch, heat-proof casserole with cover, heat oil. Add chicken pieces, browning lightly, 5 minutes per side. With tongs, remove to mixing bowl and keep warm.

To drippings in casserole dish, add onion, peppers, mushrooms, garlic and bay leaf. Sauté at low heat 2 minutes, stirring until onion is transparent. Add tomato and tomato sauce; mix well. Add salt, hot sauce and wine (I recommend Sauterne). Return chicken to casserole. Incorporate well with ingredients.

Remove casing from degreased chorizo, crumble and scatter over all. Add pimientos and olives. Stir to mix well. Cover and cook 5 minutes. Reduce heat, snap pasta into 3-inch lengths; add to casserole. Pour reserved chicken broth over ingredients. Gently press pasta down to submerge in liquids; bring to a slow boil. Cover, reduce heat again to low, and cook 5 minutes more. Stir carefully once more to make sure pasta is well-mixed.

Cover casserole, and bake 20 to 25 minutes, or until all liquids are absorbed. Remove from oven, and sprinkle with parsley or dillweed. A sprinkle of additional wine will not hurt...why not! Cover casserole and allow to rest 15 minutes before serving.

Serves: 6.

...the lovely texture of the thin pasta combined with the haunting flavors of real saffron combined with chicken and chorizo...

Angel Hair at Its Best
Fideos en su Gloria

When I prepare a recipe calling for tomatoes, I like to combine fresh tomatoes with the canned variety that, indeed, today have become such an excellent product. I remember my mother peeling, seeding and chopping tomatoes for sauces, a chore that sometimes took all morning; I was always there to help. How I enjoyed being in that spacious kitchen with her.

After homework (always after homework!), she would allow me to help, explaining as she went along the importance of peeling and seeding tomatoes, tossing in tips she had learned during her many years of cooking and serving fine food to her family. Today, I always make time to prepare fresh tomatoes like mother because they add character and distinction to any recipe. Here is a recipe simple to prepare, but don't let its long list of ingredients scare you! Gathering them will only take a few minutes.

3/4 pound angel hair pasta

4 cups cooked chicken breast meat, cubed

2 tablespoons extra virgin olive oil, divided

1 onion, minced

3 or 4 cloves garlic, minced

1 cup thinly sliced mushrooms

3 tablespoons fresh minced oregano

3 tablespoons fresh minced basil

1/2 teaspoon red pepper flakes

1/2 teaspoon crushed fennel seeds

1 teaspoon fresh minced ginger

4 ripe tomatoes, peeled, seeded and chopped

2 ounces tomato sauce

Pinch of salt

1 tablespoon extra virgin olive oil

2 tablespoons dry sherry

1 cup reserved cooking water from pasta

1/4 cup grated Parmesan cheese

¼ cup crumbled goat cheese
¼ cup fresh minced parsley or dillweed

Measure pasta and set aside.

Measure and cube chicken. In a large non-stick skillet with cover, heat 1 tablespoon olive oil. Add chicken and crisp, about 5 minutes, carefully stirring. With slotted spoon, remove to bowl. Keep warm. Do not clean skillet.

Add second tablespoon of oil to skillet, then add onion. Sauté, scraping with a wooden spoon to dislodge brown bits that may have stuck to skillet. When onion is transparent, add garlic and mushrooms. Reduce heat to low, and cook until mushrooms brown. Add oregano, basil, red pepper, fennel and ginger; cook slowly, gently stirring, until fragrant.

Add tomatoes and tomato sauce. Cook 15 to 20 minutes, until tomatoes start releasing liquid. Add reserved chicken bits to skillet. Stir to mix well. Cover and cook slowly, about 5 minutes. Meanwhile, fill a 4 or 5-quart stockpot ¾ with water, add a pinch of salt and bring to a boil. Add olive oil and snap pasta in two; drop it into the water, cooking 3 minutes only. Drain well and reserve 1 cup of cooking water.

Transfer angel hair to large mixing bowl. Combine sherry (I recommend Amontillado) with ½ cup of reserved cooking water, and pour over pasta; do not discard remaining ? cup of cooking water – you may need it to moisten pasta should it dry out. Mix well. Add chicken sauce to pasta and sprinkle with Parmesan.

Using a down-and-over motion, mix thoroughly but gently. Transfer to a large pretty platter. Scatter goat cheese, such as Montrachet, evenly over all, followed by parsley or dillweed. (When I prepare this recipe, I use as much as 1 cup of Montrachet goat cheese simply because I like it. Consider your health tolerance, as both cheeses are salty). Place in warmer a few minutes before serving.

Serves: 6.

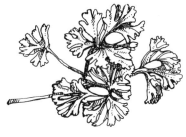

Spinach au Gratin with Angel Hair
Espinaca Gratinada con Fideos

Angel hair pasta is a comparable substitute for vermicelli pasta. Vermicelli, or fideos, is used extensively in the Spanish kitchen. A good chicken broth accompanied only by fideos creates a lovely chicken soup. Spinach and vermicelli pasta makes another legendary matchup; I am sure you will enjoy it.

³/₄ pound angel hair pasta

1 tablespoon extra virgin olive oil

¹/₂ cup finely minced onion

¹/₂ cup pine nuts

4 garlic cloves, minced

4 tablespoons fresh minced basil

2 tablespoons rice or wine vinegar

¹/₄ cup dry white wine

3 cups packed, chopped spinach, washed and spin dried

1 tablespoon olive oil plus 1 teaspoon butter

2 tablespoons unbleached flour

1¹/₂ cups skim milk

¹/₄ cup evaporated skim milk

2 tablespoons low-fat mayonnaise

¹/₂ teaspoon nutmeg

Salt and pepper to taste

1 – .4-ounce envelope dry, light ranch-style dressing

¹/₂ cup grated Gruyere cheese

1 – 2 ounce jar of pimientos, minced

1 teaspoon salt

1 teaspoon extra virgin olive oil

Parsley bouquets for garnish

Measure pasta and set aside. In a large skillet, heat oil. Add onions and pine nuts. Sauté until onion is soft and nuts turn golden. Add garlic, basil, vinegar and wine; cook 2 minutes. Add chopped spinach. Mix well carefully and cook until greens wilt slightly. Prepare a large mixing bowl; add greens to bowl. Clean skillet. Add olive oil and butter. Heat on low. Add flour. Cook to form roux,* about 3 minutes. Remove skillet from heat.

Combine the 2 milks and mayonnaise in a deep bowl. With hand whisk, beat smooth, adding nutmeg, salt, pepper and dry salad dressing. Beat 2 seconds longer. To the roux, add liquid slowly, stirring with energy to avoid flour lumps. Return skillet to heat; add cheese. Cook, stirring with wooden spoon, until cheese is absorbed and sauce has thickened. Pour sauce over spinach still in mixing bowl. Toss lightly. (Add pimientos to spinach in bowl now, before tossing with pasta).

White sauce is being prepared, bring a 4- or 5-quart stockpot $3/4$ full of water to a boil; add salt and olive oil; snap pasta in two, and cook briskly 3 minutes, stirring to avoid sticking. Drain pasta, reserving 1 cup cooking water. Mix well-drained pasta with spinach ingredients in mixing bowl. Pour $1/2$ cup cooking water over all and toss steadily, 2 minutes. Transfer mixture to serving platter. Garnish with parsley, and serve *caliente* – hot.

Serves: 6.

*For information on cooking a roux, see Page 321.

Elegant Tomato Sauce
Salsa de Tomate Elegante

Here's a wonderful tomato sauce that may be used in any number of recipes. This could make an outstanding meatless entree; or, if you prefer to add meat, use the sauce with the next recipe, my turkey meatballs. This dish is a special favorite of my grandson, Manny John, whose reaction was a big thumbs up to both recipes. I hope you like them, too. This freezes beautifully!

2 tablespoons extra virgin olive oil
1 Spanish onion, chopped
3 tablespoons fresh minced basil

3 tablespoons fresh minced oregano

3 tablespoons minced cilantro

½ teaspoon granulated sugar

5 garlic cloves, minced

1 zucchini, scraped and chopped

1 potato, cubed

2 carrots, scraped and chopped

6 cups fresh ripe tomatoes, peeled, seeded and chopped

1 – 28 ounce can whole plum tomatoes

1 – 28 ounce can tomato sauce

¼ cup full-bodied dry Burgundy wine

¼ cup grated Parmesan cheese

1 cup water

1 teaspoon hot sauce, or to taste

1 teaspoon salt

Use a large, 4- or 5-quart pot or Dutch oven with cover, heat oil; add onion, and sauté until translucent. Add basil, oregano, cilantro, sugar and garlic. Turn heat to low, and cook until fragrant, 2 or 3 minutes, stirring with wooden spoon. Add zucchini, potato, carrots and fresh tomatoes. Mix well.

Empty canned plum tomatoes into a bowl and cut in two. Squeeze out seeds, and cut solid portions into a mixing bowl. Hold a colander over the bowl and strain juices. Discard seeds. Combine with tomato sauce. Add to saucepot together with wine, cheese and water (use water to clean out tomato cans). Bring to a boil. Remove foam from surface with skimmer.

Cook, uncovered at low heat about 15 minutes, stirring to prevent food from sticking. Cover the pot and cook 30 minutes. Check seasonings. Be generous with hot sauce and stingy with salt. Cook another 15 minutes until all vegetables are cooked tender. Remove pot from heat. Cool slightly.

In an electric blender or food processor, purée in batches. As sauce is pureed, pour into a large bowl. Return sauce to cooking pot. Cover and simmer another 15 minutes or so, stirring occasionally to prevent sticking.

Yield: About 2 quarts.

Spaghetti with Turkey Meatballs
Spaghetti con Albondigas de Pavo

A good spaghetti sauce teams up beautifully with turkey meatballs. Ask your butcher to grind 1 pound of turkey breast, and a quarter pound very lean ham. Now follow the recipe carefully, for tasty, light-as-a-feather turkey meatballs.

1 pound #8 spaghetti

1 pound ground turkey breast

1/4 pound lean, ground cooked ham

1 beaten egg

1/2 cup warmed low-fat evaporated milk

1 slice whole wheat bread, crust removed

1 tablespoon extra virgin olive oil

1/4 cup finely minced onion

2 tablespoons fresh minced basil

2 tablespoons fresh minced thyme

2 tablespoons minced cilantro

1/4 cup grated, low-fat Mozzarella cheese

1/4 cup grated Parmesan cheese

2 tablespoons fresh minced parsley

3 tablespoons tomato sauce

Dash of hot sauce

Dash of salt

1/4 cup seasoned bread crumbs

Olive oil spray

Pinch of salt

1 teaspoon extra virgin olive oil

Preheat oven to 350 degrees F.

Measure pasta and set aside. In a large mixing bowl, combine turkey and ham. Toss with 2 forks lightly to mix well. Add egg, but do not mix yet. In a separate bowl, pour warm milk over the crumbled bread; set aside to soak.

(continued...)

Heat oil in a large skillet. Sauté onion, basil, thyme and cilantro until herbs are fragrant and onion is soft. Add mixture to bowl containing meat. Add both cheeses, along with parsley, tomato sauce, hot sauce, salt and bread crumbs, including the soaked crumbled bread. With 2 kitchen forks, mix lightly but thoroughly. Do not be aggressive in handling mixture. Form turkey meatballs in whatever size you wish, but make them uniform.

Spray a non-stick shallow pan or cookie sheet with olive oil and put meatballs in a single layer on it. Bake without turning until deliciously golden, 20 or 30 minutes. Transfer to a medium-sized casserole with cover measuring 12 x 3 inches. Pour $1\frac{1}{2}$ quarts of sauce (see previous recipe) over meatballs. Cover and cook over low heat for 30 or 35 minutes. Check every 10 minutes to assure food does not stick to pan.

Fill a 4- or 5-quart stock pot $\frac{3}{4}$ full of water, add a pinch of salt, and heat. When water boils, dribble oil in the water. Snap spaghetti in two, and cook briskly not more than 12 minutes; drain pasta well, reserving 1 cup cooking water; transfer to a large serving bowl. Combine with meatball sauce. Serve piping hot.

Serves: 6 to 8.

Pasta Paella
Pasta Paella

What an exciting recipe! The ideal pan to use is a paellera, a utensil especially crafted to accommodate in a leisurely fashion the extensive number of ingredients paella requires. The dark grey or black pan is attractive enough to journey directly from oven to table gracefully. It can be found in gourmet and specialty cooking shops. One shop in Ybor City, The Guava Tree, where my husband and I owned Las Novedades, has an assortment of sizes.

If a paellera is not available, use any heat-resistant glass or ceramic casserole measuring about 14 x 3 inches. It must have a lid to be used successfully for this recipe. A resounding Olé! is in order when this flamboyant entrée takes its place in the center of the dining table. Wait and see!

. . . .

1 pound angel hair pasta

1/2 pound lobster meat, cut in small chunks

1/2 pound sea scallops, each cut in half

1/2 pound medium shrimp, cleaned and deveined

1/2 pound fillet of grouper, cut in 1 1/2 inch pieces

2 dozen cherrystone clams*

2 chicken breast halves, cubed

2 center-cut pork chops, cubed

Juice of one lemon

1/4 cup dry white wine

Olive oil spray

3 tablespoons extra virgin olive oil

1 onion, minced

1/2 green bell pepper, seeded and chopped

1/2 red bell pepper, seeded and chopped

3 garlic cloves, minced

2 inner celery ribs, sliced

1 tablespoon minced fresh basil

1 tablespoon minced fresh oregano

1 tablespoon minced cilantro

3 ripe plum tomatoes, peeled, seeded and chopped

2 tablespoons tomato sauce

2 bay leaves

3 cups saffroned, defatted, low-sodium chicken broth**

Dash of hot sauce

Dash of salt

1 – 4 ounce can imported squid fillets, drained (optional)

1/4 cup dry white wine

1/4 cup water

1 – 6 1/2 ounce jar roasted red bell pepper strips

1/2 cup minced flat-leaf Italian parsley

*For instructions on cleaning clams, see Page 320.
**For instructions how to prepare stock, see Page 318, 322.

Measure angel hair pasta and set aside. Carefully clean and cut lobster, scallops, shrimp and grouper, place in bowl and set aside. Trim chicken and pork of all visible fat. Scrub clams** well.

Preheat oven to 325 degrees F.

Place clams in a medium saucepan with cover, and barely cover with water. Pour in lemon juice and wine. Place pan over heat, and bring to a boil. Cover and cook briskly 6 to 7 minutes. When clams open, remove to bowl and discard any that fail to open. Line a colander with a double layer of cheesecloth. Strain cooking liquid and reserve for later use.

Spray olive oil in the casserole you wish to use for cooking. Set aside.

In a 12-inch skillet, heat oil. Add chicken and pork. Brown well. With slotted spoon, remove to casserole or paellera you will use. To drippings left in the skillet, add onion, peppers, garlic and celery; sauté at medium low heat until vegetables are translucent. Add basil, oregano and cilantro. Stirring constantly, cook 2 minutes. Add tomatoes, sauce and bay leaves. Reduce heat to low and cook 2 more minutes.

Pour over meat in casserole. Stir to mix well. Place casserole over medium-high heat. Stir in the saffroned broth and bring to a boil. With a wooden spoon, mix all ingredients carefully. Add hot sauce and salt if needed, al gusto.

Reduce heat to low. Add lobster, scallops, shrimp grouper and squid. Stir very carefully so as not to bruise the seafood. Cover casserole and cook 5 minutes or until seafood turns pinkish. Add more hot sauce and salt to taste. Add uncooked pasta, snapped in two, scattering evenly over all. Press gently down among ingredients.

Combine reserved clam broth, wine and water. Pour over all. Place reserved clams in their shells decoratively here and there. With a long fork, poke gently through ingredients to allow liquids to flow down for better cooking. Bring to a quick boil. Stir once. Cover casserole, and bake in oven 15 minutes or until pasta has absorbed most of the liquid.

Remove casserole from oven and garnish a capricho with bell pepper strips and plenty of Italian parsley. An additional sprinkle of good dry white wine won't hurt...not one bit! Cover casserole. Allow to rest 15 or 20 minutes before serving.

Serves: 6 to 8.

VEGETABLES

Legumbres

My mother loved vegetables, and at dinnertime, two or three were always on the table. Her way of introducing a new vegetable was to serve a dressed-up version from the *"come y calla"* (eat and hush) category! However, most of the time, preparation was simple. Mother was artistic, even when preparing vegetables, and she was always a patient teacher. I can remember watching her scrape carrots and potatoes, a chore she entitled me to at a fairly early age. I remember hearing her explain, "It's better to scrape than peel, because in peeling you remove some of the nutrients found right next to the skin." To cook vegetables she used little or no water and was careful never to overcook. That was, she explained, so important nutrients would remain.

In my Orlando kitchen, I usually fill a basket with a variety of fresh nutritious vegetables, then steam them over boiling water in which fragrant fresh herbs are placed. After vegetables are cooked, (I like mine cooked), I top them with an emulsion of herbs, spices, lemon juice or rice vinegar, and a scant teaspoon of olive oil; then toss and serve. *Delicioso, pero muy delicioso!*

At other times, I prepare vegetables by sautéing or stir-frying. For this type of preparation, you need only a small amount of olive oil or a good cooking spray. And don't be afraid to experiment with an array of herbs and spices to enhance your sautéed or stir-fried veggies. Be generous with fresh herbs, greedy with salt, and cut back on fatty ingredients, like bacon or butter. If a recipe calls for two tablespoons of butter or oil, try only one or less. You may also find you can eliminate the fat completely without sacrificing quality or taste.

Be creative...*y adelante*, my friends.

Recipes

Simply Delicious Broccoli

Brussels Sprouts au Gratin

Glazed Carrots with Pineapple

My Number Two Carrot Recipe

Corn Pudding

Stir-Fried Cabbage with Onion

Cauliflower in Tomato Concasse Sauce

Eggplant Creole

Pat's Okra, Corn and Fresh Tomatoes

A Potpourri of Vegetables

Potatoes Cynthia

Tiny New Potatoes in a Skillet

Puree of Sweet Potatoes

Brown Rice with Water Chestnuts

Brown Rice with Artichokes

Fried Rice

Cilantro Rice Margaret

Spinach with Garlic

Spinach with Raisins and Pine Nuts

Acorn Squash Casserole

Crookneck Squash Casserole

Simply Delicious Broccoli
Brocoli Sencillo

Broccoli is a popular vegetable with an especially nutritious punch. Prepared in rich sauces or simply steamed, it is always a beautiful vegetable to serve. I have prepared broccoli in so many ways, but one of the best, in my opinion, is with a sprinkle of toasted almonds and grated fontina cheese.

1 bunch broccoli

2 tablespoons extra olive oil

¼ cup toasted almonds

1 onion, minced

3 garlic cloves, minced

2 tablespoons fresh minced oregano

2 tablespoons fresh minced dillweed

2 tablespoons rice vinegar

2 tablespoons lemon juice

Olive oil spray

1 – 12 ounce jar roasted bell peppers

3 ounces grated fontina cheese

¼ cup finely minced Italian parsley

Preheat oven to 325 degrees F.

Wash broccoli, pare flowerets. Place in bowl. Peel stalks, cut coarsely and combine with flowerets. Place broccoli in a large basket steamer and steam over boiling water for 5 minutes. Run cold water over vegetables to stop cooking. Set aside.

In a skillet, heat the oil. Add almonds and onion. Sauté until onion is transparent. Add garlic, oregano and dillweed. Sauté until fragrant, about 2 minutes. Pour in vinegar and lemon juice. Sauté another minute.

Spray a 13 x 9 x 2-inch glass or ceramic, heat-proof, shallow casserole with olive oil. Transfer broccoli to pan.

(continued...)

Drain roasted peppers (which you can buy in supermarkets or specialty stores); slice into uniform strips and layer over broccoli. Spoon mixture in skillet over the vegetable to cover all. Scatter cheese, and finally parsley, over all. Cover and bake 15 minutes; remove cover and return to oven for 3 minutes.

Serves: 4 to 6.

Brussel Sprouts au Gratin
Repollitos Gratinados

Brussel sprouts go well with any entree, especially broiled chicken or fish. This au gratin recipe may also be used to dress up tender green beans or broccoli.

1½ pounds Brussel sprouts, halved

1½ cups defatted, low-sodium chicken broth

1 tablespoon extra virgin olive oil plus 1 teaspoon butter

1 tablespoon all-purpose flour

¼ cup light cream or low-fat evaporated milk

¼ cup grated white cheddar cheese

4 Kalamata olives, pitted and chopped

Olive oil spray

2 tablespoons fresh minced parsley, or 1 dried

2 tablespoons dry sherry

Preheat oven 325 degrees F.

Remove ugly leaves from sprouts; wash thoroughly, and cut in half. Place sprouts in a deep pot with cover; add chicken broth, and bring to a boil. Cook until vegetables are tender, approximately 8 to 10 minutes. Drain sprouts and reserve cooking liquid.

In a skillet, heat oil and butter. Add flour and cook, at low heat, until golden. Remove skillet from heat. Combine reserved cooking liquid and cream; slowly add to roux, stirring vigorously to avoid flour lumps. Cook until thick and smooth. Add cheese and olives, and mix well.

Spray with olive oil a shallow glass casserole measuring 13 x 9 x 2 inches, and transfer sprouts. Pour sauce over vegetable. Bake 10 minutes; remove from oven, sprinkle with the parsley and the vinito (wine!).

Serves: 4 to 6.

Glazed Carrots with Pineapple
Zanahorias Con Piña

I have two carrot recipes that I must share with you. I shop for tender baby carrots to prepare these; you should, too. They produce better results because the small carrots make a great difference in eye appeal and taste. Ya veras.

1 pound, or about 4 cups, baby carrots, scraped and sliced

1 cup crushed unsweetened pineapple, partly-drained

2 tablespoons light brown sugar

1/4 cup toasted, chopped pecans

1/2 teaspoon dry mustard

2 tablespoons butter, or margarine

Salt to taste

Scrape carrots, then slice. Steam lightly in vegetable steamer, (I use mine all the time), or cook in a saucepan with very little water, 15 minutes or so. Drain and transfer to pretty deep serving dish. In a saucepan, combine pineapple, sugar, pecans, mustard and butter. Add salt. Cook over medium heat until butter melts. Pour over carrots and toss gently until carrots are thoroughly coated.

Serves: 4 to 6.

I have two carrot recipes I must share with you.

My Number Two Carrot Recipe
Zanahorias Numero Dos

1 pound, or 4 cups, baby carrots, scraped

1/2 cup defatted, low-sodium chicken broth

1/4 cup dry sherry

1 – 10 ounce package frozen peas

2 tablespoons minced onion

1 tablespoon melted butter or margarine

1/4 cup sliced manzanilla pimiento-stuffed olives

Salt to taste

Hot sauce to taste

1/4 cup finely chopped fresh parsley

Place carrots in a 2½ quart deep saucepan with cover; add broth and sherry. Cover and cook at low heat until carrots are crisp-tender. Break up frozen peas. Add to carrots, together with onion, butter and olives. Add salt and hot sauce to taste. Stir well and cook another 10 minutes at low heat. Transfer to a shallow serving platter and scatter parsley over vegetables.

Serves: 4 to 6.

Corn Pudding
Pudin De Maiz

In central Florida, we are indeed blessed with an abundance of delicious white corn, or Zellwood; it's the best corn ever. Corn pudding, fritters and chowder made with kernels cut right from the cob enliven our meals. You will notice I include cheese in many recipes simply because I love it! I use it sparingly, however, just enough to enhance a vegetable or entree, and to make that special difference in the way the dish turns out!

3 cups fresh corn, kernels cut from cob

1 cup low-fat evaporated milk

1 egg, beaten

1 inner celery rib, finely chopped

1 tablespoon plus 1 teaspoon melted butter
   or margarine

8 to 10 Saltine crackers, finely crushed

$1/2$ teaspoon hot sauce

Salt to taste

$1/4$ teaspoon granulated sugar

$1/2$ cup shredded white cheddar cheese, divided

2 egg whites

Vegetable cooking spray

Sprinkle of Spanish paprika

Preheat oven to 325 degrees F.

To cut corn from the cob, take a sharp paring knife, and slice with its blade beneath the kernels to remove them from the cob; let kernels fall in a bowl. In a mixing bowl, combine the kernels with the next 9 ingredients, ending with the cheese; use half the cheese, and mix thoroughly.

Beat egg whites to consistency of soft meringue; fold into corn mixture. Spray with vegetable oil a $2^1/2$ quart shallow, oven-proof casserole with cover. Bake, covered, 20 minutes; uncover, and bake another 10 minutes; sprinkle with remaining cheese and with paprika. Return to oven. Bake, uncovered, 10 minutes more, or until bubbly and golden.

Serves: 4 to 6.

Stir-Fried Cabbage with Onion
Coles Encebolladas

The lowly cabbage takes on an air of importance when prepared this way. This inexpensive vegetable has recently gained status. Nutritionists have found it to have important health-giving properties, among other things. Be careful not to overcook; crunchiness is ever so important.

1 white cabbage, outer leaves removed

2 tablespoons extra virgin olive or canola oil

1 Spanish onion, diced

1 cup thinly sliced baby carrots

2 teaspoons fresh basil, crushed, or 1 teaspoon dried, crushed

3 tablespoons rice vinegar or lemon juice

1 teaspoon low-sodium teriyaki sauce

Salt and white pepper

1/4 cup coarsely chopped walnuts

Wash cabbage thoroughly and cut down center; remove core; shred cabbage thinly. Heat oil in a large skillet, preferably with a domed cover, or a non-stick pot with cover. Add onions and carrots; sauté until onion is soft. Add cabbage to onion and carrots. You will have a pot full of cabbage, but don't be alarmed; it will cook down in no time. Sprinkle basil over all. Stir and mix continuously for about 3 minutes.

Combine vinegar and teriyaki sauce. Pour over cabbage. Add salt and pepper to taste. Again, mix thoroughly. Cover, cook and stir frequently for about 20 minutes; make sure you are cooking at low heat, okay? If you are using a Dutch oven, transfer cabbage to a 13 x 9 x 2-inch casserole. Sprinkle walnuts over all if you like – they are nutritious but high in fat, so use sparingly. Serve with *mucho orguello.*

Serves: 4 to 6.

Cauliflower in Tomato Concasse Sauce

Coliflor en Salsa Concassee

Concasse is a glamorous marinara sauce that provides a colorful and flavorful lift to cauliflower, as well as green beans, yellow squash, and new potatoes. It is even terrific over over pasta. The addition of fresh greated Parmesan cheese provides an Italian touch!

1 large fresh cauliflower, leaves removed

Juice of one lemon or lime

Dusting of salt

1 tablespoon plus 1 teaspoon extra virgin olive oil

3 garlic cloves, minced

2 tablespoons fresh minced oregano, crushed

2 tablespoons fresh minced basil, crushed

1/4 teaspoon nutmeg

3 ripe tomatoes, peeled, seeded and chopped

2 tablespoons fresh minced parsley

1/2 teaspoon Louisiana hot sauce

2 tablespoons full-bodied Burgundy wine or dry sherry

2 tablespoons toasted and chopped almonds

Preheat oven to 325 degrees F.

Clean cauliflower, snap off flowerets and cut into uniform pieces. Place in steamer and steam over boiling water about 3 minutes. Squeeze lemon or lime juice over cauliflower as it steams and dust with salt.

Heat oil in skillet. Add garlic, oregano and basil. Sauté at low heat until fragrant, 2 or 3 minutes. Dust with the nutmeg. Add tomatoes, parsley and hot sauce. Stir to mix well. Cook only 2 or 3 minutes, just until the mix is heated. Stir in wine or sherry.

Transfer cauliflower to a shallow, oblong glass or ceramic oven pan measuring 13 x 9 x 2 inches. Pour tomato concasse over cauliflower; sprinkle with almonds. Bake until thoroughly heated, 8 to 10 minutes.

Serves: 4 to 6.

Eggplant Creole
Berenjera a la Criolla

Eggplant gives this recipe a delectable consistency. It makes the best Creole sauce ever. The recipe may be served as a side dish, topping spaghetti or long-grain rice. A popular brunch or Tapas item.

1 eggplant, peeled and cubed

Salt to taste

Olive oil spray

2 tablespoons extra virgin olive oil

1 onion, minced

2 tablespoons fresh minced oregano

2 tablespoons fresh minced basil

2 tablespoons fresh minced dillweed

1 green bell pepper, diced

2 celery ribs, chopped

3 to 4 garlic cloves, minced

1/2 cup sliced ripe olives

1 chorizo (Spanish sausage), degreased and casing removed
and crumbled*

3 ripe tomatoes, peeled, seeded and chopped

4 tablespoons tomato sauce

1 teaspoon salt

1 teaspoon Louisiana hot sauce

1 bay leaf, crushed

1/2 cup defatted, low-sodium chicken broth**

1/4 cup full-bodied Burgundy wine

*For instructions how to degrease chorizos, see Page 318.
**For instructions how to make broth, see Page 318.

Place eggplant in colander; sprinkle well with salt. Allow to "bleed" 30 minutes. Rinse thoroughly of salt.

Preheat oven to 350 degrees F.

Spray a baking pan or small cookie sheet with olive oil, and place eggplant in a single layer in pan. Fit a sheet of foil loosely over pan to cover and place in oven. Bake, covered, 15 minutes.

Meanwhile, in a skillet, heat oil. Add the onion, oregano, basil, dillweed, pepper and celery. Stir with wooden spoon until vegetables are soft, but firm. Add garlic, olives and sausage. Stir to mix well and sauté at low heat 5 minutes. Add fresh tomatoes, tomato sauce, salt, hot sauce, bay leaf, stock and wine. Stir until well combined. Transfer sauce to a 2-quart stock pot with cover.

Remove eggplant from oven. Should be crisp, but not very tender. Add to pot, mix thoroughly and bring to a slow boil, cover and cook 25 minutes at low heat, stirring occasionally until all ingredients are soft.

Serves: 4 to 6.

Pat's Okra, Corn and Fresh Tomatoes
Quimbombo Entomatado-Patricia

What a trio. You will love this combination of vegetables. Very southern, I might add...but so is my friend Pat.

2 pounds fresh okra pods

Juice of half a lemon or lemon

1 tablespoon extra virgin olive oil

1 onion, finely minced

3 cups fresh corn, kernels cut from the cob

4 ripe tomatoes, or 4 cups, peeled and seeded

2 tablespoons fresh, finely minced parsley

Salt to taste

Hot sauce to taste

(continued...)

Wash okra and cut off ends. Slice thinly into bowl. Squeeze lemon over okra, toss and set aside.

In a deep 2-quart pot with cover, heat the oil; add onion and sauté until soft. Add okra and sauté 5 minutes. Add corn and tomatoes. Simmer for 20 minutes, covered, stirring at intervals. Sprinkle with parsley. Add salt and hot sauce to taste, stir well, and cook 5 minutes longer.

Serves: 6 to 8.

A Potpourri of Vegetables
Un Potpourri de Vegetales

This recipe is similar to the ratatouille so favored by the French. Substitute whatever vegetables you like if you're missing some listed in the recipe; however, eggplant and tomatoes are a must.

1 large eggplant, peeled and cubed

Salt to taste

2 ripe tomatoes, peeled, seeded, and chopped

2 tablespoons extra virgin olive oil

1 onion, minced

2 garlic cloves, minced

½ green bell pepper, chopped

½ red bell pepper, chopped

1 cup thinly sliced fresh mushrooms

2 ribs of celery, sliced

1 zucchini, scraped and sliced

¼ cup imported Kalamata ripe olives

2 tablespoons fresh minced oregano

2 tablespoons fresh minced basil

2 tablespoons fresh minced dillweed

1 teaspoon low-sodium soy sauce

Olive oil spray

1 cup low-fat grated Mozzarella cheese
$1/4$ cup grated Parmesan cheese
1 tablespoon butter, melted
$1/4$ cup toasted fresh bread crumbs

Preheat oven to 325 degrees F.

Place eggplant in large colander; sprinkle with salt. Allow to "bleed" for 30 minutes. Place tomatoes in another bowl; set aside. In about 25 minutes, start the preparation of the vegetables.

In a large skillet with domed cover, heat oil. Add onion, garlic and peppers; sauté at low heat, stirring constantly until onion is transparent. Add mushrooms, celery, zucchini, olives, oregano, basil, dillweed and soy sauce; stir to mix well, and cook 3 minutes. Rinse eggplant well. Add to skillet together with tomatoes. Mix carefully but well. Cover and cook, at low to moderate heat for about 5 minutes, stirring at intervals.

With olive oil, spray a shallow, $2^{1}/_{2}$ quart, oven-proof glass or ceramic casserole dish. Pour half of the vegetables into casserole, spreading evenly. Scatter mozzarella cheese over vegetables. Cover cheese with remaining vegetables.

Combine Parmesan cheese, butter and bread crumbs. Mix well. Sprinkle evenly over vegetables. Bake 15 minutes, or until golden and bubbly. The vegetables should just be crisp-tender, so don't overcook

Try this variation:

Drain completely $1/2$ cup of oil-packed, sun-dried tomatoes, chop the tomatoes very fine, and when you spread the Mozzarella over the vegetables, scatter the sun-dried tomatoes over the cheese and continue with the recipe. *Muy bueno.*

Serves: 4 to 6.

This recipe is similar to the ratatouille so favored by the French...eggplant and tomatoes are a must.

Potatoes Cynthia
Potatas Cynthia

Potatoes Cynthia is a combination of sweet onions and new potatoes that compliments any entree, especially broiled fish. You will love it.

2 pounds new potatoes, or baking potatoes, scraped,
    partly-peeled and thinly sliced
Olive oil spray
1 tablespoon extra virgin olive oil, plus 1 teaspoon butter
    or margarine
1 Vidalia or Spanish onion, thinly sliced in rings
¼ cup dry sherry
1 – .1 envelope dry Italian dressing
Dash of white pepper
1 tablespoon extra virgin olive oil
2 tablespoons finely minced fresh parsley

Preheat oven to 325 degrees F. Wash and scrape potatoes; peel around center only, then thinly slice. Spray with olive oil a shallow glass baking pan measuring 13 x 9 x 2 inches.

In a skillet, heat oil and butter; add onion rings; sauté until translucent. Spread onion rings evenly to cover bottom of prepared pan. Cover onions with the potatoes. Pour sherry over potatoes. Sprinkle Italian dressing generously over the potatoes. You don't need salt because the salad dressing has plenty, but white pepper is okay. Dribble olive oil over all. Cover casserole tightly with foil (crimp edges).

Bake, covered, 35 to 40 minutes. Potatoes should be tender. Remove from oven, uncover, and with a fork carefully pull part of the onions out to entwine with the potatoes. Return pan to oven and bake, uncovered, another 10 minutes, or until potatoes are golden. Sprinkle with parsley, and serve hot.

Serves: 6 to 8.

Tiny New Potatoes in a Skillet
Potates Nueves, Al Sarten

These tiny potatoes, slowly cooked in a skillet, take a little longer to prepare because of the low heat. The garlic is added a few minutes before cooking time is over to avoid burning.

2 pounds, or about 24, new potatoes, cut as uniformly as possible
Salted water
2 tablespoons olive oil
Salt and white pepper
1 teaspoon basil, dried and crushed
4 garlic cloves, finely minced
2 tablespoons fresh grated Parmesan cheese
1/2 cup finely minced fresh parsley

Wash and scrape potatoes; peel each around center. Place in a 2-quart, deep pan with cover. Add enough salted water to just cover potatoes. Bring to a boil. Cover, lower heat and parboil the potatoes about 5 minutes.

In the meantime in a deep mixing bowl, combine olive oil, salt, pepper and basil. Stir to mix well. Choose a large skillet with cover; spray it with olive oil. Drain the potatoes. Add these to bowl. Toss to saturate with oil mixture. Transfer the potatoes to prepared skillet. Cover and at low heat cook the potatoes. Shake and stir to avoid burning or sticking. You should not have a problem if the heat is kept low. Once potatoes are tender (test one with a skewer), add the garlic and cheese. Cover and cook 2 or 3 minutes longer.

(You can prepare potatoes without parboiling, but will take a full 40 minutes in the skillet to cook; watch them carefully, and shake the skillet to insure uniform cooking). Sprinkle with parsley, and toss gently to mix. Serve from the skillet or transfer to a fancy serving dish.

Serves: 6 to 8.

Purée of Sweet Potatoes
Pure De Boniatos

This recipe is excellent for that turkey dinner. I have trimmed considerably the butter and substituted low-fat evaporated milk for the cream. The recipe tastes as rich and smooth as its calorie-laden counterpart – You be the judge.

4 sweet potatoes
2 tablespoons butter or creamy margarine, melted
1 cup evaporated low-fat milk
$1/2$ teaspoon allspice
$1/2$ teaspoon salt
$1/2$ cup light brown sugar
$1/2$ cup coarsely chopped walnuts
1 egg, beaten
2 egg whites
Vegetable oil spray
$1/2$ teaspoon cinnamon
2 tablespoons pure maple syrup
1 tablespoon butter, melted
Marshmallows

Preheat oven to 325 degrees F.

Cook sweet potatoes, still in their skins, in a large pot of water until tender. Or, cook them in the microwave for a few minutes on each side, depending on the size of the potato; they should be soft inside when fully cooked. Cool. When you are able to handle the potatoes, peel and chop them coarsely into a mixing bowl. Add butter, and gradually add milk, mashing potatoes until they are nice and smooth.

Combine allspice, salt, brown sugar and walnuts; add to sweet potatoes together with egg. Beat egg whites to the consistency of meringue; fold into purée.

With vegetable oil, spray a ceramic or glass casserole dish measuring 13 x 9 x 2 inches, and pour potatoes into it. Sprinkle with cinnamon. Combine maple syrup and butter and dribble over sweet potatoes. Bake 20 to 25 minutes. For a fancy presentation, 5 minutes before removing from oven, top casserole with miniature marshmallows.

Serves: 4 to 6.

Brown Rice with Water Chestnuts
Arroz Prieto con Castanas de Agua

I often prepare brown rice because it is very tasty and good for you. I prefer a rice called "basmati," organically grown in the Himalayas for thousands of years, and sporting a nutty flavor and heady scent; it is found in most health stores.

2 cups uncooked basmati brown rice

2 tablespoons olive oil

$1/2$ cup onion, minced

$1/2$ cup chopped green pepper

2 garlic cloves, pressed

$1/2$ cup sliced mushrooms

$1/2$ cup chopped water chestnuts

1 bay leaf

$1/2$ cup fresh finely chopped parsley

2 tablespoons fresh, finely chopped basil

Salt and hot sauce

$3^3/4$ cups defatted, low-sodium chicken broth*

$1/4$ cup dry mild sherry

2 tablespoons chopped pimientos

*For instructions about how to make broth, see Page 318.

Measure rice.

Preheat oven to 325 degrees F.

In an oven-proof casserole with cover, heat the oil. Add onion, pepper, garlic, mushrooms, water chestnuts and bay leaf; stir with a

(continued...)

• •

wooden spoon and sauté at low heat about 3 or 4 minutes, being careful to avoid burning garlic. Add the parsley and basil. It is always better to use fresh herbs (keep dried herbs tightly covered in a cool, dry place, and use them if you must.) Add salt and hot sauce if needed. Add rice; pour in chicken broth and sherry. Bring to a boil, stir, cover, reduce heat to low; cook over direct heat 10 minutes. Stir well once again before covering and placing casserole in oven.

Bake 30 minutes. Remove from oven, cover with a kitchen towel and allow to rest 15 minutes before serving. (Rice retains heat for a long time). Decorate with pimientos.

Serves: 4 to 6.

Brown Rice with Artichokes
Arroz Prieto con Alcachofas

My second brown rice recipe is as good as the first...enjoy!

2 cups uncooked brown basmati rice

2 tablespoons olive oil

1 onion, minced

2 garlic cloves, minced

$^1/_2$ cup sliced inner rib celery

$^1/_2$ cup toasted almonds

2 tablespoons small capers

2 tablespoons finely chopped fresh parsley

8 pimiento-stuffed olives, sliced

1 bay leaf

4 cups defatted, low-sodium chicken broth*

$^1/_4$ cup dry mild sherry

Measure rice.

Preheat oven to 325 degrees F.

Heat oil in a heat-proof casserole with cover; add onion, garlic, celery and almonds and sauté until onion and almonds are golden.

*For instructions how to prepare broth, see Page 318.

Add capers and rice; mix well and cook 1 minute. Add parsley, olives and bay leaf; stir again. Now add chicken broth and sherry. Bring to a boil. Cover; lower heat, then cook over direct heat 10 minutes, stirring twice to avoid sticking.

Cover casserole, and bake 30 minutes. Stir thoroughly once during baking to insure rice grains cook evenly. Remove casserole from oven. Fluff rice with two forks; leave lid on and let stand 15 minutes. Rice will retain heat for an hour or so. Use same procedure as preceding recipe to keep rice warm.

Serves: 4 to 6.

Fried Rice
Arroz Frito

This rice recipe is one that you will prepare often; it's that good. My family loves it, and I hope yours will, too.

2 cups uncooked long-grain rice

2 tablespoons butter or margarine

8-ounce jar of canned sliced mushrooms, or

    1 cup fresh sliced mushrooms

1/2 cup sliced water chestnuts

1 cup finely chopped onion

1/2 teaspoon curry powder

1/2 cup chopped inner rib celery

1/4 cup toasted almonds or walnuts

3 3/4 cups defatted, low-sodium chicken broth*

1/4 cup dry sherry

Salt

Hot sauce

Vegetable cooking spray

*For instructions how to cook broth, see Page 318.

(continued...)

Measure rice.

Preheat oven to 325 degrees F.

In a large skillet, melt butter; add rice and cook until it starts to pop. Add mushrooms, water chestnuts, onion, curry powder, celery and nuts, and stir gently with wooden spoon until all ingredients are well-introduced and the onion is limp. Add broth and dry sherry. Add salt and hot sauce to taste. Bring to a boil.

Spray with vegetable oil an oven-proof, porcelain or glass, 2-quart casserole with cover. Transfer vegetables to it; cover and bake 30 minutes; check and fluff rice to insure even cooking. Return to oven and cook, covered, another 10 minutes. Keep covered and allow to rest 15 minutes before serving.

Serves: 6 to 8.

Cilantro Rice Margaret
Arroz Cilantro Margarita

1½ cups long-grain rice

2 or 3 tablespoons olive oil

3 green onions, chopped fine with all of the greens included

3 garlic cloves, minced

1 cup minced cilantro

¼ cup chopped red bell pepper

Water, warm

Salt

Hot sauce

Measure rice. In a non-stick shallow casserole with cover, heat oil. Add onions, garlic, cilantro and pepper. Sauté about 1 minute until fragrant. Add rice and mix thoroughly. Add enough water to cover ingredients by ½ inch. Bring to a boil and cook briskly 1 minute, stirring constantly. You can either cover, reduce heat to low, and cook 15 to 18 minutes longer on the stove-top, or cover and place in an oven preheated to 350 degrees F. for 15 to 18 minutes. The rice should be al dente.

This is your decision, whether to cook over direct heat or in the oven. However, I personally prefer the oven method, because the risk of rice sticking to the pan is minimal.

Serves: 4 to 6.

Spinach with Garlic
Espinaca al Ajillo

This method of preparing spinach may be applied to all types of greens, without exception. Delightfully easy...and deliciously good.

2¹/₂ pounds fresh spinach

Salt

Hot sauce

2 tablespoons extra virgin olive oil

¹/₄ cup pine nuts

3 or 4 garlic cloves, minced

Juice of one lemon

2 tablespoons rice vinegar

¹/₄ cup fresh grated Parmesan cheese

Stem and wash spinach thoroughly. (Soaking greens in salted water will help dislodge dirt). Chop coarsely, and pile into a large deep pot with cover, pressing down vegetable. Do not add water for cooking, as the water that clings to leaves is sufficient. Add salt and hot sauce.

While spinach cooks, watch carefully until wilted; the amount of cooking time depends on how well-done you like your greens. I like mine nice and tender, okay? Cover pot, and cook at low heat until spinach is wilted, 10 to 15 minutes. Place in a colander to drain well, pressing the vegetable to eliminate liquid.

In a large skillet, heat oil. Add pine nuts. Sauté until golden. Add the garlic, lemon juice and vinegar. Stir to mix well. Add the drained spinach to the skillet and stir gently until vegetable is well-coated with the sauté. Cover and cook at low heat a little longer. Sprinkle with the cheese and once again stir to mix well. Serve as a side dish to compliment any entree.

Serves: 4 to 6.

Spinach with Raisins and Pine Nuts
Espinaca Con Pasas y Nueces

You would never imagine that raisins and spinach are compatible until you prepare this recipe. Algo diferente.

2½ pounds fresh spinach, thoroughly washed and stemmed
2 tablespoons olive oil
2 tablespoons butter
½ cup pine nuts
½ cup dark raisins
1 tablespoon lemon juice
1 teaspoon low-sodium soy sauce
Salt
Hot sauce

Chop spinach coarsely and place in a vegetable steamer. Cook over boiling water about 5 minutes, or until wilted.

While spinach steams, pour olive oil and butter into a large skillet with a dome, if possible, as its cover. (You may further reduce oil and butter to taste). Add pine nuts and raisins; sauté until nuts are delicately golden. Pour in lemon juice and soy sauce. Stir to mix well.

Remove spinach from steamer. Squeeze dry and add to skillet. Stir gently in folding motion until spinach is involved with the sauté. Add salt and hot sauce to taste, and continue to stir carefully. Cover the skillet and cook until greens are tender – to your taste. It is an excellent fish accompaniment.

Serves: 4 to 6.

You would never imagine that raisins and spinach are compatible until you prepare this recipe.

Acorn Squash Casserole
Cacerola de Calabaza

We were traveling through New Hampshire, my husband and I, and it was a beautiful New England Sunday. We stopped at a quaint restaurant where brunch was being served. Among the many delicious items on the buffet table was an acorn squash casserole. (I went back for seconds!) I was impressed with its taste, and remembered its ingredients. I devised a recipe to delight my family and friends. It has become a popular dish from my kitchen.

2 – 1 pound acorn squash, or other similar squash
Vegetable oil spray
8-ounce can unsweetened crushed pineapple, undrained
1/4 cup unsweetened pineapple juice
1/4 cup maple syrup
1/4 cup light brown sugar
1/4 teaspoon cinnamon
1/4 teaspoon nutmeg
2 tablespoons butter, measured, then melted
2 tablespoons light rum

Preheat oven to 325 degrees F.

Cut each squash in half, lengthwise. Remove seeds and pith. Spray a shallow baking pan with vegetable oil, and put the squash in it, cut side down. Bake 25 to 30 minutes. Remove from oven. Do not peel; cut each half into slices and then cut the slices in half. Place in a wide mixing bowl.

In a saucepan, combine pineapple and the rest of the ingredients. Heat and bring to a boil, cooking 2 minutes. Pour mixture over squash, mix well, then transfer to a 13 x 9 x 2-inch casserole. Cover tightly with foil, crimping edges. Bake 45 minutes, or until squash is deliciously cooked.

Serves: 4 to 6.

Crookneck Squash Casserole
Calabacines Deliciosos

Squash should be a numero uno vegetable in our diet, because of its high nutritional value. Here, then, is a colorful combination of tender summer squash and other goodies that I am sure will delight you. This is a great introduction of squash to professed "squash haters." Also, a great buffet item.

2$^1/_2$ pounds baby crookneck squash, or
    other similar squash, thinly sliced
$^1/_4$ cup fresh toasted bread crumbs
1 tablespoon olive oil plus 1 teaspoon butter
1 onion, finely chopped
$^1/_2$ green bell pepper, cubed
$^1/_2$ red bell pepper, cubed
$^1/_4$ cup chopped water chestnuts
3 garlic cloves, minced
Salt and pepper
2 tablespoons water (if needed)
Olive oil spray
$^1/_2$ cup grated white cheddar cheese
1 teaspoon butter or 1 tablespoon margarine, melted
1 tablespoon lemon juice

Scrape and wash squash. Slice into a bowl and set aside.
Preheat oven to 300 degrees F. Put fresh bread crumbs on a cookie sheet and toast in oven 10 or 15 minutes till crunchy; set aside. Increase oven temperature to 350 degrees F.
Heat oil and butter in a large, deep skillet. Add onion, peppers and water chestnuts. Sauté at low heat until onion is translucent and water chestnuts take on color. Add reserved squash, garlic, salt and pepper to taste. Mix carefully; cover and cook at

very low heat about 15 minutes, mixing at short intervals. If needed, add 2 tablespoons of water.

Spray with olive oil a shallow glass or ceramic baking pan measuring 13 x 9 x 2 inches; transfer squash mixture.

Combine bread crumbs, cheese and melted butter or margarine. Sprinkle over ingredients in casserole, introducing some of the spread into the vegetables as well. Squeeze lemon over all. Cover and bake 10 minutes; uncover, and cook another 10 minutes or until nice, golden and bubbly.

Serves: 4 to 6.

DESSERTS

Postres

What fun it was creating these dessert recipes low in fat, cholesterol and sodium, yet still ridiculously rich and luscious in flavor. My little culinary treasure chest overflows with dessert recipes accumulated over the years. I studied these most diligently, and by adding this and that and reducing this and that, I have thoroughly been pleased with the results. I know you will, too.

In this chapter, I could have included many more recipes, but I chose to share my favorites, many of which are traditional and have been in my family forever. Most of you will agree that there is simply no substitute for that one-of-a-kind taste of butter and the velvety texture that eggs impart, especially to custards – to say nothing of thick, rich creams. So, I have modified these desserts by applying ingenuity and time-tested techniques so each dish retains its flavor essence.

There are recipes, however, that cannot be altered if you want a satisfactory outcome: Cynthia's Pick-Me-Up and Manuel's Chocolate Mousse, for instance. These you set aside for special occasions when you feel like indulging. Or just have a smaller serving.

Almost everyone has a number of dessert recipes tucked away in drawers or files. Perhaps you have abandoned them because they call for rich, caloric ingredients. Don't give up. Try experimenting by reducing the amount of fats and sugar. Then judge for yourself what miracles you can achieve.

I have included most dessert categories thoroughly. Yet, still, one of the most acceptable desserts is seasonal fruits complimented by a good cheese, such as *queso blanco (requisón)*. Fruit, whether served fresh or in compotes or cobblers is always, *el broche de oro* (literally translated – "the golden snap") served at the end of a well-planned meal.

Bon Appetit!

Recipes

Apple Crisp with Honey

Apples Parisian

Catalana Cream

Rice Pudding Navarra

Spanish Caramel Custard

Caramel Custard with Condensed Milk

Cheese and Pineapple Flan

Pretty Pumpkin Flan

An Ideal Cheesecake

Light and Easy Cheesecake

Nena's Peach Cobbler

Blueberry Bread Pudding

Simply Delicious Bread Pudding

Old-fashioned Pineapple Pudding

Lady Fingers

Angel Kisses

Incredible Angel Cake with Orange Glaze

Apple Cake a la Magnifico

Addictive Carrot Cake

Pineapple and Walnut Cake

Glazed Rum Walnut Cake

Simply Wonderful Strawberry Cake

Cynthia s Pick-Me-Up

Manuel's Chocolate Mousse

Key West Lime Pie

Maple Pumpkin Pie

Apple Crisp with Honey
Manzanas a La Miel

This rendition of apple crisp is not as rich as the original recipe, but it is wonderful! Its redeeming features are fresh crisp graham cracker crumbs and a dribble of honey – this touch provides the distinctive crisp without all the calories. Use firm, juicy apples; serve warm with dollops of frozen vanilla yogurt. You will never miss el otro.

3 pounds (about 6 to 7) Granny Smith or Fuji apples

5 tablespoons unsalted melted butter or margarine

1 teaspoon freshly grated cinnamon

1 teaspoon freshly nutmeg

$1/4$ teaspoon salt

$1/2$ cup granulated sugar

1 teaspoon tapioca

3 tablespoons honey

Butter-flavored cooking spray

1 cup (16 to 18 crackers) graham cracker crumbs

$1/2$ cup unbleached flour, or all-purpose

$1/4$ cup granulated sugar

Pinch of cinnamon

Pinch of nutmeg

$1/2$ cup pecans

Preheat oven to 350 degrees F.

Peel, core and slice apples thinly into bowl. Melt butter, and pour 3 tablespoons into a large mixing bowl; reserve the rest for later use. In a small bowl, combine cinnamon, nutmeg, salt, sugar, and tapioca; sprinkle over the apples, then dribble 1 tablespoon of honey over all, reserving the rest for later. Now, with two forks, toss apples gently but thoroughly to coat.

Spray a 13 x 9 x 2-inch oven-proof glass baking pan with butter-flavored cooking spray; arrange apples neatly and evenly to cover bottom of pan.

(continued...)

For the topping, use a medium-sized mixing bowl, and combine graham cracker crumbs, flour and sugar; mix well. Dribble the reserved 2 tablespoons of butter or margarine over mixture, and dust with cinnamon and nutmeg; toss until mixture is crumbly, then spread over apples evenly. Dribble all with last 2 tablespoons of honey. Cover pan tightly with aluminum foil, crimping at the edges. Bake in oven for 30 minutes; uncover, sprinkle pecans over all, and continue baking 10 minutes longer for crispness.

A good brand of frozen vanilla yogurt goes well with apple crisp. Serve warm, at room temperature, or chilled.

Yield: 6 to 8 servings.

Apples Parisian
Manzanas Parisien

The honey and spirits incorporated in this dessert dress up the apples, and make them mouth-watering. Just one taste, and you realize – immediately – how feelingly sweet an apple can be.

6 firm Granny apples, or other juicy apples

Butter-flavored vegetable spray

1/2 cup granulated sugar

1/2 cup cognac

1/2 cup honey

1/2 teaspoon nutmeg

1/2 teaspoon ground ginger

3 tablespoons melted butter or margarine

1/2 cup Madeira wine

1/2 cup water

Sprinkle of cinnamon

Preheat oven to 325 degrees F.

At the market, be very choosy when selecting apples; all should be as fresh, crisp and uniform as possible. Core apples on top where the stem is, and peel one inch down. Spray a shallow baking pan; place apples snugly side by side. On the cored side of each apple, place 1 teaspoon sugar; over the sugar, sprinkle $\frac{1}{2}$ teaspoon cognac.

In a bowl, combine honey, nutmeg and ginger; mix well. Drop a teaspoon of this mixture on top of cognac in each apple; divide melted butter or margarine to completely fill cored end of apples.

Combine wine, water, and any remaining of the sugar, cognac and honey mixture; mix well; pour around apples. Bake 30 to 45 minutes or until apples are tender; be careful not to overcook. Remove from oven and sprinkle with cinnamon. Return to oven 5 more minutes. Serve warm or chilled.

Yield: 4 to 6 servings.

Catalana Cream
Crema Catalana

The Catalanes claim this to be el numero uno among postres Espanoles, but of course, the Catalanes think the region of Cataluña (Barcelona) is what Spain is all about. These proud people do not mix very well with the rest of the Iberian peninsula, especially those from the capital, Madrid. They honestly believe the capital of Spain should have been Barcelona, not Madrid. Many agree. Use a quality vanilla when preparing this recipe.

3 cups 1% or 2% milk
1 cup evaporated skim milk
1 cinnamon stick
1 strip lemon or lime zest
$\frac{1}{4}$ teaspoon salt
5 eggs, or 10 ounces (1$\frac{1}{4}$ cups) egg substitute
$\frac{3}{4}$ cup granulated sugar
3 tablespoons cornstarch
1 tablespoon melted butter or margarine
Dash of nutmeg
1 teaspoon vanilla extract
$\frac{1}{2}$ cup more granulated sugar

(continued...)

Preheat broiler.

In the top of a double boiler, combine milks, cinnamon stick, lemon zest and salt. Cook until scalded (goose pimple stage). While milk heats, crack eggs or egg-substitute into a deep mixing bowl; add sugar and cornstarch; beat until well-blended. Stir in butter, nutmeg and vanilla. Slowly add the egg mixture to the hot milk, stirring vigorously to avoid curdling. Cradle the pot into the bottom pan of double boiler, where water is simmering softly. Make certain that hot water does not touch the upper pan containing the custard.

With a wooden spoon, stir constantly clockwise, until custard is thick and smooth, 10 or 15 minutes. Remove pot; discard cinnamon stick and strip of lemon. Transfer cream to a 13 x 9 x 2-inch, heat-resistant shallow casserole. Cool completely at room temperature.

Scatter sugar to cover the custard completely – real well. Place under broiler to caramelize sugar, but watch carefully to avoid burning. Remove from oven, but do not cover once sugar is caramelized. Allow to stand 30 minutes before serving.

If you wish to serve the cream chilled, then refrigerate before coating with the sugar. Remove chilled cream from refrigerator. Wait 10 or 15 minutes, then caramelize. *Estupendo* – any which way you serve it! Serve at room temperature.

Yield: 6 to 8 servings.

Rice Pudding Navarra
Arroz con Leche Navarra

One day shortly after the publication of my first cookbook, a dear member of our family called to tell me that she had made Arroz con Leche, following my recipe to the letter. The rice, said Bettie, is as stubborn as it can be. It just refuses to soften. What am I doing wrong?!

I calmly asked her what type of rice she had used. She said, "Uncle Ben's."

Short-grain rice must be used in the recipe to make it work. Converted rice will cook to a certain point, but not beyond. Bettie now knows this to be a fact. No es verdad, Bettie?

. . . .

¼ cup golden raisins

¼ cup cognac

½ cup short grain uncooked rice

1 cup water

¼ teaspoon salt

1 – 2 inch cinnamon stick

Zest of one lemon, in a long strip

2½ cups 2% milk

4 tablespoons half-and-half

½ cup granulated sugar plus 2 tablespoons

¼ teaspoon nutmeg

2 tablespoons melted butter

Dash of cinnamon

1 cup granulated sugar

Put raisins and cognac into a bowl to soak; set aside.

In the top pot of a double boiler, combine rice, water, salt, cinnamon stick and lemon zest. Bring to a boil, cover, lower heat and cook until rice totally absorbs water. Stir occasionally to prevent sticking. Stir in milk, half-and-half, sugar and nutmeg; mix well, stirring until pudding boils and sugar dissolves.

Lower heat and cook, stirring frequently, until rice thickens and has absorbed most of the liquid. Place pan over simmering water; cover and cook, until creamy thick and smooth, stirring occasionally. When rice is en su punto (thick and creamy – it could take more than an hour – add raisins and whatever remains of the cognac. Once raisins are added, cook two minutes longer. Stir in the butter until it disappears completely.

Pour creamed rice into a shallow, heat-resistant oven pan measuring 13 x 9 x 2 inches. Cool, dust lightly with ground cinnamon. Cover and refrigerate for an hour or more. Scatter sugar atop creamed rice generously, and slide beneath broiler until it browns nicely into caramel; but watch carefully to avoid burning.

Remove from oven. The pudding will now have a caramelized topping that is magnifico! Again, like in Crema Catalana, if you wish to serve the pudding chilled, omit the caramelizing. Cover and refrigerate 3 hours or overnight; remove from refrigerator 30 minutes before caramelizing.

Yield: 6 to 8 servings.

Spanish Caramel Custard
Flan de Leche Acaramelado

Spanish flan has become an international favorite. It is featured in fine restaurants throughout the world. When I experimented with its main ingredients, egg-substitutes and low-fat milk, the result was gratifying. The difference in taste is barely noticeable; it is that delicious. Should some of the caramel stick to the pan after you unmold the flan, place the pan in hot water for about 5 minutes or longer to melt the sauce; then pour over the custard.

$1/2$ cup plus 2 tablespoons granulated sugar
$2^1/2$ cups low-fat milk
$1/4$ teaspoon salt
Zest of one lemon, in a long strip
1 cinnamon stick
$1/2$ cup granulated sugar
3 eggs plus 3 egg whites; or 2 eggs and 8 ounces (1 cup)
  egg-substitute
1 teaspoon vanilla extract

Preheat oven to 300 degrees F.

In a small iron skillet, heat sugar; watch carefully, and stir with wooden fork or spoon until you produce a foamy rich golden caramel syrup. Take care not to burn. Quickly pour into a $1^1/2$ quart, heat-resistant casserole with cover; rotate and tilt until bottom and an inch up the sides of the casserole are well-coated with the syrup. Set aside to harden.

In a saucepan, combine milk, salt, lemon peel, cinnamon stick and sugar; stir to mix well. Place pot over direct heat and slowly bring to a scalding stage, stirring to totally dissolve sugar.

Pour egg mixture and vanilla into a large mixing bowl, and beat to blend well. Now, slowly and stirring vigorously, add the hot milk to the eggs. Once all is incorporated, beat with a hand beater a few seconds. Remove lemon peel and cinnamon stick.

Pour mixture into casserole coated with caramel, and prepare the bain marie. Fill a shallow pan half full of hot water, and put the casserole dish in it. (Water should come about halfway up the custard pan's side, but the water in the bain marie must not ever boil into the custard – it would be disastrous! So, every 15 minutes, place a couple of ice cubes in the water in order to stop possible boiling. See How-To, page 317 for complete directions.

Bake about an hour; the custard is ready to come out of the oven when a cake tester, inserted towards middle, comes out clean. Baking time should not exceed 1 hour. Remove custard from bain marie as soon as it comes out of the oven to avoid further cooking. Cool completely...cover and refrigerate until well chilled, 4 to 5 hours or overnight.

To serve: Remove Flan from refrigerator, and allow to stand about 30 minutes. Run a knife around sides of custard. Shake gently. Unmold upon a pretty glass serving platter about 1 inch deep. The custard sauce will drip gracefully down sides of Flan. Spoon custard into sherbet glasses or pretty dessert bowls.

Yield: 6 to 8 servings.

Caramel Custard with Condensed Milk
Flan con Leche Condensada

There are more and more varieties of flan being added to the American repertoire. Here's a quick and easy way to prepare flan. Muy bueno, tambien.

1/2 cup granulated sugar plus 2 tablespoons

14-ounce can low-fat condensed milk

1 1/2 cups 2% milk

1/8 teaspoon salt

1 – 3 inch strip of lemon, pith removed

1 cinnamon stick

3 eggs plus 2 egg whites; or 10 ounces (1 1/4 cup) egg-substitute

1 teaspoon vanilla extract

(continued...)

Preheat oven to 300 degrees F.

In a small iron skillet and over moderate heat, caramelize sugar. Stir and watch closely until it starts to foam and turn a rich amber color; pour quickly into a $1^1/_2$ quart casserole or a $6^1/_2$ cup mold. Rotate and tilt to coat bottom of pan and one inch up along the sides; set aside to harden.

In a saucepan, combine the milks, salt, lemon and cinnamon; stir well, and bring to the scalding stage (goose pimples).

In a deep mixing bowl, beat eggs and whites or egg-substitute and vanilla until well-blended (count to 25!). Slowly add the hot milk, stirring briskly to avoid curdling. Discard peel and cinnamon stick. Pour custard mixture into the casserole or mold, and place in center of a bain marie (see preceding recipe for more about bain marie).

Yield: 6 to 8 servings.

Cheese and Pineapple Flan
Flan de Queso y Piña

I call this dessert the Spanish cheesecake. It is prepared similarly to traditional flan, but is richer. It is a unique dessert, one that I guarantee you will enjoy immensely for it's smooth creaminess and tropical flavors. Using a ring mold, fill the center with colorful seasonal fruit for a festive finish.

$1^1/_2$ cup plus 2 tablespoons granulated sugar

12-ounce package low-fat cream cheese, softened

8-ounce can unsweetened crushed pineapple, drained

14-ounce can low-fat condensed milk

$1^1/_4$ cups low-fat milk

1 teaspoon vanilla extract

$^1/_4$ teaspoon salt

3 eggs plus 1 egg white; or 8 ounces (1 cup) egg-substitute

Preheat oven to 325 degrees F.

Use a $6^1/_2$ cup ring mold or a $1^1/_2$ quart casserole.

In a small skillet, heat the sugar, watching carefully and stirring until a rich golden syrup forms. Pour quickly into the casserole or mold; rotate and tilt to cover bottom of pan and 1 inch up the sides. Set aside to harden.

Into the container of a large electric blender or food processor, spoon the softened cream cheese, pineapple, condensed milk, 1 cup of the low-fat milk, vanilla and salt; blend 30 seconds. Add eggs or egg substitute; continue blending until smooth, another 30 seconds. Pour mixture into a mixing bowl. Stir in remaining 1/4 cup of milk. Mix well and pour into prepared mold or casserole.

Prepare a bain marie (For complete instructions, see the Spanish Caramel Custard recipe earlier in this chapter). Place flan in bain marie; bake one hour. Keep water in bain marie from boiling by adding ice cubes every 15 minutes as it cooks. Custard will appear soft in the middle, but it will set firmly as it cools. (See How To for complete directions. Once cheese custard is cool, cover and refrigerate until completely chilled, about 3 to 4 hours or overnight.

About 30 minutes before serving, remove from refrigerator. On a serving platter, invert custard from pan, using a hot knife to remove it; or, spoon into sherbet glasses from the mold or casserole.

Yield: 6 to 8 servings.

Pretty Pumpkin Flan
Flan de Calabaza

I use for this remarkable dessert a 6¹/₂ cup ring mold. When the flan is cooked and the moment to unmold it arrives, try a pretty stemmed cake platter with the edge about 1 inch deep to show off the dish with an elegant flourish. Use a good cognac like Cardenal Mendoza for a superior result.

1/2 cup granulated sugar plus 2 tablespoons

4 eggs, or 8 ounces (1 cup) egg-substitute

1/2 cup granulated sugar

1/8 teaspoon salt

1/2 teaspoon cinnamon

(continued...)

½ teaspoon nutmeg

1 cup fresh pureed pumpkin, or plain canned pumpkin puree

1 cup low-fat milk

1½ cups evaporated skim milk

2 tablespoons cognac

2 tablespoons melted butter or margarine

Preheat oven to 325 degrees F.

In a heavy skillet, caramelize the sugar; watch carefully, as it burns easily. When it becomes a foamy rich amber in color, immediately pour into the mold. Quickly rotate the hot syrup until bottom of pan is completely coated. Set aside to harden.

Break eggs or pour egg-substitute into a large mixing bowl. Beat until well-blended. Add sugar, salt, cinnamon, nutmeg and pumpkin. Stir well. Combine the milks; slowly pour into pumpkin mixture, stirring continually with a wire whisk until all is smooth and sugar is dissolved.

Pour cognac into a small container with handle (there is an appropriate gadget available on the market for this). Heat the cognac, then with a long match, ignite the cognac. While still flaming, pour over pumpkin mixture; add melted butter or margarine. Stir and mix thoroughly until both disappear into the custard.

Pour into prepared utensil. Prepare a bain marie (for complete instructions, see the Spanish Caramel Custard recipe earlier in this chapter). Place flan in center of hot-water pan; bake 1 hour. Do not allow water in bain marie to boil; keep at scalding stage by placing ice cubes in the water every 15 minutes.

Test for doneness at the hour by inserting a cake tester towards center of flan. It is ready to come out of the oven when tester comes out clean. Remove custard from bain marie. Cool completely. Cover loosely and refrigerate until chilled. Remove from refrigerator 15 minutes before inverting onto a pretty cake platter.

Yield: 6 or 8 servings.

An Ideal Cheesecake
Torta de Queso Crema Ideal

As you probably know, the texture of a cheesecake is often directly proportional to it's wonderful taste. The texture in this remarkable cake is heavenly. Ya verdad.

1¹/₂ cups ground graham cracker crumbs
2 tablespoons powdered sugar
¹/₄ cup melted whipped butter or margarine

    Preheat oven to 325 degrees F.
    Mix ingredients until well-blended. Remove 3 tablespoons for later use. Spread the rest upon the bottom of a springform, conditioned pan. Press firmly so crumbs will adhere to utensil. Place in oven for 10 minutes or so, until golden. Remove from oven and set aside to cool completely.

Cheesecake Filling

2 – 7 gram envelopes unflavored gelatin
1 cup granulated sugar
¹/₄ teaspoon salt
1¹/₂ cups low-fat milk
3 egg yolks or 6 ounces (³/₄ cup) egg-substitute
2 – 12 ounce packages low-fat cream cheese,
    softened to room temperature
Juice of one lemon
1 teaspoon vanilla extract
2 egg whites
2 tablespoons granulated sugar
1 cup low-fat plain yogurt

    In a saucepan, combine gelatin, sugar and salt; mix well.

(continued...)

In a mixing bowl, combine milk and eggs or egg-substitute. Stir to mix well. Add slowly to gelatin mixture. Place pan over low heat and cook about 5 minutes, stirring continually, until gelatin has dissolved and custard has thickened. Set aside to cool.

In the bowl of an electric mixer, combine softened cheese, lemon juice and vanilla extract. Beat at medium speed until smooth. Add the completely cooled custard, beating at low speed to mix well. Place the mixing bowl in refrigerator. Chill covered until partially set.

Meanwhile, place egg whites in a clean bowl. With hand beater, beat until soft peaks form. Add 1 tablespoon of sugar at a time and beat until peaks are a little firmer.

Remove custard from refrigerator and add the meringue and yogurt, in a folding motion; down and over. A rubber spatula makes this easy. Mix until meringue and yogurt disappear. Pour into prepared pan with crust, spreading evenly.

Refrigerate at least 5 to 6 hours or overnight, until cake is firm. Loosen outer sides of springform pan with metal spatula, and remove. Garnish a capriccio with seasonal fruit and sprinkle with reserved crumbs. It's a great cake...try it!

Yield: 8 to 10 nice slices.

Light and Easy Cheesecake
Torta de Queso Crema

One of the frustrations of a dieter is to be amongst people who are not dieting. They enjoy luscious desserts, while you sit there and (quietly) suffer. This need not be. Here's a solution. If I am eating with good friends de confianza – comfortably – in a restaurant, I ask for an extra spoon or fork, and I simply ask to taste my neighbor's dessert. Nine chances out of ten, that one sweet bite after a meal satisfies me. At any rate, here is a torta that will do you justice, if entertaining at home. No guilt...I promise!

1½ cups freshly-ground graham cracker crumbs
2 tablespoons powdered sugar
1/4 cup melted whipped butter or margarine

Preheat oven to 300 degrees F.

Mix above ingredients. Reserve 2 tablespoons for later use. Spread the remainder on bottom tray of a springform pan. Press crumbs so they will adhere to pan. Place in oven for 15 minutes, or until golden. Remove from oven and cool completely while preparing cheesecake mixture.

7-gram package non-flavored Knox gelatin

1 cup hot water

2 tablespoons lemon juice

12-ounce package low-fat cream cheese, softened

1 teaspoon vanilla extract

1/2 cup granulated sugar

14-ounce can low-fat condensed milk

1 cup ripe strawberries

1 ripe kiwi, thinly sliced

Dissolve gelatin in hot water. Add lemon juice. Refrigerate 30 minutes.

In large mixing bowl, whip softened cream cheese with vanilla and sugar until well-blended and fluffy. Add the chilled gelatin and condensed milk. Stir well until thoroughly incorporated.

Pour mixture into the bowl of an electric blender or food processor (you may have to do this in 2 batches). Blend each batch 30 seconds and pour into a mixing bowl. Stir vigorously, then pour mixture into the prepared pan. Refrigerate until set, about 4 to 5 hours or overnight.

To serve: Loosen side of springform pan carefully. Leave cheesecake on bottom tray. Alternate sliced fruit around edge of cake. Sprinkle reserved crumbs in center. If you wish – and what an idea! – mix 1 can of blueberries (or frozen and thawed) with 1 tablespoon cognac and 2 tablespoons of sugar. Bring to a soft boil, then lower heat and cook 3 minutes. Cool, then spread over the cake. Sprinkle with the reserved crumbs. It is one beautiful, light cheesecake.

Yield: 6 to 8 slices.

Nena's Peach Cobbler
Un postre de Nena

One of the pleasures of summer is the abundance of fragrant peaches: Ripe, sweet, juicy fruit from Georgia and North Carolina. To smell these al naturál is heaven. To eat peaches in the form of a cobbler is simply divine! And quick, too.

10 juicy ripe peaches, peeled and cut in wedges

1½ cups sifted cake flour, or all-purpose flour

¼ teaspoon salt

2 teaspoons baking powder

¼ teaspoon baking soda

¼ cup granulated sugar

5 tablespoons butter or margarine, chilled

2 egg whites, beaten

¾ cups buttermilk

¼ cup water

Butter-flavored vegetable spray

1 cup light brown sugar

¼ teaspoon nutmeg

¼ teaspoon cinnamon

2 tablespoons butter or margarine, melted

Preheat oven to 400 degrees F.

Clean, peel and cut peaches. In a mixing bowl, combine flour, salt, baking powder, baking soda and sugar. With a pastry blender or two knives, cut in the butter and mix until crumbs are about the size of peas. Make a well in the flour mixture. Add beaten egg whites, buttermilk and water. Stir to mix well without beating. Set batter aside.

With butter-flavored spray or butter, coat an 11 x 7 x 2 inch glass baking pan; set aside.

Put peaches into a large mixing bowl; add sugar, nutmeg and cinnamon, but mix carefully so as not to bruise the fruit, which is delicate. Pour into oven pan, and with care, arrange evenly to cover bottom. Dribble melted butter over all.

Spread the batter over peaches, indenting with a spoon here and there to provide breathing space. Bake 25 minutes, or until golden and bubbly. To serve, spoon warm cobbler into sherbet glasses and top each with vanilla frozen yogurt. The cobbler is best served immediately after baking, but it may be reheated effectively in a microwave. The same batter may crown any type of fruit.

Yield: 6 to 8 servings.

Blueberry Bread Pudding
Pudin de Arandanos Azul

This yummy pudding, laced with fresh blueberries, deserves a medal. A sprinkle of shredded coconut and a few just-shelled walnuts gives it a well-deserved A-plus. Important! Use a good cognac.

1 cup fresh blueberries
1/2 cup granulated sugar for caramelizing
8 slices day-old bread
1 tablespoon melted butter or margarine
2 eggs, or 1/2 cup egg-substitute
1 egg
1 cup granulated sugar
2 cups low-fat milk
1 cup evaporated skim milk
1/2 teaspoon cinnamon
1/2 teaspoon nutmeg
1 teaspoon vanilla extract
1/2 teaspoon salt
? teaspoon cream of tartar
1/4 cup chopped walnuts
1/4 cup shredded coconut
2 tablespoons melted butter or margarine
1 tablespoon cognac

(continued...)

Preheat oven to 325 degrees F.

Wash blueberries, pick out poor ones, stem and drain. Set aside.

In a skillet, caramelize sugar to a rich amber color, being careful not to burn. Quickly pour down center of 13 x 9 x 2-inch oven pan. Rotate quickly to coat bottom of pan as well as possible. Set aside.

With a kitchen brush, lightly spread the bread slices with melted butter, then cube. Spread on a cookie sheet and dry in the oven for five minutes. Do not toast. Transfer bread cubes to large mixing bowl. In a separate bowl, combine eggs or egg-substitute; whole egg, sugar and both milks. Beat with hand beater until well-blended, about 3 to 4 minutes. Add cinnamon, nutmeg, vanilla, salt and cream of tartar. Continue beating until all is well incorporated. Pour over bread in bowl. Mix well and set aside to soak 30 minutes, pressing down bread to soak evenly.

After soaking period, transfer bread mixture to prepared pan, spreading evenly. Scatter blueberries over and mix gently. Sprinkle walnuts and coconut evenly over all. Press down slightly. Combine melted butter and cognac. Dribble over the whole pudding.

Prepare a bain marie with hot water. Place pudding in center of bain marie, and bake 45 minutes. Use the ice cube method to avoid water from boiling into the pudding. (For complete instructions, see the Spanish Caramel Custard recipe earlier in this chapter). Serve hot, warm or chilled. Any which way – it's delightful!

Yield: 8 to 10 servings.

Simply Delicious Bread Pudding
Pudin de Pan Muy Sabroso

I love French baguettes. Many times when I have some leftover, I cube them and prepare bread pudding. Cuban bread, though less dense, also works well in this recipe.

1¼ ounces golden raisins

¼ cup cognac

· ·

7 cups, or about 10 slices, cubed day-old 1 French baguette or
   1 small loaf Cuban bread
4 tablespoons melted butter or margarine, divided
1 1/4 cups light brown sugar, firmly packed
1/2 teaspoon fresh grated cinnamon
1/2 teaspoon fresh grated nutmeg
1/4 teaspoon salt
4 eggs, or 1 cup egg-substitute
1/2 teaspoon cream of tartar
1 teaspoon vanilla extract
3 cups low-fat milk
2 tablespoons light whipping cream
Butter-flavored vegetable spray

Preheat oven to 325 degrees F.

In a small container, combine raisins and cognac; soak 3 to 4 hours, or overnight.

Spread cubed bread on a cookie sheet, and dry 5 minutes in oven. Remove from oven, and transfer to a deep bowl. Dribble 2 tablespoons of butter over bread and set aside. In large separate bowl, combine sugar, cinnamon, nutmeg and salt; mix well; reserve 1/4 cup for later use.

To remaining sugar mixture, add eggs or egg-substitute, cream of tartar, vanilla, milk and cream. Beat well with a good sturdy beater until sugar is dissolved. Pour this mixture over bread. Mix well. Soak for 45 minutes, pushing down bread to submerge in milk for even soaking.

Spray an oven pan measuring 13 x 9 x 2 inches with vegetable oil or butter-flavored spray.

Drain raisins, reserving cognac; scatter raisins over pudding. Combine reserved cognac with last 2 tablespoons of melted butter; dribble expertly over all. Sprinkle reserved sugar mixture over all. Bake 10 to 30 minutes; the pudding will puff up beautifully when it is ready to come out of the oven. As it cools, it will lose most of its puffiness.

Yield: 8 servings.

Old-Fashioned Pineapple Pudding
Pudin de Piña

Pineapple has long been the sign of hospitality. If you serve this pudding warm, just a few minutes out of the oven your guests will feel very welcome and so it is oh, so delicioso!

1 – 1¼ ounce package dark raisins

¼ cup white rum

4 tablespoons butter or margarine, melted and divided

Butter-flavored vegetable spray

10 slices day-old bread, crust removed

2 cups low-fat milk

1 cup evaporated skim milk

¾ cup granulated sugar

½ teaspoon cinnamon

½ teaspoon nutmeg

½ teaspoon cream of tartar

¼ teaspoon salt

3 eggs, or 6 ounces (¾ cup) egg-substitute

8-ounce can crushed, unsweetened pineapple

½ cup toasted pine nuts

Preheat oven to 325 degrees F.

Place raisins in small container. Pour in rum (I recommend Bacardi). Soak 3 to 4 hours or overnight.

Melt butter. With a kitchen brush, cover one side of bread slices with 2 tablespoons of the melted butter, then cube. Spread on single layer on cookie sheet. "Dry" in oven 5 minutes. Do not toast. Use a glass oven pan measuring 13 x 9 x 2 inches; spray pan with vegetable oil. Transfer bread to pan.

In a deep bowl, combine the milks, sugar, cinnamon, nutmeg, cream of tartar, salt and eggs. Beat with a good strong hand beater until well-incorporated; sugar must be totally dissolved. Pour the mixture over the bread and soak for 30 minutes, pushing down bread cubes to submerge completely in milk.

Drain pineapple, reserving 2 tablespoons of juice. Stir in pineapple and mix well with pudding. Drain raisins, reserving cognac soaking liquid for later use; scatter raisins over pudding with pine nuts.

Use reserved 2 tablespoons of butter: Combine with reserved rum and reserved pineapple juice. Dribble over all, making indents here and there to allow butter mixture to penetrate pudding well. Bake 30 minutes, and check to see if it's ready to come out of the oven; if it is not, bake another 15 minutes, or until it looks puffy and golden.

Yield: 8 to 10 servings.

Lady Fingers
"Polkas"

Ladyfingers (Polkas) and rich thick hot chocolate is probably the most popular merienda in a Spanish home. The famous bizcocho is made with practically the same batter. Both are widely used in the preparation of desserts. Follow me for great polkas.

4 eggs, separated
¼ cup granulated sugar
¼ teaspoon cream of tartar
½ cup granulated sugar
1 tablespoon cognac
1 cup unbleached all-purpose flour
Dusting powdered sugar

Preheat oven to 325 degrees F.

Grease and flour two cookie sheets. Separate eggs, reserving yolks for later use. Place egg whites in the large bowl of an electric mixer; beat at high speed until soft peaks form. Combine sugar and cream of tartar. Sprinkle over egg whites and beat until peaks are firmer and sugar dissolves. Set bowl aside.

In a smaller bowl of the electric beater and with clean beaters, beat egg yolks with the sugar and cognac about 15 minutes, until

(continued...)

lemon-colored and thick. With a rubber spatula, fold yolk mixture into the meringue (beaten egg whites); do not beat. Fold in the flour until it disappears and is well-incorporated. Again, do not beat mixture.

Use a pastry bag with a tube about an inch in diameter. Spoon about half of the batter into the bag. Pipe batter onto cookie sheets, making each about 3¹/₂ inches long. Spread them an inch apart. Repeat with remaining batter until all is used – each cookie sheet should accommodate about 2 dozen polkas.

Bake on separate oven racks; at 10 minutes into the baking, exchange cookie sheets upon racks to assure proper baking. Bake another 5 or 10 minutes or until golden in color. Remove with metal spatula to cake racks to cool. Dust with powdered sugar while still warm.

Yield: 4 dozen.

Angel Kisses
Besitos De Angel

Olga, a beloved member of our family, bakes these for all our family gatherings. The trouble is, you keep going back for more and more. Something as heavenly is truly irresistible.

¹/₂ teaspoon unsalted butter
1 cup walnuts, finely chopped
1 tablespoon orange zest
2 tablespoons flour
4 egg whites
¹/₂ teaspoon cream of tartar
¹/₄ teaspoon salt
1¹/₄ cups granulated sugar

Put butter in a small skillet with walnuts and toast for just a couple of minutes, until they smell good; be careful to avoid burning.

Preheat oven to 250 F.

. . . .

In a small bowl, combine walnuts, orange zest and flour. Toss to coat. Set aside. In a large clean mixing bowl, place egg whites; beat with an electric mixer at low speed until foamy. Add cream of tartar and salt. Beat until soft peaks start to form; gradually add sugar, beating continually until peaks are formed but not dry; do not over beat meringue. Fold in the mixture in the little bowl with a rubber spatula until well-blended.

Grease and flour two cookie sheets; drop meringue batter by tablespoons onto them. Place in oven, on separate racks and bake 30 minutes; reverse cookie sheets on racks to assure proper baking; bake another 30 or 60 minutes. If meringue cookies stick to pan as you attempt to remove them, they need to bake longer; return to oven and bake an additional 10 to 15 minutes.

Besitos are done when firm to the touch and golden in color.
Yield: 2 to 2¹/₂ dozen cookies.

Incredible Angel Cake with Orange Glaze
La Incredible Panetela de Angel

This cake's batter has many uses. If you prefer a jelly roll cake you're all set. Or, simply use half the recipe ingredients, and you have a cake to make the famous brazo gitano. The only difference is that you must grease the pan and use waxed paper for baking. Not so with the Angel Cake. Read on and see what I mean...

1¹/₂ cups cake flour

¹/₄ teaspoon salt

1¹/₂ cups granulated sugar

1¹/₂ cups egg whites

2 tablespoons lemon juice

1 teaspoon cream of tartar

1 teaspoon almond extract

Sprinkle of powdered sugar

Preheat oven to 350 degrees F.

Into a mixing bowl, sift the flour and salt; do it again twice. Now re-measure the 1¹/₂ cups flour.

(continued...)

Sift sugar into a separate bowl; do it again twice more, and re-measure $1^1/_2$ cups. Sift $^1/_2$ cup of the sugar and add to flour mixture. Mix well, then sift the flour with the mixture one more time! Set aside.

In a large mixing bowl, combine egg whites and lemon juice; beat until foamy. Add cream of tartar and continue beating until soft peaks start to form. Add remaining cup of sugar gradually, 2 tablespoons at a time, until all is used and peaks are formed but not dry. Remove bowl from stand. Continue beating by hand.

Add flour mixture in portions, folding each addition into the meringue before adding another. Do this gently but quickly until all is well- incorporated. Sprinkle almond extract and stir – don't beat – into batter.

Pour batter into an ungreased angel tube pan; bake 30 to 40 minutes. A cake tester should come out clean when it is done. If not, allow 5 to 10 more minutes baking time. Turn the tube pan upside down and allow cake to cool that way before attempting to remove from pan.

To remove cake from pan, use a narrow, thin spatula and carefully pry the cake loose from pan; remember to loosen it along the inner tube of the cake as well, or it will stick and fall apart. Dust a cake platter with powdered sugar; it prevents cake from sticking to the platter. Serve plain or dribble a glaze over the warm cake.

Orange Glaze

2 cups powdered sugar

2 tablespoons melted butter

1 teaspoon orange zest

$^1/_4$ cup orange juice

1 tablespoon Grand Marnier

In a small mixing bowl, combine sugar, butter, zest and juice; mix well. Heat a large pot of water and when it boils, turn heat to low and set the mixing bowl into it, stirring carefully for 3 minutes. Remove from heat, add the liqueur, and beat until smooth. Adjust the consistency of the glaze by adding more juice if necessary. Dribble glaze over the cake until it cascades over the sides. A feast for eye and mouth!

Yield: 6 to 8 slices.

Apple Cake a la Magnifico
Torta de Manzana Rallada a la Magnifico

Here's a moist cake with subtle flavors of cinnamon and apple. It's an ideal creation to serve at "high tea" with chocolate, demitasse, cortado (espresso with milk), or tea.

1 cup grated fresh apples, about 2 apples

1/2 cup unsalted butter

1/4 cup canola oil

1 1/2 cups granulated sugar

2 1/2 cups sifted cake flour

2 teaspoons baking powder

1/2 teaspoon baking soda

1 teaspoon cinnamon

1/2 teaspoon nutmeg

1/4 teaspoon salt

2 eggs, 2 egg whites; or 8 ounces (1 cup) egg-substitute

1 cup low-fat buttermilk

1 cup powdered sugar

1/4 cup skim milk

Preheat oven to 325 degrees F.

Peel, core, grate and measure apples.

In a large mixing bowl, combine butter, oil and sugar; beat until well-blended, 10 or 15 minutes. In a separate large bowl, mix together cake flour, baking powder, baking soda, cinnamon, nutmeg and salt. Set aside.

Add eggs to butter mixture, and beat at low speed, mixing well. Combine grated apple and buttermilk; to it, in 3 portions, add flour mixture, alternating with apple-buttermilk; beat at low speed. Do not over beat.

Grease and flour a non-stick Bundt pan; pour batter into pan. Bake 45 minutes; when the cake-tester comes out clean, it is done. Cool completely before turning out onto a pretty cake platter. Mix milk with powdered sugar, and dribble over cake.

Yield: 6 to 8 servings.

Carrot Cake
Pastel de Zanahoria

My son Manny says this is his favorite cake. Though it is not as rich as the original recipe, it still remains his favorite. It's simple to prepare for a quick coffee klatsch or to surprise visitors arriving at short notice. I love to surprise Manny with a fresh cake.

2 cups grated carrots

1½ ounce package white raisins

¼ cup rum

6 tablespoons soft butter

5 tablespoons vegetable shortening

1 cup granulated sugar

½ cup light brown sugar

2 eggs, plus 2 egg whites; or 8 ounces (1 cup) egg-substitute

1 teaspoon vanilla extract

1 cup crushed, unsweetened pineapple, drained

2½ cups cake flour, sifted after measuring

¼ cup wheat germ

2 teaspoons baking powder

1½ teaspoons baking soda

¼ teaspoon salt

½ teaspoon nutmeg

1 teaspoon cinnamon

½ cup low-fat buttermilk

½ cup walnuts, chopped, and lightly dusted with flour

Peel, grate and measure carrots.

Combine raisins and rum; set aside to soak.

In a large mixing bowl, place butter, shortening and both sugars; beat until well-blended. Add eggs, vanilla and crushed pineapple; mix well at low speed.

In another mixing bowl, combine flour, wheat germ, baking powder, baking soda, salt nutmeg and cinnamon; stir to mix well. At slow speed, add dry ingredients to creamy mixture in three portions, alternating with buttermilk. Beat until well-mixed; do not over beat.

Fold soaked raisins, rum and all, carrots and nuts, into the batter. When all is well-incorporated, pour into a glass oven pan measuring 13 x 9 x 2 inches, sprayed with vegetable oil. Bake 30 minutes, checking with a skewer or cake tester to assure it is done; when skewer comes out clean, remove from oven, and cool completely before preparing cream cheese frosting.

Fab Frosting

12-ounce package low-fat cream cheese
1/2 cup low-fat plain yogurt, drained
3 tablespoons pineapple juice
2 1/2 cups powdered sugar

Combine softened cream cheese, yogurt and 2 tablespoons pineapple juice in a food processor or blender until smooth. Pour mixture into a mixing bowl; add sugar and beat well; add remaining tablespoon of juice. Beat until it is the right consistency for spreading. Once cake has cooled, do not remove from its pan; ice it in the pan, and garnish with baby carrots and mint leaves.

Cut into squares to serve.

Yield: 8 to 10 servings.

Pineapple and Walnut Cake
Torta de Piña y Nuez

I have been baking this very special cake for the past 30 years for my daughter-in-law, Gerry, on her January 7th birthdate. You will like it too for special occasions. It is a great cake for a great lady, my Gerry.

1/2 cup butter or margarine
3 tablespoons vegetable shortening
1 1/2 cups granulated sugar
3 eggs; or 6 ounces (3/4 cup) egg substitute
8-ounce can crushed, unsweetened pineapple, drained

(continued...)

1 cup low-fat plain yogurt, drained, or low-fat sour cream

1/2 teaspoon baking soda

2 1/2 cups cake flour, measured, then sifted

2 teaspoons baking powder

1/4 teaspoon salt

1 teaspoon vanilla extract

Preheat oven to 325 degrees F.

Cream butter, vegetable shortening and sugar until light and fluffy. Add eggs or egg-substitute, one at a time, until they disappear. Drain pineapple, reserving half along with 2 or 3 tablespoons of juice and set aside. In a small bowl, combine the other half of the pineapple, yogurt or sour cream and soda. Mix well and set aside. In a little while the mixture will look weird!

Into another bowl, sift the flour, baking powder and salt. Now...add flour and yogurt mixture to butter-egg mixture in 3 portions, beginning and ending with flour. Reduce mixer speed to slow. Stop and scrape bowl once.

After the batter is well-blended, but without over beating, increase mixer speed, and beat while counting to 15 (or do it by hand). That is it; remove bowl from stand. Pour vanilla extract over all and gently stir into the batter.

Grease and lightly flour 2, 9-inch round layer cake pans; divide batter evenly into pans, and bake 35 minutes or until cake tester comes out clean. Allow to cool completely on cake racks before icing.

Pineapple Walnut Icing

1 cup butter, room temperature

1 box powdered sugar

1/2 cup reserved crushed pineapple

1/2 cup finely chopped walnuts

2 or 3 tablespoons reserved pineapple syrup

Sprinkle of dark rum

Cream butter. Slowly add powdered sugar, alternating with pineapple. Mix well. Add walnuts and with caution add tablespoons of pineapple juice. Mix well until consistency is correct for spreading. Turn one layer of the cake onto a pretty cake platter. Spread icing generously to cover cake. Carefully place second layer on top of filling and cover with remaining icing. When cakes are placed on cake racks, a sprinkle of dark rum (don't overdo it) will glamorize the already elegant torta.

Yield: 8 to 10 slices.

Glazed Rum Walnut Cake
Torta de Ron y Nueces

A great moist and luscious cake; one you will bake time and again. It boasts a pound-cake type taste, smooth velvety texture, and a surprise zing from the rum glaze. Excellent for company, as it has an exotic, unusual flavor.

5 tablespoons butter or margarine, at room temperature
5 tablespoons solid vegetable shortening, butter-flavored
2 cups granulated sugar
2 eggs plus 2 egg whites; or 8 ounces (1 cup) egg-substitute
3 cups cake flour
3 teaspoons baking powder
1/2 teaspoon salt
8-ounce carton low-fat plain yogurt
1/4 cup applesauce
1/4 teaspoon baking soda
1 teaspoon vanilla extract

Preheat oven to 350 degrees F.
In a large mixing bowl, cream butter and shortening with an electric mixer. Gradually add sugar, beating until mixture is nice and fluffy. Add eggs and egg whites, or egg-substitute a little at a time, beating well after each addition.

(continued...)

In a separate mixing bowl, sift together flour, baking powder and salt; in another mixing bowl, combine yogurt, applesauce and soda, and stir to mix well.

To the buttery mixture in the first bowl, add ingredients of second and third bowls, starting and ending with the flour mixture ingredients. Beat with an electric mixer at low speed, gradually increasing speed as you slowly count to 15. Do not over-beat.

Grease and flour thoroughly a Bundt pan or something similar; pour in batter, and bake. After 45 minutes, test with a wooden pick or skewer, inserted in the middle of the cake; it should come out clean. If it does not, bake another 15 minutes. Remove cake from oven; cool in pan for about 10 minutes, and carefully loosen with a knife from pan edges. Invert onto a cake platter while still warm and prepare the glaze.

Glaze

½ cup chopped walnuts
½ cup granulated sugar
2 tablespoons butter
2 tablespoons lemon juice
½ cup white rum

In a small saucepan, combine walnuts, sugar, butter, lemon juice and rum (I recommend Bacardi). Bring to a boil, stirring until sugar is completely dissolved and the mixture is foamy. With a skewer or a small sharp knife, poke the warm cake here and there. Spoon the hot mixture over the cake slowly until it is absorbed. Keep spooning mixture until all is used.

Yield: 8 to 10 slices.

Simply Wonderful Strawberry Cake
Requisima Torta de Frefas

Every one of the recipes in this chapter is unique. This strawberry cake is a very old recipe. The results, however, are very vogue. The cake is a luscious pink. Though made with a cake mix, your guests will never guess!

1 box white cake mix

2 tablespoons cake flour

3-ounce package dry strawberry gelatin dessert

$1/2$ teaspoon baking soda

1 cup frozen unsweetened strawberries, thawed

$1/2$ cup canola, or vegetable oil

$1/4$ cup butter or margarine, melted

$1/2$ cup evaporated skim milk

2 eggs, plus 2 egg whites; or 8 ounces (1 cup) egg-substitute

3 egg whites, beaten to consistency of meringue

Preheat oven to 325 degrees F.

Combine cake mix with flour, gelatin and baking soda. Mix well. To this mixture, add strawberries, oil, butter and milk, and eggs or egg-substitute. Beat by hand or with a mixer at low speed until mixture is well-blended. Fold in the meringue with a down and over motion (do not beat) until egg whites disappear and all is well-blended.

Grease and flour 2, 9-inch layer cake pans; divide batter evenly between pans. Bake 30 minutes or until a cake tester comes out clean, unless you're using a Bundt pan, which should bake 45 minutes. Cool cake on racks. Allow to cool completely before icing.

Yogurt Icing

4 ounces low-fat strawberry yogurt

3 cups powdered sugar

1 teaspoon grated lemon peel

$1/2$ cup toasted and chopped macadamia nuts

(continued...)

In a mixing bowl, combine yogurt with sugar. Beat until it is the right consistency for spreading. Fold in lemon peel and nuts. Turn one layer of cooled cake onto a pretty cake platter. Spread with icing. Place second layer over filling. Ice top and sides with remaining icing. Garnish with uniform slices of fresh strawberries dipped in sugar. Yummy...to say the least!

Yield: 8 to 10 slices.

Cynthia's Pick-Me-Up
Cynthia's Tiramisu

This sinfully scrumptious recipe does not submit gracefully to substitutions or changes in its preparation. The main ingredient is mascarpone cheese, made from sweet cream, sporting twice the fat of most cheeses. This cheese gives the dessert its distinctive flavor. Add an extra dribble of cognac if desired. Thanks to my Cynthia, for this great version of a lovely dessert.

1 tablespoon espresso coffee granules

1/2 cup hot water

30 lady fingers

6 eggs, separated

6 tablespoons granulated sugar, divided

1 pound mascarpone

4 tablespoons Marsala wine or Kahlua liqueur

2 tablespoons quality cognac

1/4 teaspoon cream of tartar

6 to 8 ounces ground semi-sweet chocolate

Sprinkle espresso granules into hot water; if you have an espresso coffee machine, 2 demitasse cups will do. Stir to dissolve; set aside to cool completely.

You can either make your own "Lady Fingers" with the recipe in this chapter, or purchase them at the supermarket, where you will find them on the cookieshelves. If the lady fingers appear soft, place them in a single layer on a cookie sheet and dry in a 325 degree F. oven 5 minutes (do not toast). Allow to cool completely, also.

Sprinkle espresso over lady fingers. Place half the lady fingers in bottom of a rectangular glass pan measuring 13 x 9 x 2 inches. Make sure the bottom of the pan is well-covered.

In a mixing bowl, beat egg yolks with 3 tablespoons sugar until thick and lemony in color. Add mascarpone, which is found in Italian specialty stores and some supermarkets; then add Marsala and cognac. Stir this mixture gently until blended (without beating).

In a large clean mixing bowl, beat egg whites until foamy. Add cream of tartar. Continue beating, sprinkling with remaining 3 tablespoons sugar, until of meringue consistency. Fold carefully into cheese mixture, very gently, in a down and over motion until meringue disappears.

Pour half of mascarpone mixture over lady fingers in pan. Sprinkle well with ground chocolate (Toll House chocolate morsels are fine to grind). Top this with rest of lady fingers. Cover with remaining cheese mixture and again sprinkle with ground chocolate. Cover with plastic wrap and chill several hours or overnight before serving.

Yield: 6 to 8 servings.

Manuel's Chocolate Mousse
Mousse de Chocolate "Manuel"

On one of many trips abroad, my husband Manuel and I took a five-week tour of beautiful Switzerland. We began and ended the trip in Lucerne. One fine restaurant "The Old Swiss House" was always one of our favorites. The food was excellent; the atmosphere quaint and friendly. We had enjoyed a superb meal there, and my husband, who was a real "chocoholic" ordered chocolate mousse for dessert.

Where, in the U.S., many restaurants serve mousse chilled in glasses, this restaurant served it on cart burdened in a large earthenware pot, brimming with chocolate mousse. Alongside, another pot was overflowing with whipped cream.

My husband looked at me, and with a gleam in his eyes, asked, "Es todo para mi?" (Is this all for me?) If that had been the case, I truly believe he would have eaten a good portion of it, and then asked for a

(continued...)

doggie bag as well! The waiter then reached beneath the serving cart, and lifted out beautiful china dessert dishes. He ladled each with mousse and then plunked huge dollops of whipped cream, which he then sprinkled with toasted macadamia nuts. Manuel asked for more. I wasn't surprised!

1½ pounds Dutch semi-sweet chocolate baking squares, chopped
2 tablespoons butter or margarine
2 tablespoons heavy cream
⅛ teaspoon salt
12-ounce can evaporated skim milk
2 cups low-fat milk
3 tablespoons cornstarch
½ cup granulated sugar minus 2 tablespoons for meringue
1 ounce Kahlua liqueur
3 eggs, separated
½ teaspoon cream of tartar
1 cup light whipping cream, whipped
½ cup toasted macadamia nuts
1 teaspoon butter or margarine

In the top pot of a double boiler pan, place chocolate, butter, cream and salt. Melt over simmering water, stirring occasionally. In a saucepan, combine milk, cornstarch and sugar. With hand beater, beat until cornstarch disappears. Cook at low heat until mixture thickens. Stir in liqueur and mix well.

Combine milk mixture and melted chocolate mixture. Mix well to incorporate all ingredients. In a small bowl, beat egg yolks well. Add a little of the hot mixture to eggs, stirring vigorously to avoid curdling. Return eggs to custard. Stir with wooden spoon constantly for 2 minutes. Set aside to cool.

In a mixing bowl, beat egg whites until foamy. Add cream of tartar. Beat until soft peaks begin to form. Sprinkle sugar over meringue and continue beating until peaks are firmer. Fold meringue into the cooled chocolate mixture, in a down and over motion (no beating!) until meringue disappears.

Pour this rich chocolate cream into a bowl with cover; chill several hours or overnight. Stir once or twice with a rubber spatula.

Just before serving, ladle mousse into dessert dishes. Beat whipping cream with a little granulated sugar until firm peaks form (do not over beat, or you will have butter). Whip the cream just before serving. If the dollops of cream are placed over the mousse ahead of time, the whipped cream tends to break down, and it will spoil the effect of this elegant dessert. Place a dollop of whipped cream over each serving and sprinkle with nuts. It sounds *delicioso*, right? It is!

Yield: 8 to 10 servings.

Key West Lime Pie
Torta de Limas de Ca-ye-jueso

A creamy, smooth and silky filling offset with a crunchy graham cracker crust makes this pie unforgettable; it is a Florida favorite. This particular version is a delicate mix of tart and sweet, the limes providing the tart and the powdered sugar providing the sweet. If you are able to find real Key Lime Juice, do use it; but if Key limes are not available, substitute Persian limes.

1 – 9 inch graham cracker crust

14-ounce can low-fat condensed milk

4 eggs, separated

1/2 cup Key lime or lime juice

Zest of one lime

4 tablespoons powdered sugar

4 egg whites

1/2 teaspoon cream of tartar

1/4 cup granulated sugar

Preheat oven to 325 degrees F.

In a mixing bowl, combine milk, egg yolks, juice, lime peel and powdered sugar. Mix well and allow to stand 30 minutes. The yolks of the eggs "cook" with the lime juice-milk combination and encourages the thickening process.

(continued...)

Beat one egg white until frothy, and fold it gently into the custard until it disappears. Pour mixture into the prepared, pie crust. Cool.

Beat remaining 3 egg whites with cream of tartar until they form a meringue; gradually add the sugar, 2 tablespoons at a time, until all is used and meringue peaks – do not over-beat meringue.

Spread meringue over the custard, piling high in center. With the back of a spoon form peaks and valleys over the meringue in a decorative manner. Bake until meringue takes on golden color. Cool before refrigerating to avoid "tear drops." Chill two or three hours or until firm. When slicing the pie, do so with a wet knife to assure neat slicing.

Yield: 6 to 8 slices.

Maple Pumpkin Pie
Pastel de Calabaza

When I was appearing on a Tampa television station for frequent cooking segments, I demonstrated this fantastic Maple Pumpkin Pie. Requests for the recipe were staggering.

1 cup all-purpose flour

$1/2$ teaspoon salt

$1/4$ teaspoon nutmeg

3 tablespoons unsalted butter or margarine, chilled

3 tablespoons solid vegetable shortening

$1/4$ cup ice water

1 tablespoon white vinegar

In a mixing bowl, place flour, salt and nutmeg. Mix well.

Cube the chilled butter and add to flour mixture, together with the shortening. Work quickly with your hands, or a pastry blender, introducing butter or margarine and shortening to the flour until particles are pea-sized.

Make a well in center of flour mixture. Pour in combined chilled water and vinegar. Using a fork and a rotating motion, stir

. . . .

the mixture lightly until it barely holds together. Gather pastry into hands and lightly press together. Form into a ball. Wrap in wax paper and refrigerate for about 30 minutes.

Remove dough from refrigerator. Allow to rest 30 minutes at room temperature. Flour the surface of a wooden board and roll out the dough from the center out (do not go back and forth) until it spreads to the right diameter for a 9-inch pie plate. Now, lift the dough onto the rolling pin and ease it into the pie plate, allowing at least 1 inch overhang. With your fingers or a fork, flute the edge artistically. Brush the crust with melted butter or a frothy beaten egg white; it prevents the crust from becoming soggy.

Filling

2 cups pureed pumpkin (canned or fresh-cooked)

1 egg, plus 2 egg whites; or 6 ounces (³/₄ cup) egg-substitute

14-ounce can low-fat condensed milk

¹/₂ cup light brown sugar

¹/₄ cup pure maple syrup

2 tablespoons cornstarch

1 teaspoon cinnamon

¹/₂ teaspoon nutmeg

¹/₄ teaspoon ginger

1 tablespoons butter, melted

Preheat oven to 350 degrees F.

In a large mixing bowl, combine pumpkin and the rest of ingredients, except butter. Stir with wire whisk until well-blended. Stir in the melted butter. Pour into prepared pie plate. Bake 1 hour or until cake tester inserted in center of pie comes out clean. Cool.

Serve with dollops of Cool Whip or whipped cream. This pie will not crack like most pumpkin pies do; I can't stand it when it cracks! Trust me, this one does not – okay?

Yield: 6 to 8 slices.

CLARITA'S HOW-TO

Bain Marie: How To Prepare and Use

Place custard dish in a shallow pan of hot water to be baked in the oven, this is called a bain marie. The water should reach halfway up the side of the dish. The water in the bain marie must not ever boil into the custard. It would be disastrous! So, every 15 minutes, place a couple of ice cubes in the water in order to stop possible boiling. The custard will be ready when a cake tester, inserted towards middle, comes out clean. Baking time should not exceed 1 hour. Remove custard from bain marie as soon as it comes out of the oven to avoid further cooking.

Butter: How To Clarify

Clarified butter is simply melted butter with the sediment removed. It is used in baking and for other dishes, such as dunking and cooking lobster. To clarify butter, melt 2 sticks or $1/2$ pound of butter in a heavy saucepan until it foams without taking on color; skim foam as it surfaces. Remove pan from heat. Milk solids will settle at the bottom of sauce pan. Carefully, without disturbing the solids, remove the clarified butter. Pour into jar and use sparingly in cooking. Even a teaspoon of clarified butter will enhance any recipe. Use in moderation.

Chicken Broth: How to Make

3 to 3½ pounds chicken breasts and thighs
1 celery rib
½ onion
½ bell pepper
2 bay leaves, crushed
1 ripe tomato
Sprig fresh parsley

To prepare chicken broth from scratch, trim, wash and dry chicken, and place in a medium Dutch oven with cover, along with the next 6 ingredients, ending with parsley. Sprinkle with salt, then fill pot ³/₄ full of water. Bring to a boil. Using a skimmer, skim off fat for about 10 minutes. Lower heat, cover and cook about 30 minutes. This should be done early in the day or the day before you plan to serve to allow time to defat chicken broth. Cool chicken in broth. Remove to a bowl. Skin and bone, removing all traces of fat. Cut into chunks, cover and refrigerate. Strain broth into a pot with cover and refrigerate.

Discard cooked vegetables. Refrigerate fully 2 or 3 hours.

Chorizo and Sausages: How to Degrease

You may degrease sausage a number of ways. I generally do this task on top of the stove or in a microwave oven. To do it on the stove, pierce chorizo sausage at intervals, then place in heavy skillet with cover. Cook on low heat turning occasionally, skimming grease as it is released. Using a microwave, pierce and place on paper towels, then cover loosely with another sheet of toweling. Microwave on high power for about 35 seconds. Drain grease on paper towels when done. Cool completely before removing casing and slicing.

Citrus: How To Zest

Using a sharp grater, carefully rub orange, lime or lemon peel across it. The zest of the fruit provides a tart, hearty flavor. Be careful not to incorporate the white pith; it is bitter.

Fish Stock: How to Make

2 pounds head, tail and fish trimmings

1 quart water

1 – .5 gram container imported saffron threads,
    toasted and crushed*

1 onion, cut in two

1 sprig of basil

1 sprig of parsley

1 sprig of thyme

1 whole ripe tomato

1 bay leaf, crushed

2 garlic cloves, crushed

1 carrot, cut in 3 pieces

2 cups dry white wine

Salt and hot sauce to taste

To prepare a fish stock, rinse fish trimmings thoroughly. Place in a large, $2^1/_2$ quart stock pot. Cover with water. Bring to a brisk boil. Skim several times. Add saffron, plus remaining ingredients. Reduce heat to low and cook covered 30 minutes, skimming if necessary until foam disappears. Strain stock through a fine sieve lined with cheesecloth layers. Discard trimmings and vegetables. Once stock is thoroughly cool, use what you need in recipe. The rest may be frozen in containers for later use.

Yield: About $1^1/_2$ quarts.

*For instructions on toasting saffron, see page 322.

Flaming Dishes: How to Flambé

Pour the liquor or liqueur you will use to flambé into a heavy saucepan and heat gently. It must be of high enough alcohol content to flame. Be careful not to get the too hot, or it will catch fire. When liquor is slightly heated, prepare to pour the liquid over the recipe you want to flambé. Have a match lit, and all in one motion, very carefully pour the warm liquor over the food and light it. Have a pan lid ready in case the flame gets out of hand and it needs to be extinguished. The liquor should turn a bluish color and diminish, but the flavor will remain. Note: special utensils for flaming foods are available at most gourmet shops.

Mussels and Clams: How To Clean and Debeard

When you are buying clams and mussels, make sure they are tightly closed. Discard any that are not closed. To allow for this, have fishmonger throw in a few extra shells. Clams and mussels in their shells are usually purged, ("cleaned") already, and are suitable to be used in a recipe. Still, once you get home, you must debeard them just before cooking, since they die soon after the beard is removed. First, place the shellfish in a large colander. With a stiff kitchen brush, scrub them under running water, one at a time, just in case sand is still lurking on the shells. To debeard mussels, use a sharp knife to cut off visible strings that grow close to the shells. Clams and mussels deteriorate quickly, so plan to use them immediately.

Nuts: How to Toast

Some nuts, like pecans or walnuts, can be toasted 5 to 8 minutes in the oven at 300 degrees F. without using butter. Others, like almonds and sesame seeds, need a teaspoonful or more of oil or butter before you sauté lightly in a skillet at moderate heat. WATCH CAREFULLY – they burn easily.

Peppers (Bell): How To Roast

Heat Broiler. Lay cleaned and halved peppers, skin side up, on a heavy broiling pan. Carefully place under broiler and cook until they are completely charred. Remove when slightly cooled, then place peppers in a brown bag, close tightly, then allow to steam 10 to 15 minutes. Now, being careful to avoid burning your hand, and scrape off clinging, stubborn blackened skin using a sharp paring knife. Rinse under cold running water, then dry with paper towels. Cut into strips if recipe so directs. You may also broil whole, then clean after broiling. This can also be done on an outdoor barbecue grill.

Rice: How to Cook

Boil water in saucepan using twice as much water as rice. For 2 cups of rice, for instance, boil 4 cups of water. When water has boiled, add 2 cups of raw rice, and stir carefully. Cover, reduce heat to low, then cook about 18 minutes. Do not remove lid, as you are trying to steam the rice, and removing it allows the steam to escape.

Roux: How to Make

Combine flour with butter or oil, and saute until flour is cooked; a nutty aroma is released and it will take on a golden color. When cooking the roux, the mixture will be crumbly and dry, and the flour will give off a nutty aroma, which indicates the flour is ready for the cold (never hot) liquid, *andantes*? The liquid should always be cold. At this point, remove from heat and slowly add liquid called for in recipe. Important: Should white sauce curdle, or annoying flour lumps appear, beat vigorously with a hand beater (I am sure you have one) to bind together again. Chances are, the sauce will not curdle again.

Saffron: How To Crush and Toast

Cut a little square of brown paper to measure 3 x 3 inches or so, and place a few strands of saffron in the center; now fold to be sure the saffron is hidden within. When you are cooking broth, place the little brown folded paper on the lid of the soup pot to allow the steam to toast it. After a few minutes, remove from the pot and without unfolding, crush between the forefingers and thumbs. Then unwrap and put into broth.

Saffron Broth: How To Prepare

Saffron is an herb of the crocus family; the dried stigmas of the plant are what s used in cooking. In our area, Central Florida, saffron is found readily in all supermarkets and in quantities in Hispanic markets. Try to find the Spanish import; in my opinion, it is better. The herb comes packed in tiny air-tight plastic containers. To prepare defatted saffroned chicken broth, pour however many cups of chicken broth the recipe calls for into a saucepan, heat to just below scalding stage (do not boil) and add toasted, crushed saffron. Steep for a half-hour or more to release the color in saffron. For 3 cups of broth, use 1 container, which weighs half a gram. Discard the stigmas if necessary.

Yogurt: How to Make Yogurt Cheese

First, read the label on the yogurt package. Two and one-half cups of plain yogurt will produce about 1 cup of yogurt cheese. Use yogurt that does not contain thickeners, such as vegetable gum or gelatin; these interfere with the release of the whey. To make the cheese, line a colander with two layers of cheesecloth. Spoon yogurt into the cheesecloth. Cover and place over a large bowl to catch drippings. Allow to drain 6 to 8 hours, or overnight. Using a large spoon, turn over the yogurt in a few hours. The cheese should have the consistency of creamy cottage cheese. Turn the cheese into a bowl with cover and refrigerate. There are any number of ingredients that can be added to the cheese to make it even more flavorful. Experiment with herbs and spices.

There are any number of ingredients that can be added to the cheese to make it even more flavorful.

· · · · ·

INDEX

Q

R